Register This New Book

Benefits of Registering*

- ✓ FREE **replacements** of lost or damaged books

- ✓ FREE **audiobook** – *Pilgrim's Progress,* audiobook edition

- ✓ FREE information about new titles and other **freebies**

www.anekopress.com/new-book-registration

*See our website for requirements and limitations.

How to Promote & Conduct a

SUCCESSFUL
REVIVAL

with SUGGESTIVE SERMON OUTLINES

How to Promote & Conduct a

SUCCESSFUL
REVIVAL

with SUGGESTIVE SERMON OUTLINES

EDITED BY
Rueben A. Torrey

with DWIGHT L. MOODY, CHARLES H. SPURGEON, AND MORE.

ANEKO PRESS

We love hearing from our readers. Please contact us at <u>www.anekopress.</u> <u>com/questions-comments</u> with any questions, comments, or suggestions.

Cover Design: Jonathan Lewis

Printed in the United States of America
Aneko Press
www.anekopress.com
Aneko Press, Life Sentence Publishing, and our logos are trademarks of
Life Sentence Publishing, Inc.
203 E. Birch Street
P.O. Box 652
Abbotsford, WI 54405

RELIGION / Christian Ministry / Evangelism

Paperback ISBN: 978-1-62245-667-3
eBook ISBN: 978-1-62245-668-0
10 9 8 7 6 5 4 3 2 1
Available where books are sold

Contents

Introduction to Fourth Edition

The first edition of this book was published the year before we began our evangelistic tour around the world. For two years or more, hundreds of us had been praying together for a world-wide revival and we had reached the point where we were absolutely sure that the revival was coming, and this book was prepared as a preparation for that revival and as a help to it. I had not decided at that time to go around the world. The decision was made shortly afterwards. In looking over the book since my return home, I have been surprised to see how closely we have followed the lines of action suggested in this book, and have rejoiced to see how God has set His seal upon the principles enunciated in the book.

At the time that the book was given to the public, I was known more as a Bible teacher and as a pastor than as an evangelist. My evangelistic activity had been largely confined to those churches of which I was pastor. Since the publication of the book, God has seen fit to lead me out into the evangelistic field and I've had the privilege of applying on a very wide scale the principles which are enunciated in this book and I have found that these principles work successfully, even beyond my own anticipation. I am more firmly convinced than ever of the truth of the statement found on the eighteenth page of the book:

"When any church can be brought to the place where they will recognize their need of the Holy Spirit, take their eyes off from all men, surrender absolutely to the Holy Spirit's control, give themselves to much prayer for His outpouring, present themselves as His agents – having stored the Word of God in their heads and hearts, and then look to the Holy Spirit to give it power as it falls from their lips, a mighty revival in the power of the Holy Spirit is inevitable."

R. A. Torrey.

Preface

At the time of this writing, revival is in the air. Thoughtful ministers and Christians everywhere are talking about a revival, expecting a revival, and, best of all, praying for a revival. There seems to be little doubt that a revival of some kind is coming, but the important question is, What kind of a revival will it be? Will it be a true revival, sent of God because His people have met the conditions that make it possible for God to work with power, or will it be a spurious revival gotten up by the arts and devices of man? A business man who is in touch with religious movements in all parts of the country said to me recently, "There is little doubt that a revival of some kind is coming, and the revival that is coming will be either the greatest blessing or the greatest curse that has ever visited the church of Christ."

There are many who are trying to promote a revival by pushing to the front doctrines that have never produced a revival in all the history of the church of Christ. These doctrines are called new, but they are in reality as old as the early heresies that crept into the church. They have never had power in the past to produce conviction of sin, conversion, or regeneration, so presumably they will not have that power today.

Others are advocating a forward movement along lines utterly untried, and that seem to have little promise in them. Some of the methods described in this book will doubtless appear novel to many, but they are methods that have been tried and proved effective. There is no mere theorizing in the book. Men whom God has used in winning souls to

Christ and building up believers, have been asked to write out of their own experience. No one who has been asked to write has declined. Such a book as this seems to be an absolute necessity of the hour. There are thousands of ministers and other Christian workers in the land longing for a true revival of God's work, but with no experimental or even theoretical knowledge of how to go to work to promote such a revival. It is our earnest prayer and confident expectation that this book will prove helpful to all such.

Chapter 1

The Holy Spirit in a Revival

R. A. Torrey

Two passages of Scripture might well form the watchwords of every true revival, watchwords that should never for a moment be forgotten. The first is a portion of Zechariah 4:6, "'Not by might nor by power, but by My Spirit,' says the LORD of hosts"; the second is, "It is the Spirit who gives life; the flesh profits nothing" (John 6:63). In the conduct of any real revival, the Holy Spirit must occupy the place of supreme and absolute control. Revival is new life, and only the Holy Spirit can impart life.

I. The Holy Spirit's Part in a Revival

Let us look at the Holy Spirit's part in a revival, or, in other words, at what the Holy Spirit must do if there is to be a true revival.

1. In the first place, the Holy Spirit must inspire us to and guide us in prayer. In regard to the great revival that is to someday come to Israel, God says, "'I will pour out on the house of David and on the inhabitants of Jerusalem, *the Spirit of grace and of supplication*" (Zechariah 12:10) So also, if there is to be a true revival in any church or community or nation, God must pour out upon them the spirit of grace and of supplication.

The work must begin with Him. We are living in a day when there are many indications that God is doing His part to do this very thing for us. Prayer is the vital breath of a true revival. Prayerless revivals are a sham. But we know not how to pray as we ought, and if there is to be acceptable and effective prayer, the Holy Spirit must help our infirmity and teach us how to pray (Romans 8:26-27). We need to cry to God that He will not only pour out upon us a spirit of grace and of supplication, but that He will also by His Holy Spirit teach us how to pray. Doubtless He is already doing this in a measure, but we need a larger measure.

2. *The Holy Spirit must have the oversight and direction of all the revival activities.* It was so in the apostolic church, which was a revival church. The Holy Spirit chose the officers (Acts 20:28). He directed where His chosen servants were to preach and work (Acts 13:1-2). He oftentimes directed in a most minute way, and in ways that those directed did not altogether understand (Acts 16:6-8). All the plans for the revival, and all the details of the plans, should be submitted to the Lord for His guidance; He should be the recognized chairman of every committee.

3. *The Holy Spirit must give power to the preaching and to the testimony.* When Jesus gave to the disciples the great commission to go out and evangelize the world, He said, "...you will receive power when the Holy Spirit has come upon you" (Acts 1:8). Paul, in writing to the church at Corinth, said, "I was with you in weakness and in fear and in much trembling, and my message and my preaching were not in persuasive words of wisdom, but in demonstration of the Spirit and of power, so that your faith would not rest on the wisdom of men, but on the power of God" (1 Corinthians 2:3-5). Again, in writing to the church in Thessalonica, "... our gospel did not come to you in word only, but also in power and in the Holy Spirit and with full conviction" (1 Thessalonians 1:5). Whoever does the preaching in the revival, whether it be the pastor or the evangelist, the whole dependence for results from the preaching must be upon the Holy Spirit. Whoever testifies, we must look to the

Holy Spirit to give power to the testimony. Many a preacher of very small gifts has been mightily used of God because he and the people looked to the Holy Spirit, and many a man of naturally large gifts has accomplished nothing of real and permanent value because the dependence was upon him and not upon the Holy Spirit.

4. *The Holy Spirit must convict men of sin.* Jesus said in promising the Holy Spirit to the disciples, "He, when He comes, will convict the world concerning sin" (John 16:8). A revival without conviction of sin – deep, pungent, overwhelming – is not a true revival. It is true that a great many may be converted and born again without the deep and overwhelming conviction of sin that others have. They may come in as quietly as Lydia, whose heart the Lord opened (Acts 16:14), but when there is a deep and true work of grace, there will be a deep and overwhelming conviction of sin on the part of many. It was so on the day of Pentecost; as Peter preached in the power of the Holy Spirit, a loud cry went up from men who were pricked in their heart, "Brethren, what shall we do?" (Acts 2:37) There has been similar conviction of sin at every genuine and lasting revival since. This is beginning to be so in the church today. From all directions come reports of deep conviction of sin. Now it is the work of the Holy Spirit to convict men of sin, and we must depend upon Him to do it. We must ask Him to do it. We must expect Him to do it. Nothing is more futile than to try to convict men of sin by any unaided powers of reasoning that we may possess. The natural heart is so blind, and especially so blind as to its own condition, that the supernatural grace of the Spirit is necessary to open the eyes of the soul to its real condition. But the Holy Spirit, where dependence is placed upon Him, is constantly administering His power to convict even the most careless of sin.

5. *The Holy Spirit must regenerate.* Revival is new life, and new life to the unsaved comes through regeneration. It is the Holy Spirit's work to regenerate. Men are saved not through works of righteousness which they themselves have done, but according to God's mercy, who saves us by the washing of regeneration and renewing of the Holy Spirit

(Titus 3:5). ""Truly, truly, I say to you, unless one is born of water and the Spirit he cannot enter into the kingdom of God" (John 3:5). If there is to be a mighty revival in any church, ministers and people must look to the Holy Spirit to regenerate men. He can do it; He is doing it every day where dependence is placed upon Him. He is touching the hearts of men and women seemingly almost beyond the reach of the grace of God and quickening and transforming them by His almighty power. Let us ask Him and expect Him to do it in our own community. What He did in Saul of Tarsus in Damascus, He can do in many another Saul of Tarsus in Chicago, or in any city or village of the land.

6. *The Holy Spirit must sanctify, consecrate, and fill.* A revival means not only life for those dead in trespasses and sins, but, furthermore, new life – life more abundant for those who already have some life. It means complete surrender to God, a setting apart for God, a filling with God for Christians, and all this is the Holy Spirit's work. He is the sanctifier and the filler (1 Peter 1:2; Ephesians 5:18). Many are trying to cleanse and fill themselves. No! No! Look to the Spirit to do it for you and for others.

II. How to Secure the Holy Spirit's Work with Power

We have seen how much in a revival depends on the Holy Spirit's work and how, in fact, everything depends upon Him. Someone might think, then, that all we have to do is sit down and wait for the Holy Spirit to work, but this is not so. The Holy Spirit is always willing and anxious to do His work if the proper conditions are supplied. It is true that the Holy Spirit, like the wind, bloweth where He willeth (John 3:8), but He always willeth to blow where He can consistently, that is, where certain conditions are supplied. What are these conditions, or, in other words, what must we do to secure the Holy Spirit's work with power?

1. *First of all, we must recognize our need of Him.* The Holy Spirit only works with power when men deeply realize their need of Him. In many so-called revivals, men feel that they are themselves quite sufficient for the work in hand. They think that if they can only have the right

plans, the right machinery, the right advertising, and the right sort of singing and preaching, the desired results will follow. For some years in our country, we have been trying these machine-made revivals, and the result is a sorry and sickening failure. We must feel our utter help-lessness and dependence upon the Holy Spirit. Do we feel that today? Much that is said and written about the coming revival would seem to indicate that we do not.

2. In the next place, we must take our eyes off from men. If we get our eyes on any man, or any company of men, the Holy Spirit cannot work. God tells us that He has chosen the foolish things of the world to con-found the wise, and the weak things of the world to confound the things that are mighty, and the base things of the world, and things which are despised, and things which are not, to bring to naught things that are. Then God tells us why He has chosen the foolish things; in order that no flesh should glory in His presence (1 Corinthians 1:27-29). God will not give His glory to another, and if we get our eyes fixed on any man, God will withhold His power and blessing. "Men of low degree are only vanity and men of rank are a lie; In the balances they go up; They are together lighter than breath" (Psalms 62:9). Power belongs unto God and to Him alone, and if our dependence is upon men of low degree or men of high degree, the almighty power of God will not be manifested.

If we wish the Holy Spirit to do His glorious work, we must keep our eyes fixed upon Him, and Him alone.

3. We must surrender absolutely to the Holy Spirit's control. We have already said that He must control everything, but we on our part must gladly recognize His right to control and submit whole-heartedly to it. God gives the Holy Spirit to them that obey Him (Acts 5:32). If we would see a mighty work of God's grace, the deepest longing of our hearts should be that in all our meetings everything about them should be surrendered absolutely to the control of the Holy Spirit. Then shall we see great things.

4. We must pray. If there is anything absolutely clear in the Word of God, in Christian history, and in individual experience, it is that the Holy Spirit is given in His fullness in answer to definite prayer (Luke 11:13). The Holy Spirit was given at Pentecost after a ten days' prayer meeting; and if He is to come in mighty power in these days, there must be much private and much united prayer.

5. We must furnish someone for the Spirit to work through, and something for the Spirit to use.

(a) The Holy Spirit works through men. When Cornelius was to be converted and there was to be a revival in Caesarea, the Holy Spirit did not go directly to Cornelius; He sent Peter, and Peter presented himself as an agent for the Holy Spirit's power. So must we. The Holy Spirit convicts men, but He convicts them through us. In speaking to His disciples Jesus said, "But I tell you the truth, it is to your advantage that I go away; for if I do not go away, the Helper will not come to you; but if I go, I will send Him to you. And He, when He comes, will convict the world concerning sin" (John 16:7-8). So it is evident that the Holy Spirit who convicts the world does it through the believer. He comes to the believer and convicts the world through him. Will we now present ourselves to the Holy Spirit as the agent through whom He may do His glorious work any way He chooses? It may be in invitation work, in tract distribution, in personal work, in singing, in preaching, in any way He will. There is a great revival coming. The Holy Spirit wants agents for this work. How many of us are willing to be His agents, absolutely at His disposal?

(b) The Holy Spirit not only works through men, but He works through a certain instrumentality, that is, the Word of God (Ephesians 6:17). If the Holy Spirit is to work mightily, we must get the Word of God into our heads, into our hearts, and upon our lips. On the day of Pentecost, the Word of God which Peter had been storing in his heart for years, got onto his lips, and a mighty revival followed. In Acts 6:4, Peter and the rest of the disciples decided to give themselves to prayer and the ministry of the Word. What the result was, we read in verse seven, "The word of God kept on spreading; and the number of the disciples continued to increase greatly in Jerusalem, and a great many of the priests were becoming obedient to the faith" (Acts 6:7).

When any church can be brought to the place where they will recognize their need of the Holy Spirit, take their eyes off from all men, surrender absolutely to the Holy Spirit's control, give themselves to much prayer for His outpouring, present themselves as His agents – having stored the Word of God in their heads and hearts, and then look to the Holy Spirit to give it power as it falls from their lips, a mighty revival in the power of the Holy Spirit is inevitable.

Chapter 2

The Place of Prayer in a Revival

R. A. Torrey

The first great revival of Christian history had its origin on the human side in a ten-days' prayer-meeting. We read of that handful of disciples, "These all with one mind were continually devoting themselves to prayer" (Acts 1:14). The result of that prayer-meeting we read of in the second chapter of the Acts of the Apostles: "And they were all filled with the Holy Spirit and began to speak with other tongues, as the Spirit was giving them utterance" (Acts 2:4). Further on in the chapter, we read that "there were added about three thousand souls" (v. 41). This revival proved genuine and permanent. The converts "were continually devoting themselves to the apostles' teaching and to fellowship, to the breaking of bread and to prayer" (v. 42). "And the Lord was adding to their number day by day those who were being saved" (v. 47).

Every true revival from that day to this has had its earthly origin in prayer. The great revival under Jonathan Edwards in the eighteenth century began with his famous call to prayer. The marvelous work of grace among the Indians under Brainerd had its origin in the days and nights that Brainerd spent before God in prayer for an enduement of power from on high for this work.

A most remarkable and widespread display of God's reviving power was that which broke out at Rochester, New York, in 1830, under the labors of Charles G. Finney. It not only spread throughout the State, but ultimately to Great Britain as well. Mr. Finney himself attributed the power of this work to the spirit of prayer that prevailed. He describes it in his autobiography in the following words:

"When I was on my way to Rochester, as we passed through a village, some thirty miles east of Rochester, a brother minister whom I knew, seeing me on the canal-boat, jumped aboard to have a little conversation with me, intending to ride but a little way and return. He, however, became interested in conversation, and upon finding where I was going, he made up his mind to keep on and go with me to Rochester. We had been there but a few days when this minister became so convicted that he could not help weeping aloud at one time as we passed along the street. The Lord gave him a powerful spirit of prayer, and his heart was broken. As he and I prayed together, I was struck with his faith in regard to what the Lord was going to do there. I recollect he would say, 'Lord, I do not know how it is; but I seem to know that Thou art going to do a great work in this city.' The spirit of prayer was poured out powerfully, so much so that some persons stayed away from the public services to pray, being unable to restrain their feelings under preaching.

"And here I must introduce the name of a man, whom I shall have occasion to mention frequently, Mr. Abel Clary. He was the son of a very excellent man, and an elder of the church where I was converted. He was converted in the same revival in which I was. He had been licensed to preach; but his spirit of prayer was such, he was so burdened with the souls of men, that he was not able to preach much, his whole time and strength being given to prayer. The burden of his soul would frequently be so great that he was unable to stand, and he would groan in agony. I was well acquainted with him and knew something of the wonderful spirit of prayer that was upon him. He was a very silent man, as almost all are who have that powerful spirit of prayer.

"The first I knew of his being in Rochester, a gentleman who lived about a mile west of the city called on me one day and asked me if I knew a Mr. Abel Clary, a minister. I told him that I knew him well. 'Well,' he said, 'he is at my house, and has been there for some time, and I don't know what to think of him.' I said, 'I have not seen him at any of our meetings.' 'No,' he replied, 'he cannot go to meeting, he says. He prays nearly all the time, day and night, and in such agony of mind that I do not know what to make of it. Sometimes he cannot even stand on his knees, but will lie prostrate on the floor, and groan and pray in a manner that quite astonishes me.' I said to the brother, 'I understand it: please keep still. It will all come out right; he will surely prevail.'

"I knew at the time a considerable number of men who were exercised in the same way. A Deacon P. of Camden, Oneida County; a Deacon T. of Rodman, Jefferson County; a Deacon B. of Adams, in the same county; this Mr. Clary and many others among the men, and a large number of women partook of the same spirit and spent a great part of their time in prayer. Father Nash, as we called him, who in several of my fields of labor came to me and aided me, was another of those men that had such a powerful spirit of prevailing prayer. This Mr. Clary continued in Rochester as long as I did and did not leave it until after I had left. He never, that I could learn, appeared in public, but gave himself wholly to prayer.

"I think it was the second Sabbath that I was at Auburn at this time, I observed in the congregation the solemn face of Mr. Clary. He looked as if he was borne down with an agony of prayer. Being well acquainted with him and knowing the great gift of God that was upon him, the spirit of prayer, I was very glad to see him there. He sat in the pew with his brother, the doctor, who was also a professor of religion, but who had nothing by experience, I should think, of his brother Abel's great power with God.

"At intermission, as soon as I came down from the pulpit, Mr. Clary, with his brother, met me at the pulpit stairs, and the doctor invited me to go home with him and spend the intermission and get some refreshments. I did so.

"After arriving at his house, we were soon summoned to the dinner-table. We gathered about the table, and Dr. Clary turned to his brother and said, 'Brother Abel, will you ask the blessing?' Brother Abel bowed his head and began, audibly, to ask a blessing. He had uttered but a sentence or two when he broke instantly down, moved suddenly back from the table, and fled to his chamber. The doctor supposed he had been taken suddenly ill and rose up and followed him. In a few moments he came down and said, 'Mr. Finney, brother Abel wants to see you.' Said I, 'What ails him?' Said he, 'I do not know, but he says that you know. He appears in great distress, but I think it is the state of his mind.' I understood it in a moment and went to his room. He lay groaning upon the bed, the Spirit making intercession for him, and in him, with groanings that could not be uttered. I had barely entered the room, when he made out to say, 'Pray, Brother Finney.' I knelt down and helped him in prayer, by leading his soul out for the conversion of sinners. I continued to pray until his distress passed away, and then I returned to the dinner table.

"I understood that this was the voice of God. I saw the spirit of prayer was upon him, and I felt his influence upon myself, and took it for granted that the work would move on powerfully. It did so. The pastor told me afterward that he found that in the six weeks that I was there five hundred souls had been converted."

Mr. Finney, in his lectures on revivals, tells of other remarkable awakenings in answer to the prayers of God's people. He says in one place, "A clergyman in W – n told me of a revival among his people, which commenced with a zealous and devoted woman in the church. She became anxious about sinners and went to praying for them. She prayed, and her distress increased, and she finally came to her minister, and talked with him, and asked him to appoint an anxious meeting, for she felt that one was needed. The minister put her off, for he felt nothing of it. The next week she came again and besought him to appoint an anxious meeting; she knew there would be somebody coming, for she felt as if God was going to pour out His Spirit. He put her off again. And finally, she said to him, 'If you do not appoint an anxious meeting I shall die, for there is certainly going to be a revival.' The next Sabbath he appointed a meeting and said that if there were any who wished to converse with him about the salvation of their souls, he would meet them on such an evening. He did not know of one, but when he went to the place, to his astonishment he found a large number of anxious inquirers."

In still another place he says, "The first ray of light that broke in upon the midnight which rested on the churches in Oneida County, in the fall of 1825, was from a woman in feeble health, who, I believe, had never been in a powerful revival. Her soul was exercised about sinners. She was in agony for the land. She did not know what ailed her, but she kept praying more and more, till it seemed as if her agony would destroy her body. At length she became full of joy and exclaimed, 'God has come! God has come! There is no mistake about it, the work is begun, and is going over all the region!' And sure enough, the work began, and her family were almost all converted, and the work spread all over that part of the country."

The great revival of 1857 in the United States began in prayer and was carried on by prayer more than by anything else. Dr. Cuyler in an article in a religious newspaper some years ago said, "Most revivals have humble beginnings, and it starts in a few warm hearts. Never despise the day of small things. During all my own long ministry, nearly every work of grace had a similar beginning. One commenced in a meeting gathered at a few hours' notice in a private house. Another commenced in a group gathered for Bible study by Mr. Moody in our mission chapel. Still another – the most powerful of all – was kindled on a bitter January evening at a meeting of young Christians under my roof. Dr. Spencer, in his 'Pastor's Sketches' (the most suggestive book of its kind I have ever read), tells us that a remarkable revival in his church sprang from the fervent prayers of a godly old man who was confined to his room by lameness. That profound Christian, Dr. Thomas H. Skinner, of the Union Theological Seminary, once gave me an account of a remarkable coming together of three earnest men in his study when he was the pastor of the Arch Street Church in Philadelphia. They literally wrestled in prayer. They made a clean breast in confession of sin and humbled themselves before God. One and another church officer came in and joined them. The heaven-kindled flame soon spread through the whole congregation in one of the most powerful revivals ever known in that city."

In the early part of the sixteenth century there was a great religious awakening in Ulster, Ireland. The lands of the rebel chiefs, which had been forfeited to the British crown, were settled up by a class of colonists who were for the most part governed by a spirit of wild adventure. Real piety was rare. Seven ministers, five from Scotland and two from England, settled in that country, the earliest arrivals being in 1613. Of one of these ministers named Blair it is recorded by a contemporary, "He spent many days and nights in prayer, alone and with others, and was vouchsafed great intimacy with God." Mr. James Glendenning, a man of very meager natural gifts, was a man similarly minded as regards prayer. The work began under this man Glendenning. The historian of the time says, "He was a man who never would have been chosen by a wise assembly of ministers, nor sent to begin a reformation in this land. Yet this was the Lord's choice to begin with him the admirable work of God which I mention on purpose that all may see how the glory is only the Lord's in making a holy nation in this profane land, and that it was "'Not by might nor by power, but by My Spirit,' says the LORD of hosts" (Zechariah 4:6). In his preaching at Old-stone, multitudes of hearers felt in great anxiety and terror of conscience. They looked on themselves as altogether lost and damned, and cried out, "Men and brethren, what shall we do to be saved?" They were stricken into a swoon by the power of His Word. A dozen in one day were carried out of doors as dead. These were not women, but some of the boldest spirits of the neighborhood, "some who had formerly feared not with their swords to put a whole market town into a fray." Concerning one of them, the historian writes, "I have heard one of them, then a mighty strong man, now a mighty Christian, say that his end in coming into church was to consult with his companions how to work some mischief."

This work spread throughout the whole country. By the year 1626, a monthly concert of prayer was held in Antrim. The work spread beyond the bounds of Down and Antrim to the churches of the neighboring counties. So great became the religious interest that Christians would come thirty or forty miles to the communions and continue from the time they came until they returned without wearying or making use of sleep. Many of them neither ate nor drank, and yet some of them professed that they "went away most fresh and vigorous, their souls so filled with the sense of God." This revival changed the whole character of Northern Ireland.

Another great awakening in Ireland in 1859 had a somewhat similar origin. By many who did not know, it was thought that this marvelous work came without warning and preparation, but William Gibson, the moderator of the General Assembly of the Presbyterian Church in Ireland in 1860, in his very interesting and valuable history of the work, tells how there had been preparation for two years. There had been constant discussion in the General Assembly of the low estate of religion, and of the need of a revival. There had been special sessions for prayer. Finally, four young men, who became leaders in the origin of the great work, began to meet together in an old schoolhouse in the neighborhood of Kells. About the spring of 1858, a work of power began to manifest itself. It spread from town to town, and from county to county. The congregations became too large for the buildings, and the meetings were held in the open air, oftentimes attended by many thousands of people. Many hundreds of persons were frequently convicted of sin in a single meeting. In some places, the criminal courts and jails were closed for lack of occupation. There were manifestations of the Holy Spirit's power of a most remarkable character, clearly proving that the Holy Spirit is as ready to work today as in apostolic days, when ministers and Christians really believe in Him and begin to prepare the way by prayer.

Mr. Moody's wonderful work in England and Scotland and Ireland that afterwards spread to America had its origin on the man-ward side in prayer. Mr. Moody made little impression until men and women began to cry to God. Indeed, his going to England at all was in answer to the importunate cries to God of a bedridden saint. While the spirit of prayer continued, the revival abode in strength, but in the course of time less and less was made of prayer and the work fell off very perceptibly in power. Doubtless one of the great secrets of the superficiality and unreality of many of our modern so-called revivals, is that more dependence is put upon man's machinery than upon God's power sought and obtained by earnest, persistent, believing prayer. We live in a day characterized by the multiplication of man's machinery and the diminution of God's power. The great cry of our day is work, work, work – new organizations, new methods, new machinery – but the great need of our day is prayer. It was a master stroke of the devil when he got the church so generally to lay aside this mighty weapon of prayer. The devil is perfectly willing that the church should multiply its organizations, and deftly contrive machinery for the conquest of the world for Christ if it will only give up praying. He laughs as he looks at the church today and says to himself, "You can have your Sunday Schools and your Young People's Societies, your Young Men's Christian Associations and your Women's Christian Temperance Unions, your Institutional Churches and your Industrial Schools, and your Boys' Brigades, your grand choirs and your fine organs, your brilliant preachers and your revival efforts too, if you don't bring the power of Almighty God into them by earnest, persistent, believing, mighty prayer."

Prayer could work as marvelous results today as it ever could, if the church would only betake itself to it.

There seems to be increasing signs that the church is awaking to this fact. Here and there God is laying upon individual ministers and churches a burden of prayer that they have never known before. Less dependence is being put upon machinery and more dependence upon God. Ministers are crying to God day and night for power. Churches and portions of churches are meeting together in the early morning hours and the late-night hours crying to God for the latter rain. There is every indication of the coming of a mighty and widespread revival. There is every reason why, if a revival should come in any country at this time, it should be more widespread in its extent than any revival of history. There is the closest and swiftest communication by travel, by letter, and by cable between all parts of the world. A true revival of God kindled in America would soon spread to the uttermost parts of the earth. The only thing needed to bring this revival is prayer.

It is not necessary that the whole church get to praying to begin with. Great revivals always begin first in the hearts of a few men and women whom God arouses by His Spirit to believe in Him as a living God, as a God who answers prayer, and upon whose heart He lays a burden from which no rest can be found except in importunate crying unto God.

How Can We Get Our People to Praying?

First of all, we as ministers should begin praying ourselves. Those who read this book who are not ministers should also begin praying themselves. It is recorded of a young minister that there came to him such a burden for the salvation of the lost that he offered this prayer to God, "O God send us a revival or let me die." This seems extravagant, but is it any more extravagant than Moses' prayer in the mount? "'But now, if You will, forgive their sin – and if not, please blot me out from Your book which You have written!" (Exodus 32:32) Is it any more extravagant that Paul's expression of love for his unsaved brethren? "For I could wish that I myself were accursed, *separated* from Christ for the sake of my brethren, my kinsmen according to the flesh" (Romans 9:3). Extravagant or not, God answered this young minister with a mighty outpouring of His Holy Spirit. When we as ministers have something of a similar burden of prayer for the perishing, revivals will soon appear.

Having been brought by God's Spirit into such a place of earnest prayer ourselves, we should seek out the more spiritual members of our flock and gather them around us for prayer. Then, in due time, the whole church can be gathered for prayer. There should be prayer meetings at the church, but not only at the church; there should be prayer meetings in the homes. Cottage meetings should be instituted, where neighbors gather together to pray for a revival. In country districts, neighborhood meetings should be held in the schoolhouses, or wherever the farmers and their families can be gotten together. The godly ones, who are sick and shut in, and the very aged ones, who may not be able to get out, should be especially enlisted in this ministry of prayer. Others at a distance can also be enlisted by correspondence. Not a little of the marvelous results of Mr. Newell's great Bible classes in Chicago, Detroit, and St. Louis is due to the fact that he secured from all his friends the names of the godliest people they knew, far and wide, and began writing to them and thus enlisting them in a work of prayer in behalf of these classes.

Let each one get to praying, and get as many others as possible to praying for his own community and then for the world at large.

Chapter 3

The Preaching Needed in Revivals

Louis Albert Banks, D. D.

First, revival preaching must be positive to be effective. The doubter never has revivals. The man who finds it necessary to be all the while hedging and explaining and apologizing for the Gospel message which he brings, will never arouse revivals under his preaching. A revival is a revolution in many important respects, and revolutions are never brought about by timid, fearful, or deprecatory addresses. They are awakened by men who are cocksure of their ground, and who speak with authority. So the men who arouse revivals by their preaching are men who believe the Bible and who hold its great message to not only be true but infinitely important. And they preach it with the positive force of a man who is certain that he stands on solid rock. The message is true. The man who believes it shall be saved; the man who does not believe it will be damned. Eternal destiny hangs upon it. Christ is able to save the sinner. No one else can save him. The sinner can be saved now. These great facts must be central and positive in the preacher's mind and heart, and he must utter them with positive emphasis.

Second, revival preaching must be direct. It must be addressed to the people right then and there before the preacher. He is not giving out a message to be diffused around through the community. He is a messenger from heaven with a free pardon in his hand for a man condemned to die, and that man sits right there in the pew before him. He must get the man to see the pardon, to feel his need of it, and to accept it before he leaves the house. He must get on to some basis by which he can make that man feel, as well as understand, the message.

Third, revival preaching must be sympathetic. If it is not, it may arouse men and yet fail to win them. It must get at men from their human side. The preacher must find a man's heart and warm it to himself, as well as to the Christ whom he preaches. There are many people who can be won largely through personal reasons. They are just as certainly won as though they were won in another way. But they come to know Christ through the preacher who proclaims Him. The sympathy, tenderness, and love of the preacher's heart which show forth in his sympathetic words and manner, attract them like a magnet, and they are drawn away from their sins and drawn toward Christ.

Fourth, revival preaching must be directed toward the heart and not the head. In spite of all that is said about agnosticism and infidelity, there are very few who, down at the heart, are really unbelievers in the divine power of Jesus Christ to forgive sins and save the soul. Where there is one such, there are a hundred who are believers (so far as a wicked man is ever a believer), but whose heart-lusts and sinful passions hold them away from Christ and righteousness. The conviction of the head will never win them to Christ. The heart must be aroused; they must feel the baseness of their ingratitude; they must see the heinousness of their sins; they must appreciate the certainty of punishment and feel that, hanging over their guilty heads, even now, is the weight of condemnation and guilt. Get hold of the heart, and the head yields easily. Men continue in sin because their hearts are evil. Make the heart feel its guilt, let the heart see Christ as the One who is "wholly desirable" (Song of Solomon 5:16), and as the helm turns the course of the ship in the hands of the pilot who has just been taken on from the pilot-boat, so the life will change just as suddenly from the changed heart to which you have made your appeal.

Fifth, revival preaching must be simple and clear. There is no time to let a man study about it for a week and reason out what you have told him. You are like a lawyer before a jury, on the last day of the trial, when he knows that the jury is to go out to make its decision immediately on the close of his speech. All his desires to make a great impression on the jury that may help him in some future case are thrust aside. What he must do is to make the jury understand the case now and look at it from his standpoint. He will not use a word, if he knows it, that is not comprehended at a glance by the jury. What he says must be absolutely clear and simple and stand out distinct in their minds if he is to win his verdict. Revival preaching is like that. No man who wants immediate effect in the conversion of sinners ought ever to say anything in a sermon that a boy ten years old, brought up in a Christian family, would not easily comprehend. There is perhaps as great a weakness at this point as at any other among preachers who try to have revivals. They want to preach too big sermons. I had a man come to me once who was very serious and deeply anxious to have results in the conversion of sinners under his ministry. During the conversation, he made this remark: "I cannot get the consent of my mind to so lower the literary and philosophical standard which I have set for myself, to do the kind of preaching which seems to win men to decision for Christ." That was a real confession. He had hit the root of the matter. He always reminded me of that moral, rich young man who came to Christ and who was such a good young fellow that Christ loved him, and yet he went sadly away with a frown on his brow from the very door of the kingdom. This man of whom I have spoken has never got the consent of his mind to do the right kind of preaching, and as a result has never had a revival. And he never will until he surrenders to Christ to do the kind of preaching that will accomplish the result he desires.

Sixth, revival preaching must be illustrative. It must be in pictures. It must seize hold of the imagination. The Master used pictures. His sermons are full of stories and parables. He made men see His message as well as hear it. His message lived again in the imagination. We can bring men to action in the same way. No man has ever been a great revivalist who scorned a generous use of illustrations. It is a common thing for the great evangelists and the pastors who have great success in winning men to Christ to be criticized by the so-called eloquent and profound preachers, who never have any revivals of their own, as being only story-tellers and not being "strong" preachers. This is all nonsense. A sermon is strong only when it is powerful to produce the effect for which a sermon is made. If the great end of a sermon is to arouse a man to hate his sins, see in Christ a divine Savior, and so awaken him as to cause him to immediately accept Christ and find forgiveness, then that sermon is a strong sermon which brings about that result, and the man who attempts to do it in any other way, and fails, has preached a weak sermon, no matter how scholarly nor how splendid its rhetoric, nor how profound its thought, nor how dignified its delivery. Sermons are strong that pull down the works of the devil and capture sinners for Jesus Christ.

Seventh, revival preaching must be intense. It must be more than earnest; it must be charged with suppressed moral electricity. A man must be excited in his emotions, and yet hold them in restraint. He must so feel his message that he could cry aloud on the street-corner, and yet must hold himself in leash, as a hunter holds back his dog that quivers with excitement and yet keeps silent until the proper moment. So the man who is seeking to win souls by his message must hold his emotions in leash, but they must be there, and if they are not there the sermon will fail of its highest effectiveness. If there is any lack of this feeling, it can only be brought about by putting himself in the place of the man to whom he is preaching until he feels like Paul – that he is in prison with him, bound with him in like chains – and thus his message will become real.

Eighth, to preach effectively in revivals, the preacher must absorb a great deal of the Bible. The sermon must be saturated with the Bible. God has promised to bless his own Word, and the people to whom we preach must feel that we are loyal to the Word of God. Illustrations drawn from the Bible are peculiarly effective in times of revival.

Ninth, the preacher must be conscious that he is God's man. He must feel like Elijah did when he strode into the presence of Ahab and his wicked queen, and said, "'As the LORD, the God of Israel lives, before whom I stand, surely there shall be neither dew nor rain these years, except by my word" (1 Kings 17:1). He must feel as Nathan did when he stood before David, and told him the story of the ewe lamb until David has committed himself, and then, with whitened cheek and flashing eye and accusing finger, says to the startled and astounded king, "'You are the man!" (2 Samuel 12:7). If the preacher feels sure that God is with him and that he stands in the presence of the living God, there will be a glorious independence of speech, mingled with a deep and tender love for the people to whom he speaks, that will be marvelously effective.

Tenth, he must be sensitive to the Holy Spirit. He must be in the frame of mind and heart that Philip knew when he was caught away from the city into the desert, and which he felt and yielded to when he climbed into the chariot of the Ethiopian treasurer and preached to him Christ (Acts 8:26-35). The presence of the Spirit of the living God in our hearts, giving holy unction to the message, is the crowning glory of the revival preacher. I have not time to speak of many other things, but must not fail to say that here, as everywhere else, true manhood, unspotted life, and genuine character, frank, open, and read of all men, is tremendously powerful.

Chapter 4

The Minister as an Evangelist

William Patterson

The work of the Minister, according to the teaching of the New Testament, is threefold.

First, he is to feed the church of God – the babes with the sincere milk of the Word, and those who are more advanced with the strong meat of its doctrines (Hebrews 5:13-14).

Second, he is to care for those over whom he has been placed as an overseer or under-shepherd. This twofold aspect of the work was very clearly brought out by our Savior on that early morning when He stood by the Lake of Gennesaret and commanded Peter to feed the sheep and the lambs and to shepherd them (John 21:15-17). We are all agreed as to the importance of these two departments in connection with the minister's work; in fact, we can hardly overestimate the importance of building up Christian people in faith and in knowledge, and also in caring for them as the shepherd cares for the sheep, by leading them to the green pastures and the quiet waters.

Third, he is commanded to do the work of an evangelist; in other words, to reach out after the unsaved and to bring into the fold those who are outside. This part of the work was surely referred to when Christ called the disciples and told them that, if they would follow Him, He would make them "fishers of men" (Matthew 4:19), that as they had in the past drawn the fish out of the sea by the net, they would in the future draw men from the sea of iniquity to the rock of safety.

If we look at our Lord as the great example, we will see that while He was the greatest of all teachers and the One who was preparing His disciples for their life work, yet His great mission to this world was the saving of the lost. His very name meant Savior, and He Himself said that the Father sent Him into the world that the world might be saved through Him (John 3:17), and He informed the murmuring Pharisees that the Son of Man came to seek and to save that which was lost (Luke 19:10). Paul, speaking of the Savior's work in after years, said that Christ Jesus came into the world to save sinners; but it is not necessary to multiply passages of Scripture in order to prove that the great mission of the Master was to save the lost.

In commanding the disciples, He told them that as the Father had sent Him into the world, in like manner He was sending them (John 17:18). They were to be the saviors of men – not in the sense in which He was, by making an atonement for sin, but by telling to the lost ones that an atonement had been made, that God was reconciled, and that for them there was redemption if they would turn to the Savior. Again, before He ascended on high after His resurrection, He commanded His followers to go into all the world and to preach the Gospel to every creature; to preach repentance and the remission of sins in His name, beginning at Jerusalem.

The great work of the church is the evangelizing of the nations and the saving of the lost through proclaiming the Gospel of the Son of God. We are not discussing the question of evangelists. Some say they have a place in the New Testament, and some say they have not. We know that many of them have been instrumental in accomplishing great good, that God has set His approval on their work, and that today there are multitudes rejoicing in the salvation of Christ through the labors of evangelists. We know on the other hand that some of them, through lack of grace or lack of wisdom, have been the means of breaking up congregations, but what has been said of evangelists could be said of ministers with equal truth. Many of them have been wonderfully blessed in advancing the cause of God, but is it not true that some of them have broken up congregations and injured the cause they were representing? The question we are discussing is, "The Minister as an Evangelist."

At the very beginning, we are met with the assertion that many ministers have not the evangelistic gifts. It is true that some ministers are better adapted for preaching the deep things of God and for edifying the church of God than they are for reaching the unsaved, while others are better adapted for evangelistic work than for the work of teaching and edifying the church, but while this is true, every minister should be able to show the unsaved the way of salvation. If we expect our Sabbath School teachers to bring their scholars to Christ through their teaching, we should expect the ministers to be able to bring sinners to a knowledge of Christ as their Savior through their preaching. It will not do for a minister to say, "I have not the evangelistic gift, and therefore the lost are not being saved in my congregation." If a minister is not qualified to preach to sinners, he is not qualified to be a minister, and he should never be set apart for that work by a pastor, church, or college.

What is evangelistic preaching? Or what does it mean to do the work of an evangelist? It is not being able to tell anecdotes in an interesting manner, or to clothe stories with beautiful language, but it is the presenting of the truth to men in such a way that they will see themselves as sinners and then presenting Christ to them as the Savior of sinners in such a way that they will receive Him as their personal Savior and thus be saved.

If we glance back at the history of the church, we shall see that this has been done by men who are not designated as evangelists. John the Baptist, for example, was an evangelistic preacher for he was calling men to repentance, and on the Day of Pentecost, Peter's sermon was evangelistic. He did two things in that sermon – he convinced the multitudes that they were sinners, that they had with wicked hands crucified the Son of God, and when they came to see themselves as sinners, lost and condemned, Peter presented unto them the way of salvation through Christ. Three thousand of them believed his words and were baptized. Surely this was an evangelistic sermon, and, if we follow through the Acts of the Apostles, we will discover that not only

Philip, who was called an evangelist, but that the apostle and teachers as well were evangelistic preachers and were instrumental in bringing men into the Kingdom of God.

If we come down to the days of the reformers, we will find that men like Luther and Knox were evangelistic in their preaching, for they preached justification by faith. Coming down further in the history of the church, we see men like Rutherford and McCheyne, who were wonderfully gifted for edifying Christians, yet these men were great evangelists, for through them many were brought to a saving knowledge of the truth. Again, Chalmers, while he was a great philosopher and wonderful theologian, was also an evangelistic preacher, and the same could be said of Jonathan Edwards, under whose preaching men trembled and cried out, "What must we do to be saved?" Then, if we turn to Spurgeon, we will meet a man who was a preacher to preachers, and yet one of the greatest evangelists of the century, for his tabernacle was spoken of as a "soul trap," a place where many sinners were caught and brought out of the darkness of sin into the light of God.

Dr. John Hall, of New York, was also evangelistic, and presented the truth in as forcible and clear a manner as any evangelist ever did. On one occasion, when the audience were going out of the church on Fifth Avenue, a man was heard to say, "The old man gives a fellow no chance to dodge." In other words, Dr. Hall closed up every false way of escape with such thoroughness that the sinner could see no way of refuge, save in Christ.

The question now comes, are the ministers of this country and of this age doing the work of evangelists, and, if they are, how shall we account for over fifteen hundred congregations in one denomination reporting no additions to the church by profession of faith during the year, and over nineteen hundred in another denomination who could not say they had been instrumental in saving any during the twelve months of the year? This is a terrible state of affairs. Can it be that ministers are leaving the work of soul-saving to those who are called evangelists? The evangelist should be to the minister and congregation what the Sabbath School is to the home, or what it should be to the home. But if the Sabbath School takes the place of the home, it fails to accomplish its mission, and that is not the fault of the Sabbath School. If the evangelist is taking the place of the minister in his work as a soul-winner, he is not fulfilling his mission, and the fault is not his, but the minister's.

It may be that this is true to a certain extent, and that ministers do not look for or expect conversions except when they are having what are called "special meetings." The minister should expect conversions at every service where the unsaved are present. Do not let us blame the evangelists unless we are sure that they are to blame, and that we, as ministers, have done our duty in this respect. There is still a little bit of the old Adam left in us which leads us to roll the blame over on others, or try, like the young lawyer, to justify ourselves.

I hear a great deal of discussion in this country about the evening service. The question is, how are we to reach the people, and how are we to get them to come out to the evening service? I do not wonder that the evening congregations in many churches are very small when I see advertised the subjects upon which the ministers preach. So many of these subjects are sensational trash or semi-religious topics. Some ministers seem to think that if they are to draw a congregation, they must discuss some political or scientific subject, but they never made a greater mistake, for there is nothing that will draw an audience and interest an audience like the evangelistic truth contained in the Scriptures. A woman who was speaking to a minister concerning the crowds of people who went to hear him, said, "It must be the Lord who is bringing them, for it is not the singing, and I am sure it is not the preaching." It was rather a strange way of putting the case, and yet it was true, for singing will not fill an empty church, that is, the classic singing we hear so much about will not. It has been tried in this country and it has failed. There are churches which pay a great deal of money for singers, and yet the pews are not crowded, neither is it the preaching which will draw, apart from the truth of God, for we have many preachers who are bright scholars, cultured men, gifted and fluent speakers, and yet their churches are far from full.

On the other hand, there are churches where the ministers could not be called scholarly, or eloquent, and where the singing is not by any means classic, and yet they have large congregations; and men are being saved week after week because the Gospel is preached in sincerity, in simplicity, and with power.

I take it for granted that those who shall read these pages are anxious to be instrumental in bringing sinners to a knowledge of the Savior, and I shall now refer to what I consider a few essentials in the accomplishing of this. First of all, we must have power with men if we are to reach and win them, and in order to have this power we must be right with God. I believe that there are many ministers and Christian workers whose names are in the Book of Life, and yet have no power because there is something wrong in their lives. It is probable that Jacob was a child of God from the night when he first met the Lord at Bethel (Genesis 28:12-22), yet for twenty years, as far as we can gather, his life was powerless and fruitless. But when he met with the angel who changed his name from Jacob to Israel, he was informed that he would have power with men because he had power with God (Genesis 32:24-28); and that power made itself manifest on the following day, when the wrath of his brother, Esau, was turned away.

David was a man who had power with God and power with men, yet he lost that power through sin and, in Psalm 51, he prays for a restoration of the joy of salvation for cleansing (v. 12), and he adds that, as a result, sinners will be converted unto God (v. 13). It has pleased God to save sinners by what may be called the foolishness of preaching (1 Corinthians 1:21). God is reaching the unsaved through those already redeemed – through His Church, which is the one and only divine institution in the world. Men and women who have put their confidence in Him are the channels through which His salvation is to reach all who are outside the Kingdom of God, and, if there is anything wrong with that channel, to that extent the work of saving the world will be affected.

We may take an illustration to make this plainer. Suppose we have a great reservoir full of water on a hill and a city in the valley, and pipes connecting the reservoir with the homes of the people. The water which they receive from the reservoir will come through these pipes as the channels. Something may happen to the pipes, they may be frozen by the cold atmosphere surrounding them or they may become choked with sand or earth getting into them, but in either case the water will cease to flow and the inhabitants will suffer. The same may happen to those who are the channels conveying the love and forgiveness of God to the sinners who are unsaved. Christians may become so cold and so indifferent or they may become so engrossed with science or philosophy or the things of the world that they may cease to be the channels through which God's forgiveness will reach men, and as the water-pipes to which we have referred cannot thaw themselves nor cleanse themselves, neither can men who have got into this state restore themselves to a state of usefulness. The power to do this must come from without; and so we find David calling upon God to cleanse him and to stay him with His free spirit so that sinners might be converted (Psalms 51:12-13).

The first essential, then, is to see that we are right with God – that we are in perfect fellowship with Him – and then we can be the channels through which He can reach the ungodly and the sinful.

Another essential in this work is love. In speaking of the gifts which were given to men in 1 Corinthians 12, Paul exhorted them to choose the best gifts, and then he went on, in chapter 13, to show them the more excellent way. There he speaks of love as the greatest and most enduring of all the gifts, and without it, he says, a man is as sounding brass or tinkling cymbal (1 Corinthians 13:1) We will never reach men nor be instrumental in saving them unless we love them, and the more of Christ we have in our hearts, the more compassion we will have for the lost.

How many wonderful pictures of Christ are presented to us in the Gospels. At one time we see Him looking with compassion upon the multitudes because they are as sheep without a shepherd (Matthew 9:36), and at another time we see Him beholding the great city through His tears, and hear Him cry out, "'Jerusalem, Jerusalem, who kills the prophets and stones those who are sent to her! How often I wanted to gather your children together, the way a hen gathers her chicks under her wings, and you were unwilling" (Matthew 23:37). If we look at Paul, His greatest Apostle, we will see this same truth made manifest. Before his conversion, he hated men and consented to the stoning of Stephen (Acts 8:1). After his conversion, he said that his heart's desire and prayer to God for Israel was that they might be saved (Romans 10:1).

Though these very people were persecuting him, He could say with all his soul, "Grace be with all those who love our Lord Jesus Christ with incorruptible *love*" (Ephesians 6:24). But, in addition to this love for the saints, he had a passion for the souls of the lost. When our hearts become full of love to Christ, they will go out in compassion and in love to the lost sheep who have wandered from the fold and, like the faithful shepherd, we will be anxious to go after them, though the night be dark and though difficulties lie in the way. The work will be a pleasure if our hearts are in it and we will be anxious to bring back those who have gone astray, but without this love, the work of the minister is the greatest drudgery and the fruits will never be made manifest.

Another essential to success is obedience, and it is a proof of love, for Christ said, "'If you love Me, you will keep My commandments" (John 14:15). Now, I believe that some of us are failing in the work because we have not obeyed the voice of God in all things, and there is nothing that will take the place of obedience. If we go back to the history of the Old Testament, we shall discover that the failure of Saul was due to his disobeying the voice of the Lord. He had everything in his favor at the start, yet he made shipwreck of himself and of the nation, and we know, from Samuel's message to him, that all his failure was brought about through his disobeying the voice of the Lord. On the other hand, if we look at David, who seemingly had everything against him at the start, we see that he overcame all difficulties, gathered together the scattered fragments of the nation, established a throne so great and so glorious that the Son of God was spoken of as the Son of David, and the key to David's success we find in the prayer, "Make me know Your ways, O LORD" (Psalms 25:4). He had his failings and some of his sins were grievous, but all his strength and all the success he ever attained lay in his obedience to the voice of God.

Take as another example the prophet Jonah. He was commanded to go to Nineveh and preach to the people, but for reasons known to himself and only guessed at by us, he turned his back upon the great city and made for Tarshish. While in the path of disobedience, he was unhappy himself and brought sorrow to the sailors and great loss to those who had sent their merchandise on the vessel in which he took passage; but just as soon as he got into the path of obedience and went to the city as he was commanded, he was instrumental in bringing the whole city to repentance and in turning away the wrath of an angry God.

If we turn to Saul, or Paul, the greatest Apostle of New Testament times, we get the key to his wonderful success in the second question which he asked the Lord, when he said, "What wilt Thou have me to do?" (Acts 9:6). If we follow him all through his missionary journeys, we will see that his desire to obey the divine will makes itself manifest continually. If God tells him to leave Asia he will go, no matter what the result may be. If God tells him to enter into Europe, he will go, no matter what the difficulties may be which stand in the way. Like a faithful soldier, he was continually awaiting the command of his captain, and his delight was to obey.

If God sends any of us to a certain field, and if, for reasons known to ourselves, we refuse to go, we need not expect to be instrumental in saving the lost. God has a plan for every man and a field for every worker, and if we are where He wants us to be and are doing the work that He wants us to do, success will surely crown our efforts. To obey is better than sacrifice (1 Samuel 15:22) and, if we commit our ways to Him, He surely will direct our steps. If we are anxious to do His will, we will hear a voice saying, "This is the way, walk in it" (Is. 30:21). Whether the field be large or small, whether the work be popular or obscure, if we are in the place where He has put us, we can look to Him for the power and the help without which our efforts would be in vain.

Another essential for soul-saving is wisdom, or tact. When the Savior was sending His disciples out, He told them to be wise as serpents. In trying to reach men, we must know how to deal with them. Looking at some of the figures which our Savior used will help us to understand it more fully. He spoke of Himself as the physician and, in a certain sense, His disciples and followers are physicians for the healing of the souls of men. Now, it is not only necessary for a physician to understand the remedy, but he must also understand the patients and diseases for which these remedies are intended, because what would give healing to one might bring death to another, so he must make a diagnosis of the cases and treat the man accordingly. It is so in dealing with men spiritually; it is not enough for us to know the Word of God and to be thoroughly acquainted with its doctrines, but we must know something of the spiritual condition of the people with whom we are dealing. Understand, there is no use talking to a man who has had no sense of sin about the salvation from sin. He does not want a Savior because he has never felt his need. We often err by bringing men to Mt. Calvary who have never seen Mt. Sinai. The first thing to do with a man who has never seen himself as a sinner is to convince him, by the use of God's Word, that he is lost, and then salvation will have some meaning for him, or, when we have a man who is being crushed through a sense of his sins and who is almost in despair, it would not do to bring that man the passages of scripture that speak about the wrath of God. We must reveal to him the remedy and show him God as a refuge for those who are in trouble.

Then we are spoken of as "fishers of men" (Matthew 4:19) and, if the figure means anything, it means that wisdom and skill are necessary to accomplish this work. A fisherman must in some way come in contact with the fish before he can catch them. He must go to where they are, or else get them to come where he is. He must study their ways so as to know how best to catch them. There are two kinds of fishermen who never catch any fish – one class takes nothing with them but the hook, and the fish look at it and pass on, and another class takes no hook, but a considerable amount of bait. As a general thing, the latter have a large following. The fish enjoy and appreciate such men; they swallow their bait and go their way, and the fisherman congratulates himself upon seeing so many fish in the clear stream that go after his bait, but he has not made a catch. How often this is done by ministers! Some present the truth in such a bald, bare way that men keep clear of them. Others give the people nothing but bait: stories, anecdotes, and a lot of stuff that people seem to be pleased with, but there is no divine hook, and the preacher fails to save men. The true method is to have the hook and the bait, to be all things to all men (1 Corinthians 9:22), like the Apostle Paul, that we may gain some. It is true that the wise fisherman, having everything that is necessary, may fail to catch all the fish in the stream, and it is just as true that the wise or faithful minister may fail to reach all the unsaved in the community, but surely it is equally true that as the fisherman cannot catch any fish without complying with certain laws and fulfilling certain conditions, neither can the minister reach men if he violates the laws according to which the Spirit of God works in the conviction and salvation of men. God has promised wisdom to those who ask, and if we are wise to win souls the reward will be glorious, for we shall shine "like the stars forever and ever" (Daniel 12:3).

Another essential in this work is realizing the value of a soul and what it means for a soul to be saved or to be lost. Our Savior informed us that there is joy in the presence of the angels of God over one sinner who repents (Luke 15:10). This joy is not among the angels but in their presence, and it must mean that the joy is in the Father's heart, as the joy was in the shepherd's heart when he found the sheep (Luke 15:4-7), in the woman's heart when she found the coin (Luke 15:8-10), and in the father's heart when the lost son was found (Luke 15:11-24). God doesn't rejoice over trifles, and we see the other side of this when we look at the tears of Christ over the doomed city and we may rest assured that Christ never wept over trifles. We have God the Father rejoicing over a sinner being saved, we have God the Son weeping over sinners who are perishing, we have God giving His Son to save sinners, and we have Christ bearing the agony of Gethsemane and the shame of Calvary that the lost might be saved. Surely this ought to convince us of the value of a soul in the sight of God, and if once we realize this, we shall then have a passion for souls, but we shall never be satisfied with our efforts so long as the unsaved are around us or in our congregations. This thought will help us in preparing our sermons; it will help us in delivering the sermons; it will give us a goal to strive after; it will enable us to reach the highest and truest result – the bringing of these men to the feet of the Savior.

Now, a word about methods. I have tried as a pastor to do the work of an evangelist for fourteen years in one congregation. As a general rule, the morning sermons were more for building up Christians, and the evening sermons were intended to reach sinners. Of course there were exceptions, because there are the unsaved who come to the morning services, and there are many Christians who come to the evening services, and this has to be taken into account, but, as a general rule, I think it is well to have most of the preaching in the morning for the Christians, and most of the preaching in the evening with a view to reaching the unsaved. I have never resorted to any sensational methods, never advertised subjects, but preached the Gospel in its simplicity as I knew it and as I believed it, and those in connection with the church to which I refer would bear me testimony that during the fourteenth year of my ministry the audiences were larger, and more people were unable to gain admittance to the evening services during that winter than ever before. During these years, 2,750 people united with that congregation, of which number 1,449 united by profession of faith, and a large number, during these years, who were converted at the regular services, united with other churches. This was the regular work of a minister who at the same time was trying to do the work of an evangelist.

I have been frequently told that methods which are successful in Toronto might not be successful in other cities, but I have tried the same style of preaching in the city of Boston in the month of August and in the month of January, with the same results which I had in Toronto, and at the present time I am trying the same methods in the city of Philadelphia, with the same results which I had in Toronto. I make this personal reference for the purpose of showing that I am not talking theory, but in this chapter I'm speaking of things about which I know.

When a student at college, I believed in the power of the Gospel to attract men and to save men. I went out of college more than fourteen years ago into the ministry, and I am now more thoroughly convinced than ever that the Gospel is the power of God unto salvation. If it is presented in sincerity and in simplicity it will interest the people, and it is our business as ministers not only to study the Word of God, but to prepare and to deliver our sermons in such a way that people will be interested and that sinners will be saved. I fully realize the meaning of what our Lord said to the disciples in the fifteenth chapter of John, "… apart from Me you can do nothing" (John 15:5), but I am sure that if we are doing our best in His name and in His cause that He will own our efforts.

The question now comes, are we doing our best, or are we offering to Him our second best? Are we resting satisfied if the finances and other things in connection with the congregation are satisfactory, while all around us the souls of men are dying and the Master is calling for us, not only to build up His people in faith, but to do the work of an evangelist? Surely, if He died that men might be saved, we should put forth every effort to make known unto men the way of life through the crucified, risen, and exalted Redeemer.

Chapter 5

Organizing for Revival Work

Len G. Broughton

To have a successful revival in any community, whether city, village, or country, there is needed a certain amount of organization. The fact is, nothing goes well today without organization. I once knew a man who represented his district in Congress four consecutive sessions, and never had any kind of organization and never made a speech in the district. He simply would announce himself a candidate, and that was the end of it so far as his work was concerned. But this was a long time ago. In that same district today, if that man desired to go to Congress he would have to organize his forces into one large club, and it would be divided into smaller clubs, and they would split up into still smaller bands, and these divide up into personal workers. This would be necessary to find every voter in the district. I saw a statement some years ago to the effect that during one presidential campaign there could not be found a single doubtful voter who had not been seen by somebody with reference to his vote. What thorough organization these politicians have! And what a lesson the church today ought to get from studying their methods. Jesus Christ himself was a man of organization. He had His disciples and then divided them up and sent them out two by two.

Not long after I entered the ministry, I went to a certain town to hold a series of meetings. It was one of those good old Southern towns, the inhabitants of which banked on aristocracy and fed their souls upon the glory of departed days. Sadly, they had never known what it was to be spiritually warm. The first night I was there, I preached to a large audience. That was in my early ministry, when I made many propositions. The first one I made that night was for anyone to stand who wanted prayers offered for his friends. As soon as I made it, a boy got up and walked out into the aisle, where he stood looking me square in the face. I said, "God bless you, little man!" and he sat down. I then asked anyone who wanted the prayers of God's people to rise. That boy got up in the aisle again and looked me in the face, and again I said, "God bless you!" I asked if there was anybody present who was willing to accept Jesus. That boy stood up again and looked me in the face, and again I said, "God bless you!" Nobody else stood up that night, and I began to think I had struck the hardest and coldest crowd I had ever run up against.

The next night I preached as hard as I knew how to sinners and, when I finished, I asked anybody who wanted to be prayed for to stand up. That same little rascal popped out into the aisle as he had done the night before and stood looking at me till I saw him, and said, "God bless you!" I thought I'd vary the thing a little, so I asked if anybody present was willing to come forward and give me his hand as an indication that he would accept Jesus. That same boy came shuffling out of his seat, straight down the aisle, and gave me his hand. I saw smiles on the faces of some in the congregation. Nobody but the boy showed any interest, and I went off somewhat disheartened. The third night I preached, and when I asked all who wanted prayer to rise, that boy popped out into the aisle. The people had begun to regard it as a joke, and they nudged each other with their elbows, while a broad smile flared from one side of the house to the other. When I asked anyone who was willing to accept Jesus to come and give me his hand, that boy came, and the congregation smiled broader than before, and some actually tittered. After the meeting, the deacons came to me and told me that the boy must be stopped, as he was mentally challenged, and was throwing a damper on the meeting. I said "Stop nothing! How are you going to throw a damper on an ice-house?"

For the whole of that week, the boy was the only person in the house who showed any interest in the meeting. Then he wanted to join the church. The pastor was absent, and I was to open the doors of the church. I said, "Look here, brethren, I want to take this responsibility on my hands. I'm going to put that boy on you, and if you choose to reject him, his blood be on your hands." At the conclusion of the morning service, I invited all who desired to unite with the church to come forward. That boy came. I asked him if he had accepted Christ for his personal Savior. That's all I ever ask. He said he had. "Brethren," said I, "you hear what this boy has to say. What will you do with him?" An ominous silence fell on the congregation. After a time, from way back by the door, I heard a muffled and rather surly, "I move he be received." Another painful silence followed, and then from the middle of the church I heard a muffled, "I second the motion." When I put the motion, about half a dozen members voted "Aye" in a tone so low that it seemed as if they were scared. I gave the boy the right hand of Christian welcome awaiting baptism, and then dismissed the congregation.

The next day the boy went out to see his old grandfather, a man whose whitened head was blossoming for the grave, and whose feet were taking hold upon the shifting sands of eternity. "Grandfather," said he, "won't you go to church with me tonight and hear that preacher?" We always feel kindly towards those who are afflicted, you know, and we are willing to please them, so the old man agreed to go.

That night I saw the boy and the old man sitting away back near the door. When the sermon was finished, one of the members of the church arose and said, "I have a request to make. We have with us tonight Mr. Blank, one of the oldest and most respected citizens, but he is out of Christ. I want special prayer offered for this, my special friend." With that he laid his hand upon the head of the old man, down whose furrowed cheeks the tears were streaming. The next night I saw the old man sitting halfway down the aisle. When all who wanted to accept Jesus were invited to come forward and give me their hand, I saw the mentally challenged boy coming down the aisle leading the old man by the hand.

That little boy's father kept a saloon. The following day the child went there, and climbing up over the high counter, he peeped down upon his father and said, "Papa, won't you go to church with me to-night to hear that preacher?"

"You get out of here, child. Go out of here," said the father. "Don't you know you mustn't come in here?"

Strange, so strange, how fathers will keep places into which their children cannot go!

"But, papa," continued the boy, "won't you go to church with me tonight?"

"Yes, I'll go, but you get out of here."

That night the man came with the mentally challenged boy and sat about where the old man had sat the night before. When I asked all who would accept Christ to come forward, he walked down the aisle and gave me his hand. He asked if he could make a statement, and when I said "Yes," he faced the congregation and said, "My friends, you all know me, and I want to say that so long as I live I will never sell another drop of whiskey, for I have given my heart to God tonight, and from this day forward I propose to serve Him." The meeting warmed up at last, the town was largely won for God, every saloonkeeper was converted, and every saloon for seven miles in the country was closed and the keeper was converted to God. This experience taught me a valuable lesson at the very beginning of my ministry, and I thank God for every blessing that has come to me through the exercise of it till this day.

How Shall We Organize?

Of course, every man has his method and every community will have to vary according to the local conditions. But, generally speaking, I would insist first of all upon at least a week of united prayer on the part of the church or the general movement which may be made up of any number of churches. Let the burden of the prayer be for the enduement of power for the workers, and guidance of the Holy Spirit in the details of the work. I would suggest at these meetings of prayer that special Bible studies directed to the deepening of the spiritual life of the Christians, the salvation of the souls of the unsaved, and the Holy Spirit's work be given.

After this week of prayer on the part of the church or the group of churches, let the church or general movement appoint a general committee, making it large enough to meet the emergency and yet not so large as to be cumbersome. This committee is to carry on for a week a series of cottage prayer-meetings. This can be done in country districts almost as easily as in cities or villages. By this committee, the territory is to be divided and a superintendent appointed for each division. Then he will group around him a certain number of men and women who will agree to stand by the meetings, from house to house, rain or shine. The homes of the rich as well as of the poor are to be taken in and every section at all in touch with the church or churches should be covered in this way. At these cottage meetings, not only should there be Bible-study along the lines already suggested for the week of prayer by the church or churches, and not only prayer for the work and the workers, but a carefully prepared list of the unsaved and the backsliders and all lukewarm Christians should be taken. At the close of this week of prayer, which will be seen to have been also a week of the very best advertisement and of gathering statistics concerning the very matter that is desired in the meeting which is to be held, these names, taken by these workers in their respective meetings throughout the various sections of the community, are to be turned over to the chairman of the cottage meetings who will carefully arrange them to be used by the workers when the meeting proper has begun.

The Revival Starts

Now, then, when this preparation has been made, we will suppose the meeting to begin on Sunday. At the first general service of the meeting, the preacher or evangelist in charge would find it greatly to the advantage of the meeting to have an after-meeting for the purpose of conferring with and further organizing the workers. The pastor or pastors connected with the work should then appoint as many special personal workers, both men and women, as will be needed to thoroughly look after the work in the church or place where the meeting is held. Of course, those who have already been in the organization would do good work in this capacity. What he wants is workers whose sympathies are thoroughly enlisted and who are filled with the Spirit.

I would say in an ordinary church meeting there should be from fifty to a hundred men, and the same number of women, appointed to do this work. A chairman is to be selected for each group. They are then to be assigned to their places throughout the audience. Try as far as possible to put them within ten feet of each other. The chairmen of these groups will of course be expected to keep the number up to the point of necessity. If more are needed, they must find more. If some drop out, others must take their places. These men and women are expected to bring their Bibles and are to be given instructions as to how to use them in pointing the unsaved to Christ. After the sermon, when an effort is made to reach the unsaved, these workers, thus arranged, are able to begin doing personal work at once. When someone stands up or comes forward confessing Jesus, they are in close enough touch to reach him and give him a handshake and a hearty, "God bless you!," furnish him with a card, obtain his name and address, and perhaps his church preference.

Thus organized, the meeting will always move with smoothness from start to finish. Meanwhile, the list of names of the unsaved and lukewarm is being looked after by the chairman of the cottage committee, and these cottage workers who obtained them are of course expected to see to it that those obtained by them come to church and are reached if possible.

Objections Answered

Now, in this connection, it seems to me to be proper to give the workers a list of objections that they will most assuredly meet with in doing their personal work. The following arrangement, which I invariably use in meetings, will be found very helpful.

1. *"I'm not such a sinner."*

> Romans 3:23 – "… for all have sinned and fall short of the glory of God"
>
> 1 John 1:8 – "If we say that we have no sin, we are deceiving ourselves and the truth is not in us."
>
> John 3:18 – "He who believes in Him is not judged; he who does not believe has been judged already, because he has not believed in the name of the only begotten Son of God."

2. *"I'm not good enough."*

> Mark 2:17 – "And hearing this, Jesus said to them, "It is not those who are healthy who need a physician, but those who are sick; I did not come to call the righteous, but sinners."

3. *"I've got too much to give up."*

> Matthew 16:25 – "For whoever wishes to save his life will lose it; but whoever loses his life for My sake will find it."

4. *"I see too much inconsistency in others."*

> Luke 13:3 – "I tell you, no, but unless you repent, you will all likewise perish."
>
> Romans 14:12 – "So then each one of us will give an account of himself to God."

5. *"I can't hold out."*

> Romans 8:38-39 – "For I am convinced that neither death, nor life, nor angels, nor principalities, nor things present, nor things to come, nor powers, nor height, nor depth, nor

any other created thing, will be able to separate us from the love of God, which is in Christ Jesus our Lord."

6. *"I'm afraid He won't save me."*

Revelation 22:17 – "The Spirit and the bride say, 'Come.' And let the one who hears say, 'Come.' And let the one who is thirsty come; let the one who wishes take the water of life without cost."

7. *"There's time enough yet."*

Proverbs 27:1 – "Do not boast about tomorrow, for you do not know what a day may bring forth.

Closing Up the Meeting

In closing up the meeting, there is nothing that I know of that will be so helpful to Christian workers, and, indeed, to all concerned, as a sort of spiritual love-feast, a meeting of testimony. The workers who have been blessed in the meeting will readily respond, many who have been saved will be glad to testify, and the church or group of churches conducting the work will find themselves greatly uplifted and all ready to settle down to the business of training and developing themselves into still further usefulness.

Singing

I have said nothing about the music. This is no small part of a revival. There is nothing that equals spiritual, devotional singing. I would always have, if possible, a chorus choir, and secure the very best leader possible. If I could not get a good soloist and congregational leader combined, I would do without the solo, although where this combination can be found, a good devotional solo now and then will be found very, very helpful. There should always be plenty of songbooks or card-slips, which can easily be prepared for the occasion, and everybody should be urged to take part in the singing.

Christian Literature

I have also found that it works well in a meeting of this character for the church or churches engaging in the work to provide a good selection of Christian literature. Such books as are furnished by the Colportage Library Association will be found exceedingly helpful, not only to the meeting while it is in progress, but to the good of the work when the meeting is over. These books are very cheap, and people can easily be induced to buy them. Let them be sold practically at cost, or make the usual profit and let the money go to some definite work of charity in the community or to the general expenses of the revival movement. It is not the money that we are trying to make; it is the good we want to establish in a permanent way by Christian literature.

Chapter 6

The Sunday-School Teacher as a Soul-Winner

M. Lawrance

The government has two ways of saving life on the ocean. One takes a number of men who are planted in a certain place and told, "You are to conduct a life-saving station." They have all the apparatus for that sort of work, but they must wait until the ships are on the rocks, until the men are struggling in the water for their lives, before they can send men out to save them.

Then the government has another way – the lighthouse. It plants this house and says to someone, "You live in this house, and before the ships get onto the rocks, you warn them off and show them from the place of danger into a place of safety." The rescue-mission work that these dear brothers are giving their lives for is the life-saving station, but the Sunday School is trying to save life by the *lighthouse* plan rather than the *life-boat* plan. We are trying to keep these boys and girls off the rocks.

I was in Pacific Garden Mission not long ago, and saw a bleary-eyed, drunken man come staggering in, and I knew that that man had once been an innocent little boy. In the Jerry McAuley Mission, where I spent an evening a while ago, I saw a woman in the same condition and I knew she had once been an innocent little girl. Our work is for the boys and girls, and your hearts are all interested in these. I was sitting one day with Mr. Wannamaker, and he said, "We have the best end of it. When you save a man or a woman, you save a unit, but when you save a boy or a girl you save a whole multiplication table." It is a great thing to save a soul at any age, but it is the greatest thing to save a soul, plus a life. The child is the center of the world. That little child Jesus put in the midst has been in the midst ever since, and the world revolves around it. The little child is king and queen. We are glad to do the bidding of the baby. I have known of people walking the floor all night because the baby wanted it that way. Some time ago there was a little child lost in New York City in Central Park, and the papers were full of it. A short time after that, the child was found and the papers came out in great headlines announcing the finding. In a few months, there was a great battle, the battle of Santiago where many precious lives were lost, and the papers again came out in great headlines announcing that, but there were more newspapers sold in New York when they announced the finding of that child than there were at the time of the battle of Santiago. Everyone is not interested in war, but everyone is interested in a little child.

There are 25,000,000 in the Sunday School army, and it is a wonderful power. Out of all the people that join our churches by conversion, 83 percent come out of the Sunday School. Dr. John Watson was dining in this country once, and was asked, "What is it, in your judgment as a foreigner, that does most to make America great among the nations of the earth?" He said, "It is the Sunday School."

I am to talk to you about the teacher. I know you are all either teachers or interested in Sunday School work. I want to talk practically along the line of the teacher's work. The office of teacher is a divine office. Jesus chose to be a teacher because He thought it the most important business in the world. His last command, in Mark 16:15, was a command to you and to me to go and teach, and that command is on every man and woman, everyone that has the ability to teach and the opportunity to teach. I believe, as a superintendent, that the teacher is the most important factor in any Sunday School. The teachers really do the work for which the Sunday School is held. I know of no place on the footstool so fraught with opportunity and responsibility as to stand with the open Bible before a class of children and try to bring them to the Savior. Daniel 12:3 reads, "And they that be wise shall shine as the brightness of the firmament; and they that turn many to righteousness as the stars for ever and ever" (KJV). If you will take a reference Bible, you will see that the word translated "wise" may with equal correctness be translated "teachers." In Proverbs 11:30, we read,

> "The fruit of the righteous is a tree of life,
> And he who is wise wins souls."

Knowledge is how much we know; wisdom is the use we make of it. The purpose of all teaching is primarily instruction; in Christian work, it is primarily for edification and salvation.

I want to speak very briefly of the use of the Bible. This is a very much neglected part of our work. We try to teach too much without the Word of God. The Word of God has its mission and place and it should be used. Psalms 119:130 reads, "The unfolding of Your words gives light." God wants the darkness of the world driven away, and there is only one way to get darkness out, and that is the very way the janitor drove the darkness out of this room tonight – by putting in the light – and this is the only way to drive sin out of the world. The Word of God is the light.

> "Your word is a lamp to my feet
> And a light to my path" (Psalms 119:105).

When God wants anything done, He has an agency to do it.

> "'For as the rain and the snow come down from heaven,
> And do not return there without watering the earth
> And making it bear and sprout,
> And furnishing seed to the sower and bread to the eater;
> So will My word be which goes forth from My mouth;
> It will not return to Me empty,
> Without accomplishing what I desire,
> And without succeeding *in the matter* for which I sent it"
> (Is. 55:10-11).

If God wants the earth watered, He has a way. If He wants the earth saved, He has a way. Take the Bible into your Sunday School work, into the teaching of your lesson.

Let us look a little further at the teacher's work, and what kind of work we do as teachers. We need the teacher and the teacher must be a living teacher; we want the living teacher. That was what God meant when He took Philip away from the promising work in Samaria and led him away down that desert road and pointed out to him the eunuch. The eunuch was reading the Word, but he needed the touch of the living heart. We need the teacher, and so we must have some qualifications and some helps for our teachers. First of all, I would like to name some of these. We must prepare. It is not a general preparation that is needed, but specific study. Prepare early. If you begin in the early part of the week to prepare your lesson for the coming Sunday, then all through the week you are looking at everything through your Sunday School spectacles. The very best illustrations are those that come from your own observation and reading and interaction with your friends. I heard one the other day that I thought was really good. It was not intended as an illustration, but I used it. One time a young lady was presented with a book by an older lady friend. The young lady took the book home and tried to read it, but found it so dry she gave it up. She said to herself, "I wonder why my friend gave me such a dry book." The next day she saw this friend, and was so afraid that she would ask her if she had read the book that she was very uncomfortable while in her presence, and made up her mind she would go home and read that book even if it was dry. So she tried again, and again she was compelled to give it up. Three times she tried, and then laid the book away. Sometime after, she met a young man in whom she became very much interested. He became interested in her, too, and in due time they became engaged. Shortly after this, she happened to pick up this book and noticed that the name of the author was the same as that of her lover. The next time he came to see her she said, "I have a book here which has your name in it, initials and all." He blushingly acknowledged himself to be the author. That night she sat up all night to read it and wondered why she had ever seen a dry line in it. What was the difference? *Why, she was in love with the author.* It is the same way with the Bible. Who loves God's book and who does not? When do we love God's book and when do we not?

Prepare more than you expect to teach. You cannot teach all you know and teach with power. Another thought: Prepare from the Bible. I think the Bible is the best commentary in the whole world. I have seen some commentaries upon which I think the Bible would throw a great deal of light. We want more of the Scripture in our Sunday School teaching.

I believe in lesson helps, but I do not believe they ought to take the place of original Bible study. At the world's Sunday School Convention in London, I heard Richard Glover give three rules for the use of helps: (1) Use lesson helps, but don't depend solely on lesson helps, (2) Use them with the Bible, and not apart from the Bible, and (3) those lesson helps are the best helps which *set* you to thinking and not *save* you from thinking.

We need to study methods of presenting the lessons, and we need to study the scholars. It pays to stop and get the tools in order. The following illustration was once given me. A man was shoveling sticky clay. Beside him he had a pail of water. He would dip his shovel into the water, and then into the clay, then go back and dip it into the water, and then into the clay, and it took him just as long to keep his shovel in condition to do the work as it did to do the work. But did the man who hired him complain? No, indeed! For if he had not taken the time to keep his shovel in the proper condition, it would soon have been so covered with the clay as to be useless for the work which he was hired to perform. It is always best to take time to keep the tools in order and so we need to study methods and principles of teaching.

The essential conditions of a good teacher are regularity of attendance, punctuality, and cheerfulness. There is mighty little religion in a whine. We need more of the gospel of a shining face and an open hand. Mr. Reynolds once told me of a man in his Sunday School who did not have the ability to teach, but he used to stand in the door and shake hands with everyone who went in or out, and Mr. Reynolds said that man shook more boys and girls into the kingdom of heaven than any of his teachers taught in. There is power in a smile. A little boy once said: "Please, Mister Superintendent, let me go over to that class where the teacher smiles so much."

In the twenty-second verse of the ninth chapter of 1 Corinthians, Paul said, "I have become all things to all men, so that I may by all means save some." The successful teacher adapts himself to the situation. That is tact. This business takes tact. It does not do to ask a man if he is saved when he is running to make a train. You must know the persons in your class and adapt yourself to the disposition and need of each.

A teacher, to be a success, must have beyond his teaching the spiritual life. For, after all, it is what the teacher *is* that really tells. Emerson said, "How can I hear the words you *say*, when what you *are* is thundering in my ears." One boy said to another, "I don't take any stock in my teacher anymore." "Why?" said the other. "Because when you add him up there is nothing to carry." Teachers, you are more than instructors. You want to be what you seek to have your scholar become, and a good lesson is absolutely spoiled by a bad life. The Gospel gets into a man's heart not so much by words as by wedges.

A man told this story of his conversion. He said, "I was a gambler, and I went into Pacific Garden Mission one night and heard a man testify who said, 'Jesus Christ saved me, and I was a gambler.' The next night I went again, the same man got up and said, 'Jesus Christ saved me, and I was a gambler.' I listened to that testimony for six straight weeks, forty-two nights in succession, and I made up my mind if that story was true for six weeks it was true for me, and I was saved." It is what we are that tells the story.

Look for results. Would it be a surprise to you if a dozen of your scholars should come to you and say, "What shall I do to be saved?" One of Mr. Spurgeon's students went to him and said, "I am discouraged, I don't see any results from my work." Mr. Spurgeon said: "You don't expect to see results coming along all the time, do you?" "Why, certainly not." "Well, that is the reason you don't have them."

But do not be discouraged if you do not see results. Some will say, "I have taught, and I have not seen my girls saved." It does not say, "Be thou successful," but, "Be faithful" (Revelation 2:10). Some folks seem to be such good seed-sowers that God lets them do the sowing and someone else do the reaping. A dear Christian man who had been teaching a class of boys for some time was about to go out into the next world. He called his wife to him, and spoke of his boys, and said, "Oh, not one of my boys has been saved!" She comforted him by telling him that he had been faithful. When that man's body was laying in the casket, those boys came and dropped bitter tears upon it, and shortly after every one of them gave his heart to Christ.

The Christian world had prayed and prayed for a single woman to go away to the cannibal islands to be a missionary. Finally, Harriet Newell volunteered to go. Much money was spent on her training. They had a great jubilee meeting in New York City when she started. There was great rejoicing. But before the ship landed on those islands, she died. The letter that came back with the sad news brought sorrow and disappointment to the Christian world. But that letter had not been on American soil three months when fifty young women were ready to go. Harriet Newell's life was a magnificent success, though she never did one moment's work in her chosen field. Fidelity is success.

Do personal work if you want to be successful. I have had teachers come to me and say, "I have only one scholar in my class today. Don't you think I had better let him go in some other class, and I will go home?" On nineteen different occasions, Jesus sat down and taught one scholar. Our scholars are not won by classes, but one by one. It is hand-picked fruit we want. Andrew is only mentioned separately three times in the Bible, but one time it is said he brought in his brother Peter, and do you know, it seems to me that Andrew will get a whole lot of stars in his crown for the three thousand souls Peter won on the day of Pentecost.

One time in Toledo, there came a knock at my door, just as we were sitting down to breakfast. I opened the door, and there stood a young man seventeen years of age. He said, "You did not feel very much encouraged over the work in Sunday School yesterday. I want to tell you that it was your words that led me to Christ." That boy is Tracy McGregor, now superintendent of the McGregor Helping Hand Mission in Detroit. I believe it was the best day's work I ever did, and I don't know when I spoke the word.

Love is the hammer that breaks the heart. Our scholars are drawn by the power of love. Love will do what nothing else will do. These boys and girls want to know right away that we love them and are interested in them. My daughter teaches a class of little girls. One morning there was a knock at the door and when Louise went to the door, there stood one of the little girls in her class crying most piteously. When Louise put her arms around her and asked her what the trouble was, she said, "My little baby brother died last night, and I wanted to tell you and have you cry with me." That scholar knew the teacher loved her. Love is the hammer that breaks the stony heart.

Decision-Day in the Sunday School

A mistake which many Sunday School teachers make is that of trying to develop the fruit of the Spirit from an unregenerate life. They teach their scholars to love one another, to be joyful, patient, and unselfish before they have been converted. They might as well hang oranges on a Christmas tree and expect it to bear that kind of fruit. The fact is, one cannot evolve the fruit of the Spirit from a life in which there is no Holy Spirit.

I have a friend who has fifty greenhouses and about five acres under glass. A large part of his business is the culture of roses. He imports the wild rose stock from Ireland and France, and buds or grafts it with scions from the choice roses which he wishes to produce. It requires two men several months to do the budding. Now this florist is not foolish enough to put the wild stock into the green-houses and spend thousands of dollars in cultivating it. If he did, the result would be only wild Irish roses which would not sell for ten cents a thousand. On the contrary, the first thing he does is to insert a new life in the wild stock. Then he puts it in the greenhouse and applies all the methods known to modern science, and the result is those elegant Marechai Niel and General Jacque roses which sell for several dollars a hundred.

Many a teacher is trying to evolve the fruit of the Spirit from a life in which there is no Holy Spirit, because the scholar has never either consciously or unconsciously accepted Christ as his Savior. The first thing to aim at is conversion and, after that, what might be called Christian culture may properly follow.

The attention of the writer was called to the value of Decision Day in the following way. He was spending a Sunday in a Presbyterian church, and was asked to address the Sunday School. He suggested to the pastor that as it was the last Sunday in the year it might be well to explain to the boys and girls just how to become a Christian, with the idea of leading them to begin the new year with a new life. The result was that twenty-five or thirty accepted Christ as their Savior. Apparently, they were just waiting for an opportunity.

The next Sunday he was in another city, in a Baptist church. When asked to speak to the school, he told the superintendent what occurred the Sunday before, and was urged to use the same method. He did so, and quite a number of conversions followed. So much interest was awakened that they wished to continue the services through the week. The next Sunday he was in a Congregational church and had a similar experience. In this place, the officers of the school were so surprised at the results that they tried the plan themselves the following Sunday and had several more conversions. They then planned for a series of meetings in which some of the worst men in town were converted, and out of which grew a Men's Band and a Gospel Mission.

The experience of these three Sundays in churches of different denominations, in both city and country schools, led me to realize the importance of giving young people a definite opportunity to accept Christ. I said to myself, doubtless there are thousands of schools in the land which are in precisely the same condition that these were. They have had faithful preaching and teaching, but for some reason there has been no effort to gather in the harvest which years of seed-sowing should have produced. Since then I have seen the same method employed in scores of schools, and I can hardly recall an instance in which conversions have not occurred.

Mr. Moody often said that what led him to give up business and devote all his time to Christian work was an experience which he had with one of his Sunday school teachers. This teacher was taken seriously ill and was obliged to leave the city. He came to see Mr. Moody and expressed great sorrow at leaving his class of young women, since none of them were Christians. Mr. Moody proposed to him to take a carriage and go and visit each of them and tell them just how he felt. He did so, and the result was that every one of those young ladies gave her heart to God. Mr. Moody, who went with him, was so impressed with the possibilities of definite hand-to-hand work in winning souls that he resolved to devote his whole time to it.

In the State of Iowa, the fourth day of February, 1900, was observed as Decision Day. The reports were incomplete, but the 172 schools which did send in returns reported 3,476 conversions, including three Sunday School teachers. This was an average of over twenty for each school. In their report, they said nothing has ever so stirred the teachers and revealed to them the possibility of winning souls. In Philadelphia not long ago, about three hundred schools observed the day, with the result that about five thousand young people decided for Christ. Over two hundred entered the new life in one school alone. In another city, I know of a class in which fifty-five young ladies accepted Christ on a single day as the result of an earnest plea by one who taught the class for that day only.

Method

1. Announce to the school some weeks in advance that a Decision Sunday will soon be observed, not stating, however, which Sunday it will be. This will set the scholars thinking and, very likely, will lead to decisions before the day arrives. It will also increase the prayerfulness of parents and teachers and those scholars who are Christians already.

2. On the evening before, let all the teachers be called together for special prayer and conference. Let the pastor explain precisely what is involved in becoming a Christian and just what steps to pursue in leading a soul to Christ. Many a teacher has no idea how to go about it. Let each teacher have a list of all the unconverted members of his class, and let each one be prayed for by name, taking one class after another. Then let all unite in earnest prayer for a special anointing of the Spirit

to fit them for the work of the coming day, and let no one leave the place until assured of it (1 John 5:14-15).

3. When the day arrives, let the pastor preach a sermon which will prepare the way for the service which is to follow. When the school is in session, let the attendance be marked and the offering taken at the very outset, so as to have nothing to distract attention from the main object. It would be better to dispense with library books altogether for that Sunday. Let the superintendent announce that the lesson study will be omitted for today as there is more important business, and then state what the object of the meeting is and in a tender, loving way show how anxious he is that every unsaved member of the school should decide for Christ that very hour.

Select hymns which are personal and persuasive, such as, *"There is a Green Hill Far Away," "Almost Persuaded," "Just as I Am,"* etc. Arrange for several prayers by the most spiritual teachers. Then let an address be given by the pastor or whoever seems best qualified to do it. In this address, I would especially emphasize three things. First, the fact that all have sinned against God; second, the suffering which Christ endured for our sins, and our debt of gratitude to Him; third, explain very clearly just what one needs to do in order to become a Christian.

For the sake of those who have had no experience in such a service, we give an outline sketch of one which has been found useful.

Suppose you ask the scholars how many of them have ever seen a flock of sheep. Then remind them that although sheep are very tame and docile, they are also quite stubborn and willful; they like their own way. Furthermore, they are great imitators. If one of the flock jumps over the wall, all the rest will go tumbling after it, and you cannot stop them. You may catch them by the head or the heels, but they will go, and you will go too, unless you let go.

Now, God says that we are very much like sheep – we are determined to have our own way. In Isaiah 53:6, He says, "All of us like sheep have gone astray"; and in the next sentence He explains what He means by going astray: "Each of us has turned to his own way." That is the real essence of sin – that the sinner is determined to have his own way. It may not be a dishonest way, or an immoral way, or an untruthful way. It may not be nearly so bad as someone's else way, but it is *his* way, and not God's way.

What do we say of a sheep that has gone astray? Why, we say it is lost. Yes, and that is what God says about those who have had their own way and refused to walk in His way. They are lost, and that applies to all of us, doesn't it? For we have all had our own way. Adam was a kind of black sheep who jumped over the wall, and the whole race has gone tumbling after him.

However, there has been just one person who did not have His own way, but always walked in God's way. Who can tell who that person was? Jesus. Yes, Jesus, the Lamb of God.

Suppose you had a flock of sheep and wished to drive them in a certain direction, but they all ran off another way, except one good lamb who stayed by your side. You would not take a whip and punish that innocent lamb instead of those which ran away. And yet, do you know something almost like that has occurred in your case and mine? God has allowed His Son Jesus, the only innocent Lamb in the whole flock, to suffer for the sins of all the rest of us who went astray.

> "All of us like sheep have gone astray,
> Each of us has turned to his own way;
> But the LORD has caused the iniquity of us all To fall on Him" (Is. 53:6).

> He is the Lamb of God who taketh away the sin of the world (John 1:29).

Then I would turn to the twenty-seventh chapter of Matthew and show what Jesus suffered for our sins. I would paint that picture, if possible, so that they would remember it to their dying day. Show how the soldiers stripped Him and put a scarlet robe on Him as if He were a king. One of them said, "A king ought to have a golden scepter," and another ran out and brought in a piece of reed and placed it in His hand. "What else does He need?" "A crown, of course. Who ever heard of a king without a crown?" "Surely, I will get one," said another, and he ran out and broke off a piece of thorn bush, twisted it up in the form of a crown, and brought it in and placed it on the head of Jesus. Now, the king has a royal robe and a crown and a golden scepter, and they began to mock Him and say, "Hail, King of the Jews!" Then some of them took the reed out of His hand and struck Him on the head with it, and others went up and actually spit in His face. Think of it! It is enough to make one's blood boil with indignation, the way they treated our dear Lord, and it was all for our sins too.

Then show how they stripped off the royal robe and made Him carry His cross up Calvary's hill, how He fainted and broke down, and how Simon took His place. Then describe the crucifixion briefly, avoiding all that is ghastly and gruesome, but making it as vivid and realistic as possible, in order that each one may see the picture, and realize clearly the relation of Christ's death to his own sins.

Many people, both old and young, have never stood at the foot of the cross and looked up into the face of the dear Lord, and said to themselves, "That Man died in my stead." Make them stand there – for once in their life, at least – and feel the full force of that thought.

A friend of mine, who had a Working Girl's Club in New York, was showing them some photographs of famous paintings. Among them was a Crucifixion scene by Tintoretti. At the right of the picture is to be seen one of the thieves who has been nailed to the cross, and the cross has been erected. On the left is the other thief. The soldiers have laid him on the cross and have driven the nails through his feet. The thief is resisting with all his might, and is trying to raise himself from the cross, while one soldier is brutally crowding down his arm, and another is trying to drive the spike through his hand. In the center of the picture you see the Lord Himself. They have laid Him down upon the cross – no, I think He laid Himself down and suffered them to drive the nails through His hands and feet. The thieves doubtless made the air hideous with groans and curses, but Jesus did not groan, did not complain, did not even open His mouth.

"Like a lamb that is led to slaughter,
And like a sheep that is silent before its shearers,
So He did not open His mouth" (Is. 53:7).

Then the soldiers took the cross, with its precious burden, and dropped it into the deep hole prepared for it. As the cross went down, it brought a strain upon the hands and feet which produced an agony which no mortal words can describe, but the artist has brought it all out in the expression of the countenance and, as you look into the face of the dear Lord, you see what unearthly suffering He is enduring for the sins of the world.

As this picture came into the hands of one of the girls, she drew back with an expression of horror, saying, "Oh, Mrs. P, you don't mean to say that Jesus was crucified alive, do you?"

"Yes, my dear," said the teacher.

"Why," said the girl, "I never realized that before. Oh, it is awful!"

"Yes, my dear," said her teacher. "Jesus suffered all that and much more, for your sins and mine."

"Well," said the girl, "if Jesus suffered all that for me, then I want to live for Him." Then and there, she gave her heart to the Lord.

Many of you doubtless feel as that girl did; you are grateful for what Christ has done for you, and you want to give your heart to Him, but you do not know just how to do it. Listen, then, and I will try to make it plain.

Salvation is a two-sided thing. On God's part it consists in giving something, and on our part it consists in receiving something, but the thing given by God and received by us is not a thing at all, but a Person. "And the testimony is this, that God has given us eternal life, and this life is in His Son. He who has the Son has the life; he who does not have the Son of God does not have the life" (1 John 5:11-12).

Then show how simple a thing it is to receive a gift. Here is a leaflet. I will give it to anyone who will accept it. Someone takes it and I ask him whose it is now.

"It is mine."

"How do you know it is yours?"

"Because I accepted your offer."

"That is right, but why does it not belong to that other boy? I offered it to him as much as I did to you."

"Yes, but he did not accept your offer and I did."

"Very true. Now God has given His Son to be the Savior of all sinners who will accept Him. Some of us have accepted God's gift and we have a Savior. Some of us have not accepted God's gift and we haven't a Savior, and we see the reason why, do we not? It is simply and solely because we have not been willing to accept God's gift. How long did it take that boy to become the owner of that leaflet?"

"Not a quarter of a minute."

"It would not take you any longer to accept God's gift and obtain a Savior."

Nor is it a question of feeling, as many suppose. Turning to the boy who accepted the leaflet, I would say, "Did you have any special feeling of joy when you took that leaflet?"

"No, I can't say that I did."

"Have you had any particular joy since you became the owner of it?"

"No, I do not even know what it is, for I have not read it."

"But suppose you should open it and find a hundred-dollar bill in it, would you have any feeling then?"

"I think I should."

"Quite likely, but would that tract be any more yours with all the feeling that came from finding a hundred-dollar bill in it than it is now without any feeling?"

"Not at all."

"You see, then, that the question of feeling has nothing to do with the ownership. It was the acceptance of my offer which made it yours. So, one may accept Christ with feeling or without it, as the case may be. God does not say, 'As many as felt happy, or as many as felt sinful were saved'; but, 'as many as received Him, to them He gave the right to become children of God' (John 1:12).

"Perhaps you are saying, 'Suppose I should receive Christ as my Savior right here and now, what would happen to me?' In the first place, He would forgive your sins, for He says, in 1 John 1:9, 'If we confess our sins, He is faithful and righteous to forgive us our sins.' But that is not all He would do. He would also come into your heart and take possession of your life, for He says, in Revelation 3:20, 'Behold, I stand at the door and knock; if anyone hears My voice and opens the door, I will come in to him.'

"You see, then, that if any of you should invite Christ to come into your heart and be your Savior, He would do it, because He says He will. You would not go home alone today, you would not sleep alone tonight, because you would have the constant company of the Lord Jesus. '... lo, I am with you always, even to the end of the age' (Matthew 28:20)."

"But how can we know that Christ is in our hearts, if we accept Him?"

"Well, in the first place, you have His word for it, which ought to be sufficient, but in addition to that, He promises to reveal His presence to those that obey Him. In John 14:21, He says, "He who has My commandments and keeps them...I will love him and will disclose Myself to him." In other words, when you pray to Him He will seem to answer back; when you read His Word, He will speak to you out of it; and every time you make any real sacrifice for Him, there will come a thrill of joy into your heart and His blessed, 'Well done, good and faithful slave' (Matthew 25:23), will ring in your ears.

"Here, then, is a definite promise that if you confess your sins, He will forgive them (1 John 1:9), if you invite Him into your heart He will come (Revelation 3:20), and if you obey His commandments, He will manifest Himself to you (John 14:21).

"In view of these promises, how many of you are willing to accept Christ as your Savior now? You all expect to do it sometime, of course, but there is no time so good as the present. Will all the school please bow their heads?

"Now we will have a few moments of prayer, in which I wish that every unsaved person in the house would confess their sins and receive Christ as their Savior. I will pray for you, and I will put it in such a way that if you will make my words your prayer, it will bring Jesus Christ into your heart."

After the prayer, made just as simple and direct as possible, I would assume that some of them had accepted Christ. Then I would say, "The first step in beginning the Christian life is to accept Christ as one's Savior, and that I am sure some of you have done. The second step is to confess Christ as your Savior. In Romans 10:9, we read, 'if you confess with your mouth Jesus as Lord, and believe in your heart that God raised Him from the dead, you will be saved.' You have accepted Christ, and the next thing to do is to tell someone of it. If I were you, I would tell my teacher that I had settled the question and had decided to live a Christian life."

At this point, give the school five minutes for this purpose, saying, "Now, teachers and scholars, just have a free talk with each other about this important matter."

After a suitable interval, let the leader say, "I would advise those of you who have accepted Christ today to tell your parents what you have done, and ask them to help you in your Christian life. If you care to come and tell me, I should be glad to give you a Life Card, which I am sure you will find very helpful." On the first page is a covenant which I would read to them, and suggest that after they arrive home they read it carefully, and then kneel down and ask God to help them keep it, and then sign it with pen and ink, putting down also the date when they signed it, and the place where they live. Say to them, "You will find this covenant useful in many ways. For instance, the devil will very likely come around tomorrow morning and try to make you think you are not a Christian. He will say, perhaps, 'You thought you became a Christian yesterday, but you were mistaken, for this morning when your brother hid your shoes under the bed and made you late for breakfast you lost your temper, now didn't you?' and perhaps you may have to confess that you did. 'Well,' he will say, 'that proves that you are not a Christian, for if you were you would not lose your temper.' This statement is not true, as I can show you by a simple illustration. Suppose you should go to work tomorrow for a man whose name we will call Mr. Johnson. Mr. Johnson is now your new master, is he not? Suppose that the first day you should spoil a yard of cloth or break a machine. Would that prove that Mr. Johnson is not your new master? By no means. Have you left his employ? No. Do you intend to leave it? No. What does it prove then? The fact that you have damaged his work or broken his machine? It only proves that you have not been as careful to please your new master as you should have been, or that you did not fully understand his work – that is all. So, if you have taken Christ as your new Master today, and tomorrow morning should lose your temper, what does that prove? That Jesus Christ is not your new Master? By no means. Has He discharged you? No. Have you left His service? Certainly not. Do you want to leave it? By no means. Then what does it prove? The fact that you lost your temper the very first day? Why, it only proves that you were not as careful to please your new Master as you should have been – that is all. I hope you will not do it, of course, but if you should, the thing to do is to kneel right down and confess your sin, and He will forgive it instantly. Then be more careful to please Him in the future.

"Now, suppose you had taken one of these Life Cards and signed it, see what a help it would be to you. Perhaps ten years from now you might open your Bible and find this covenant, and it would bring back this hour to your mind, and you would say, 'I haven't been as faithful to Christ as He has been to me, but, thank God, I haven't withdrawn from that position which I took in that Sunday School, and that position is the Christian life.' And thus your weak faith may often be strengthened by this outward and visible evidence of the covenant which you made with God a few moments ago."

Having offered to give a Life Card to any who come for it, I would then dismiss the school. The teachers, who have been previously instructed, will encourage their pupils to come and get the Life Card, and, if necessary, will come with them. Often a teacher will come bringing a whole class of boys or young men with her. As they come, the leader can ask each one personally if they have really accepted Christ as their Savior, and when they did it. In many instances, they will say, "I did it while you were praying, or while my teacher was talking with me." It is a good plan to ask them to shake hands with you as a token of their sincerity and make them promise to sign the Life Card as they take it. Then say to each one, "There is one thing more I wish you to do, and that is to go and tell your pastor just what you have told me. Will you do it?" In this way, you pass them on to him and commit them to their purpose still more. Occasionally one will come for a card who has not really accepted Christ, but is only thinking of it, but usually he can be persuaded to settle the question in a moment or two, if one is wise and tactful.

After all have come who are likely to, I would suggest that all kneel down and tell the Lord audibly what they have said before in their heart, and to make it easy for them it would be well to lead them in prayer, asking them to follow you in concert, sentence by sentence. It is a great help to them to hear their own voice as they enter into covenant with the Master, and you also make sure that they say the things you wish them to say.

I would then lead them in prayer, making sure that they confess their sins, and invite Jesus to come into their heart and take possession of their life.

When they had risen, I would question each one something after this fashion, "Henry, you knelt and confessed your sins and asked God to forgive you for Christ's sake. Did you really mean it?"

"Yes, I did."

"Do you think He has forgiven you?"

"I don't know that I am sure."

"What did He say He would do, if you confessed your sins?"

"He said He would forgive me."

"Do you think God has lied to you?"

"Of course not."

"Then where are your sins?"

"They must be forgiven."

"What makes you think so?"

"Because God says so."

Or I would say, "Jesus says in Revelation 3:20, 'Behold, I stand at the door and knock; if anyone hears My voice and opens the door, I will come in to him...' I heard you ask Him to come into your heart. Did you really mean it?"

"I did."

"Do you think He has come into your heart?"

"I do."

"Why do you think so?"

"Because I feel better, because I am so happy."

"Very well, but suppose you wake up in the morning with a headache. You wouldn't feel happy then, would you?"

"I suppose not."

"Then where would your hope of salvation be? Do you not see that if your hope of acceptance depends upon your feelings it will vary from day to day?" Then show him that if he has honestly invited Jesus to come into his heart, he has His promise that He would come, which is the best evidence that a Christian can have.

If one has time, it is well to give the converts some instruction concerning the dual nature of the Christian life. Show them that while the unsaved person has only one nature, the selfish, sinful nature, the Christian has in addition a new Divine nature which is Jesus Christ. Let them understand that the old nature is not one whit better now than it was before their conversion, and that all their temptations will come from this source. However, "greater is He who is in you than he who is in the world" (1 John 4:4). And, "God is faithful, who will not allow you to be tempted beyond what you are able, but with the temptation will provide the way of escape also, so that you will be able to endure it" (1 Corinthians 10:13).

In holding such a service, it is best to exclude the smaller children from the main room and have a separate service with them if desired. Some may also prefer to call for an expression by rising, or by entering an inquiry-room, but do not fail to deal personally with each one and see that they have a scriptural reason for their hope of salvation.

Following Up Results

This is very important. Indeed, it is a question whether it is wise to hold such a service unless it is to be carefully followed up. A Decision Day opens the way for conversation with every person in the parish, and a careful canvass should follow to lead to Christ those who did not accept Him during the service. The parents of all who decided should be visited, and their cooperation secured. In some instances where the parents were not Christians, such a visit has led to their conversion.

A class for the converts should be formed for instruction in the duties and doctrines of the Christian life, and in due season they should be received into the Church. The Life Card is a four-page leaflet which contains many useful hints on Christian living, how to grow in grace, how to use the Bible, etc. It may be obtained of the Bible Institute Colportage Association.

The covenant which the converts are asked to sign and keep in their Bibles, where they may often see it, reads as follows:

In obedience to *God's command,* I do here and now turn from every known sin, and believe *the Gospel* that Christ died for my sins, was buried and rose again. *I receive Jesus* as my Redeemer, who bore my sins in His own body on the cross (2 Corinthians 5:21; Galatians 3:13; 1 Peter 2:24), and who has power to forgive my sins (Mark 2:10; Acts 5:31), as my teacher to whom I will submit all my thoughts (John 6:68), as my guide to whom I will commit the direction of my life (Acts 9:6), as my risen Savior whom I will trust to keep me from falling (Jude 24) and save me to the uttermost (Hebrews 7:25) and, resting upon *God's assurance,* I believe all my sins are forgiven and *I have eternal life.*

(Signed)_____

Date: _____ Place:_____

Chapter 7

The Conversion of Children

E. P. Hammond and R. A. Torrey

No revival is what it ought to be if a good deal of attention is not given to the children, and much prayerful effort put forth for their conversion. If Christian people use the divinely appointed means to lead souls, young or old, to Christ, they may confidently expect God's blessing, but this is preeminently true in dealing with children. Dr. Duff, of Scotland, went to India and labored for the conversion of the heathen, yet with all his eloquence, I heard him say in the Free Church Assembly Hall of Edinburgh that his labors were a comparative failure until he turned his attention to the children, and held up Christ as the atoning sacrifice for the sins of the world. Then their hearts were touched, and many repented and believed in the Lord Jesus. From that time on, he began to speak of certainties instead of continuing to speak of possibilities. "See, said Jesus, "that you do not despise one of these little ones" (Matthew 18:10). The word translated "despise" is a very suggestive word. It means literally to think down, to think little or nothing of. Take heed that ye think not down one of these little ones. The conversion of a child may be of very little importance in our sight, but it is of immense importance in Jesus's sight.

I. The Importance of the Conversion of Children

1. The conversion of a child is important in the first place because children oftentimes die. The majority in Chicago die in childhood.[1] For everyone who dies between twenty and forty, there are many who die between birth and twenty. So, with very many of the children at any time upon the earth, they must be converted in childhood or pass into eternity unconverted. In spite of the large number of children's caskets that pass us in hearses, it is hard to bring people to realize how likely children are to die. We look at the whitehaired man and say he is likely to die soon, but we look at the little child and think that child has many years before it. That is not at all sure. We have very rude awakenings from this dream. Mothers and fathers, do you realize that your children may die? Up quick, then, and lead them to Christ before that day comes. If you do not, it will be the darkest day you ever knew, but if you have led them to Christ it will not be a dark day. Lonely it will be, but not dark. Nay, it will be glorious with the thought that the voyage is over and the glory land reached quickly by one you love. Sunday School teachers, do you realize that any one of the boys or girls in the class you teach may die any day? Up, then, and win them to Christ as speedily as you may.

2. The conversion of children is important, in the second place, because it is much easier to win a child to Christ than an adult. I once heard Dr. E. N. Kirk, of Boston, say, "If I could live my life over again, I would labor much more among children." During a series of meetings lasting sometimes five or six weeks, I have seen more children converted the first week than adults in all the weeks following. Children have no old prejudices to overcome as many grown people have. With the help of the Holy Spirit, they are easily led to feel the great love of Christ in giving Himself to die for them, and when the simple story of His suffering and death is read and explained from God's Word, they believe it, exercise saving faith, and there and then the Holy Spirit effects a change of heart. Mr. Spurgeon once said in my hearing, "I could spend days in giving details of young children whom I have known and personally conversed with, who have given evidence of a change of heart." And he added,

---

1   At the time of this writing.

"I have more confidence in the spiritual life of such children whom I have taken into my church, than I have in the spiritual condition of adults thus received. I will go further and say that I have usually found a clearer knowledge of the Gospel and a warmer love toward Christ in the child convert than in the man convert. I may astonish you by saying that I have sometimes met with a deeper spiritual experience in a child of ten or twelve than in some persons of fifty or sixty. I have known a child who would weep himself to sleep by the month together under a crushing sense of sin. If you would know deep and bitter and awful fear of the wrath of God, let me tell you what I felt as a boy. If you want to know what faith in Christ is, you must not look to those who have been be-muddled by the heretical jargon of the times, but to the dear children who have taken Jesus at His word, and believed on Him, and therefore know and are sure that they are saved."

Every year that passes over our heads unconverted, our hearts are less open to holy impressions. Every year away from Christ, our hearts become harder in sin. That needs no proof. The practice of sin increases the power of sin in our lives. God, heaven, Christ, and holiness lie very near childhood, but if the child remains away from Christ, every year they become farther and farther away. When I see a child walk into the inquiry room of a Sunday evening, I feel quite certain that if a worker of any sense gets hold of that child it is going to be converted, but when I see a man or a woman walk in there I do not feel at all as sure. The adult has become so entangled in sin, the mind has become so darkened by the error and skepticism that arise out of sin, there are so many complications added by each year, that the case of an adult is very difficult as compared with that of a child. The fact is, that with very many if they are not converted in childhood, they will never be converted at all. Fathers and mothers, that is true of the children in our homes. Sunday School teachers, that is true of the children in your Sunday School classes. It is now or never.

3. Conversion of the children is important, in the third place, because converted children are among the most useful workers for Christ. They can reach persons who are inaccessible to everyone else. They can reach

their schoolmates and playmates, the Jewish children, the Catholic children, the children of worldly parents and infidels. They can bring them to Sunday School or to children's meetings, and to Christ. You and I cannot get close enough to them to show them how beautiful Jesus is, and what joy and blessing He brings. They can. Then they can reach their parents oftentimes when we cannot. Parents who will not listen to us, will listen to their children.

There was a rough, drunken gambler in Minneapolis, MN. He often went by the mission door, but when a worker invited him in, he repelled him with rude insults. But his child, about ten years old, was gotten into the Sunday School and won for Christ. Then she began to work and pray for her drunken papa, and a cottage meeting was at last held in his wretched home. The father took down his overcoat to go to the saloon. Little Annie asked him if he would not stay to the meeting. He roughly answered, "No."

"Won't you stay for my sake, Papa?" The man hung up his coat. The meeting began, and the man was surly and wished he was out of it. They knelt in prayer while he sat on the end of the sofa. One after another prayed. Then all were silent. Then Annie's little voice was heard in prayer something like this, "God, save my papa." It broke the wicked man's heart, and then and there he accepted Christ. He afterwards became a deacon in my church. When New Year's Day came and many had testified for Christ, Annie arose and said, "Papa used to drink and Mamma used to drink, Grandpa used to drink and Grandma used to drink. But Papa is a Christian now, and Mamma is a Christian now, and Grandpa is a Christian now, and Grandma is a Christian now, and Uncle Joe is a Christian now, and Auntie is a Christian now. I guess we are all Christians down to our house now." But the little girl herself led the way. Wasn't the conversion of that child important? Many a hardened sinner and many a skeptic has been led to Christ by a child.

When in Scotland I heard a touching story, showing how a child's simple question was used in leading a scoffing skeptic to the feet of Jesus. It is a true story. I was acquainted with the father of the child. Let the skeptic tell the story:

"As I stepped upon the platform at the railway station, a hand was laid upon my arm, and a voice said, 'Norman, is this you?'

"I turned and looked at the speaker. It was an old classmate, Richard, with whom I had agreed to pass a few weeks and had not seen for years. After we had pushed our way through the noisy crowd and were seated in his carriage, I looked at him again and exclaimed, 'Richard, how you have altered! how different now from the wild youth of old!'

"'Yes, Norman, there have been many changes with me since we parted; but the greatest has been here,' said he, smiling and gently touching his breast.

"'Humph!' was my exclamation, which elicited no reply.

"That evening, as he, his wife, and myself were walking in the conservatory, and I was admiring some Jessamines, he said to me, 'Norman, I have yet a little treasure to show you, and, although it is small, it is greater than all these, almost the greatest one I have. Can you guess?'

"When we went back to the drawing-room, he introduced me to his beautiful little girl, his only child, his little Bessie. I was not fond of children, but strangely did the little maiden win her way to my heart. Eight cloudless summers of her sunny life had passed, and had each one as it gently glided by left with her all its charms, she could not have been more beautiful.

"That evening, sweet in memory to me, we became firm friends. She loved me because, when she asked papa, he said he did.

"The next day we all went out for a drive. Little Bessie was bright and beautiful as the day, but sometimes there was a strange thoughtfulness of expression upon her face which troubled me as being beyond her years.

"As I was talking to her father, I said something jeeringly about Him Who had led the only pure life on earth. Richard said not a word in reply but motioned me to look at Bessie. She was looking into my face with a gaze of mingled horror and surprise – an expression such as I never saw before nor since, and which I shall never forget. It was for a moment. No one spoke. Then the little maid burst into a flood of uncontrollable tears, and I felt a certain shame that in the presence of one so pure I should have spoken what she had never heard before. Then she looked at me in a sort of pitying way and said, 'I thought you loved my Jesus; oh, how could you have said that of Him?' During the rest of the drive, she lay upon her father's bosom in perfect silence.

"The next morning, I was alone in my room thinking of all that had occurred, and a strange unaccountable feeling of seriousness was creeping over me, a sort of longing to be like her, when suddenly the little one was at my side. I started as I saw her and met the tender gaze of love and pity which she bent upon me. Her head was laid upon my arm, and for a moment both were silent. Then the silence was broken with the words, 'Won't you love my Jesus?' and she was gone.

"I could not ridicule that lovely spirit. The next morning, and the next, and the next, the little girl came in the same way, said the same words, and disappeared. I never answered her and at no other time did she allude to the subject, but she never failed to come at that morning hour.

"One day I said to her, 'Tell me how, Bessie.' She looked at me a moment, and the next was seated on my knee, and the words that flowed, those simple, childish words in which she told the story of Christ's love, never shall I forget. My eyes were far from dry when she went away, but there was less sorrow on her face than usual. Morning after morning she came, and never seemed weary of telling the sweet tale. But one morning she did not come, and I waited a long time in vain. No little feet came pattering along the hall; no little hand was clasped in mine; no little words of instruction were lisped in my ear. Presently there came a hurried knock at my door. It was opened without waiting for permission, and her father was with me.

"'Norman,' said he, 'she has just waked from a long and heavy sleep and is fearfully ill. Will you come? Tell me if you know what it is.'

"I went. There lay the little one with eyes closed, and in a sort of stupor. I knew at a glance it was scarlet fever. How I told those two aching hearts I know not, but they were wonderfully calm in their anguish. The doctor soon confirmed my statement, but there was so painfully little to be done for the dear sufferer that two days passed almost in silence as we watched over her precious form. We knew from the first that she was no longer of the earth and, indeed, it was a heavy burden for us to bear to think that she no longer would be the light of our hearts. I say we, for, though I was perhaps mistaken, the little one had so taken possession of my heart, that it seemed to me that she could not be dearer to those who had the first earthly claim upon her affections. At the end of the second day, her life seemed partially to return. She opened her eyes and, smiling, said, 'Dear Uncle Norman, won't you love my Jesus? Mamma loves Him, Papa loves Him, and I love Him, and am going to Him, and I want to tell Him that you will love Him.'

"'Bessie,' said I, 'tell Him my heart and life are His forever more.'

"'Mamma, Papa, I am so happy now. Now I have all I want. Now I come. I come, Lord Jesus!' and the youthful spirit, so pure, so holy, returned whence it came. God's little messenger had turned a soul to righteousness and was called home."

4. The conversion of children is important because persons converted in childhood make the best Christians. If one is converted when he is old, he has learned many bad tricks of character and life that have to be unlearned and it is generally a pretty slow process. But when one is converted in childhood, character is yet to be formed and it can be formed from the beginning on right lines. If you wish to train a tree into a thing of beauty and symmetry, you had better begin when it is young. If you want to form a character of Christlike symmetry and beauty, you had better begin in childhood. That Christlike man of the olden time, Polycarp, who ended his life as a martyr at ninety-five, was converted at nine. That fine young man of the New Testament, Timothy, was brought up on Scripture from a babe. I rejoice with all my heart when an old broken-down drunkard is brought to Christ. It means so much. But it means so much more when a child is brought to Christ.

5. The conversion of children is important once more because there are so many years of possible service before them. If one is to live to eighty, say, if converted at seventy, there is a soul saved plus ten years of service. When the boy Polycarp was converted, there was a soul saved plus eighty-six years of service. I think enough has been said to show that the conversion of the children is tremendously important, in fact, the most important business the Church of Christ has on hand. Surely

it was well that Jesus said, "See that you do not despise one of these little ones" (Matthew 18:10).

II. Who Is Responsible for the Conversion of the Children?

Now we come to another question: *Who is responsible for the conversion of children?* An easy question to answer.

1. First of all, the parents are responsible for the conversion of the children. The first and greatest responsibility of parents regarding their children is their salvation. The responsibility to feed and clothe and educate our children is nothing to our responsibility to bring them to Christ and bring them up in Christ. The parent who fails to bring his children to Christ has failed at the main point of parental responsibility. Yet parents are willing to leave the conversion of their children to others: to the minister, to the Sunday School teacher, or even to chance. What would you think of yourself if you left the feeding of your children and the clothing of your children to others or to chance? You would despise yourself, and well you might, but you would not really be as despicable as if you left the salvation of your children to others. This is your highest and most solemn obligation as a parent – to bring your children to Christ. Have you done it? If not, then go at it at once. I sat in the station at Evansville, Indiana, one day waiting for a train. A man and wife came in with two babes, one a year and a half old, the other three. They sat down to wait for another train. I turned to the man and said, "Are you a Christian?"

"No, sir."

"Then," I said, "you are not fit to be the father of those children. God has laid a solemn responsibility upon you in giving you those children to bring up for Him." And I say to every parent who is not a Christian, an out and out Christian, you are not fit to be a parent. The highest responsibility of fatherhood and motherhood you are unfit for. Get fit today by taking Christ and then begin at once to lead your children to Christ. And you who are professed Christians, seek power for this work and begin at once.

2. In the next place, the responsibility for the conversion of the children rests upon all pastors, evangelists, and preachers of the Word. We are too exclusively occupied with the grown-up people. But Christ's first direction to the great preacher Peter was that he was to prove his love by feeding the *lambs* (John 21:15). The minister or evangelist who overlooks the young is disobeying Jesus Christ, and the warning of Christ should come to him with great power: "See that you do not despise one of these little ones" (Matthew 18:10). The fact is, that it is our pride that leads us to neglect the children. It is gratifying to our vanity to think that the grown people, and especially the men, flock to our ministry. Anyone, we fancy, can interest the children, but it takes men of our own great mental caliber to interest the men. Oh, take heed, take heed! In the eyes of our Master, the children are of first importance.

3. In the third place, the responsibility for the conversion of the children rests upon the Sunday School teacher. The first and highest duty of the Sunday School teacher is to lead his scholars to Christ. The Sunday School teacher has not done his whole work when he interests his scholars or even when he instructs his scholars with good, sound, orthodox, Biblical doctrine. His business is to convert them, to win them to Christ. Sunday School teacher, the probability is that there are scholars in your class that will be led to Christ by you or else will never come. Do you realize that? When you next sit before your class, let this thought sink deep into your heart – some of these scholars are to be won to Christ by me or lost forever. Oh, it is a glorious thing, but it is a solemn thing to be a Sunday School teacher. What an opportunity! What a responsibility! Yet many and many a Sunday School teacher allows scholars to drift into their class and drift out of their class without any definite word to convert and save them! Under the first sermon I ever preached in Chicago, a young woman was deeply stirred. She was elegantly dressed and occupied a respectable place in society, but only because her history was not yet known. She was as truly a sinner as

any woman of the street. The next night, in conversation, she told me all her shameful story. I pleaded with her to accept Christ, and have her vileness washed away. She said that I was the first person who had ever spoken to her about her soul. Her mother was worldly, but for six years she had been a regular attendant at one Sunday School, but never once had her teacher approached her personally about accepting Christ. And she had gone out into the world to sin and shame. What a responsibility rests upon the heads of that young woman's Sunday School teachers! Oh, teachers! Be soul winners, realize the immense importance of the conversion of the children to Christ, and feel deeply your own responsibility for those in your class.

4. After Sunday School teachers, the responsibility for the conversion of the children rests upon all workers. We must save the old if we can, and, thank God, in many cases we can, but we must save the children anyhow. In church, in inquiry meeting, on the street, in the home, everywhere, look out for the children, and take every possible opportunity to bring them to Christ.

III. How to Convert the Children

We come now to the last question and the all-important one: *How can we convert the children?*

1. First of all, by prayer. True conversion and regeneration is the Holy Spirit's work. It is He who convicts of sin and righteousness and judgment (John 16:8-11). It is He that leads to saving faith. It is He that makes children as well as adults new creatures in Christ Jesus. And He works in answer to prayer. There must, then, be very definite prayer for the conviction and conversion and the regeneration of the children. We had one child that did not seem naturally as religiously inclined as the rest. One night I was led to ask prayers for that child. That very night (or perhaps the next) when I went home, I was told that the child burst into tears as she went to bed, and when her sister asked her what was the matter she replied, "Oh, I am afraid I shall die and go to hell!" She did

die, but, thank God, before the hour came, prayer had been answered and she was trusting Jesus and went to be with Him forever. Oh, parents, pray for your children. Sunday School teachers, pray. Pray definitely, pray earnestly, pray expectantly. Of all that I heard in my own Sunday School days, nothing impressed me so as a story of a teacher who prayed earnestly for all her scholars and all were converted. I was a mere boy when I heard it, but when in later years I got back into Sunday School as a teacher I remembered it and I prayed. My class was composed of reckless boys, but I saw every one of them, with possibly one exception, make a profession of faith in Christ.

2. The second step towards the conversion of the children is the use of the Word of God. The Word of God is the instrument God has appointed for conviction, conversion, and regeneration (1 Peter 1:23; James 1:18). Fathers, mothers, Sunday School teachers, study your Bibles to find out just how to use them in leading a soul to Christ, and then use them in that way with the children in the Sunday School class, in the home, in the inquiry room, and everywhere.

3. If we are to convert the children, we must be baptized with the Holy Spirit. Jesus said, "You will receive power when the Holy Spirit has come upon you" (Acts 1:8). Holy Spirit power is what every parent needs and must have. Holy Spirit power is what every Sunday School teacher needs and must have. I once met a gentleman and lady who had read an address on the Baptism with the Spirit and they had sought and received this baptism, so when I visited the city where they lived, they came to see me. Their hearts were full of joy. The man told me what wondrous things God had done for him by the Holy Spirit's power. Then the wife broke in and said, "Yes, and the best part of it is that I have been able to get into the hearts of my own children, which I was never able to do before." Ah! that is what we want, parents – to get into the hearts of our children. The baptism with the Holy Spirit is the secret. It is not enough that we can interest and amuse and instruct the children. It is not enough that we can draw pretty pictures on the blackboard, play kindergarten games, sing bright songs, and get texts of Scripture and

pretty notions into the children's heads. We must get Christ into their hearts. We must get them to take Jesus as their own Savior, to trust in the shed blood of Calvary, to surrender to Christ as their Lord and Master, and confess Him as such before the world. We must get them saved. Much of our Sunday School work and of all our children's work in this day is tomfoolery and an abomination in the sight of God. We get the children – yes, *we get* them in droves – and we amuse them, we instruct them, we delight them, we send them home happy and resolved to come again, and then we fancy we have done a good work for God, when in reality we have done nothing for God but much for the devil. If the children are not converted, your work is a failure. The conversion may not always be immediate. It takes time to effect real conversion, and sometimes the fruit may not appear until years after, but if there is not converting power in your work either now or ultimately, your work has been a failure. That there may be converting power in our work we must have the Holy Spirit. It is not enough that we know the lesson, it is not enough that we understand all these new-fangled ways of teaching and interesting the scholars – we must have the Holy Spirit. Ah! the teacher that knows nothing about using the blackboard and that sort of thing, but knows the power of the Spirit, is worth a hundred who have gone to all the schools of methods and can draw as well as Frank Beard himself, but don't know the power of the Holy Spirit.

4. We should hold special meetings for children. In these meetings, as the children come in, they should be placed in classes of four or five, with a teacher at the end of each class. There should be first a class of boys and then a class of girls. This will prevent disorder and noise. There should be a good deal of singing, and the hymns should be bright and fresh and of a character that the children can understand. They should be taught the hymns verse by verse, and the meaning of the hymns should be explained. Hymns setting forth God's love and the atoning death of Christ should be especially used. Children enjoy singing the same verse over and over again until the truth has sunk itself way down into their hearts.

The sermon should be short and simple, emphasizing the great facts, that all, including children, are sinners, and that Jesus has borne our sin in His own body on the tree. It should be made very clear just what one must do to be saved. When the sermon is over, there should be a few moments of silent prayer, then the conductor of the meeting should lead in a simple, direct prayer to God, having the children follow him audibly, sentence by sentence. When this is done, each teacher of a class should deal personally with each child in the class, seeking to bring each one to an immediate and intelligent acceptance of Christ as Savior. I have found this prayer, that is simple and easily remembered, of great help:

> "Jesus take this heart of mine,
> make it pure, and wholly thine.
> Thou hast bled and died for me,
> I will henceforth live for thee."

(For further description of how to conduct children's meetings, see the chapter on "Decision Day in the Sunday School.")

Chapter 8

Open-Air Meetings

William Evans

I. The Importance of Open-Air Work

This is seen by the indisputable fact that the greatest and most influential preachers and teachers of ages past, and the age in which we now live, have made constant use of it.

The messages of the prophets were delivered in the open air. God's call to the prophet was, "Proclaim all these words in the cities of Judah and in the streets of Jerusalem" (Jeremiah 11:6). The sublime evangelical predictions of Isaiah, the mournful dirges of Jeremiah, the symbolical and picturesque visions of Ezekiel – all these, for the most part, were announced in the streets of the great cities of Jerusalem and Babylon. Throughout the streets of Nineveh resounded the warning voice of the prophet Jonah. The message of Micah, Nahum, and the rest of the minor prophets was, without question, "a song of the winds." Nehemiah's great revival sermon – a sermon which resulted in an almost national revival – was preached in the street of Jerusalem, close to the water-gate (Nehemiah 8:1-3).

The open-air worker and preacher of today, then, is in "the goodly order of the prophets." The apostles of Jesus Christ were noted open-air workers. The command of their Lord and Master was to "go out into its streets and say" (Luke 10:10). Paul's greatest sermon – that master-stroke of homiletics – was delivered in the open air, preached on Mars Hill (Acts 17:22-31). Peter's "Magnum Opus," that great Pentecostal sermon, was delivered in the streets of the great metropolis of Palestine (Acts 2:14-36). The apostles of our Lord were great street-preachers, and the open-air workers of today are not only in "the goodly order of the prophets," they are also "in the goodly fellowship of the apostles."

Our Lord Jesus Christ, the great Exemplar of Christianity, was a great open-air worker. His greatest sermon – the "Magna Charta" of our holy religion, that incomparable code of Christian ethics, that Sermon on the Mount – was delivered with the hillside for a pulpit and with the sky for a sounding-board (Matthew 5-7). That our Lord was noted for street-preaching is implied from the fact that in the record of the last judgment, recorded in Matthew 25, those being judged exclaimed, "Didst thou not preach in our streets?" He who engages in street-preaching and open-air work is following in the footsteps of his Master. Beloved, the call to open-air work comes to us one and all just as new and just as true today as when the sands of Galilee were fresh with His footprints and the temple's marble pavement echoed with His tread.

The Church of England sustains a great many open-air preaching-stations.[2] Noted among the men who preach at these stations are the Bishop of Bedford and Lord Radstock. Many of the prominent ministers and laymen of the Established Church are often to be seen conducting these services. In Whitechapel, London, there is a pulpit built in the wall from which some clergyman addresses those who come to hear.

The Presbyterians of London are also very aggressive in this line of work. They have a standing committee appointed to take charge of open-air work there. The famous Presbyterian preacher, John McNeil, may be heard preaching in the open-air meetings.

Spurgeon, the greatest preacher of the century, was an indefatigable open-air worker. Read his lectures to students and see what rousing talks he gives them on this kind of work. When asked one day what he thought of this kind of work, he said, "Give us all you can of it; the

---

2   At the time of this writing.

more the better." Whitefield, Wesley, Moody, Meyer – in fact, the best men and preachers the age has produced for the ministry of the Gospel – have been and are open-air workers.

One of the laws of the Presbytery of Glasgow is that every minister, once a month, shall obey the command of the Lord Jesus Christ and "'Go out into the highways and along the hedges, and compel them to come in" (Luke 14:23). I feel constrained to say that I think this would be a good thing for all our Theological Seminaries, our Bible Institutes, and our Training Schools for Christian work to insist on. I hope to see the day – yea, I believe it is not far distant – when every such institution shall have in its possession and for its constant use a Gospel wagon and a Gospel tent; that a place shall be provided in their faculties for a teacher and professor of open-air work; and that it shall be considered a part of the training of every student for the ministry of the Evangel of Jesus Christ to go out into the streets and preach the Gospel to the masses, and thus follow the example of Him who brushed the dew from the Judean lilies as He went about doing good and preaching the Gospel of the kingdom.

II. The Value of Open-Air Work

I use the word value, not in the sense of the comparative worth of this kind of Christian work to that of any other branch of the same work, but I use the word in the sense of utility – as to what its value is to everyone who engages in it.

1. It will enable you to reach people you could not otherwise reach.
This is true with regard to both quality and quantity. Your audiences will be composed of people moral and immoral, church-going and non-church-going, righteous and unrighteous, honest and dishonest, the father and the debauchee, the mother and the harlot, old and young, male and female, national and international. There will be a goodly representation of all sorts and conditions of both men and women. Such a heterogeneous assembly, such a motley crowd, would not and

could not be gathered into any church in the land – no, not even in our so-called institutional churches.

Then, as to quantity, to numbers. Just look at the crowds you can reach! Some of our ministers who have only a handful to preach to might have hundreds if they would go out into the open-air and preach. There is no need, in this day of our Lord, of our ministers complaining because they cannot get a large congregation to preach to. If you want an audience, you can find one anywhere. I think that when our evening services are so poorly attended during the excessive heat of the summer months, it would be a good thing to close the church that contains but the handful and go out into the parks, into the streets, where the multitudes are and there preach to them the Gospel of the grace of God. This, then, is one value of this feature of Christian work – you will reach people you would not and could not otherwise reach.

2. It will enable you to reach men.
That is the great problem every minister of the Gospel has to face today – how to get hold of the *men*. Our audiences are composed very largely of women. They are in the great majority. We are glad the women are there. We thank God for the godly women of the churches, and we esteem it to be a glorious privilege to preach to these mothers of the nation. But we want, and we ought to have, *men*. When Jesus Christ called His disciples to follow Him in His work and labor of love, He said: "From henceforth ye shall catch *men*." (Luke 5:10) We ought to have as many men as women in our audiences each Lord's Day. This may not be a possibility in some towns and states where the census shows many more women than men, but it is possible in this city. If you cannot get hold of the men in your church, then go out into the streets and get hold of them there. You will find your audiences to be composed almost wholly of men.

3. It will give you freedom of speech not always
possible in the pulpit of your church.
How often we preachers have to take the sharp corners off some of our sentences because such might offend Mr. Brown, or Mrs. Smith! How

aimless are some of our sermons because of that very thing! I remember reading of a plain but godly preacher being asked to preach in a fashionable city church. Just before the hour for the service, one of the church people came to him and said, "Brother Williams, I understand that you preach against Christians playing cards. May I suggest to you that you refrain from mentioning that this morning, because Deacon G. indulges in the game and has a weekly card-party at his house. He might be offended and leave the church if you were to speak against card-playing." Hardly a minute had passed before another one came and asked him not to preach against the dance, and another not to preach against the theater.

Feeling somewhat at a loss to know what to do and say, he said to one of these men, "What would you suggest that I preach about, then?"

The church-member turned to him and said, "Give the Jew's 'Hail Columbia'; there's not one within forty miles of here."

This story may be true, or it may not be. It illustrates my point, however, and that is, that we oftentimes are restricted in our speech from the pulpit. In the open-air work, you need not be so sparing. You can be more pointed in your preaching. You can say things there that you would not dare say, and which would not be wise to say, from the pulpit of your church. That may be the only time you will have the privilege and opportunity of speaking to or seeing those people, hence you can say some striking things to them.

4. It will give you good development of the lungs.

This is not a thing to be lightly esteemed. More than you or I have ever imagined depends on possessing good lungs. I feel no diffidence in saying that if we had more open-air preachers, we would have fewer consumptive preachers. Instead of the weak, thin, squeaky, collar-button voice characteristic of so many preachers today, and which is an intolerable nuisance to listen to, you would have good strong lungs and a voice rich, full, and resonant – one which it would be a pleasure rather than a pain to listen to.

III. The Nature of the Open-Air Meeting

Under this heading, I will also include the Speaker, the Time, the Place, and the Order of the Meeting.

I. The Speaker.

He ought to be the best man that can be had for the place, or that the place can afford. The Bible says, "Wisdom shouts in the street" (Proverbs 1:20). Mark that. Wise ones, not fools, cry aloud in the streets. If there is one place in the world that you need to have a man of tact, it is in the open-air meeting. Banish from your minds the false thought that any kind of an inexperienced man will do. Such a man will never hold a crowd on the street-corner. He might possibly hold one in a church where, for propriety's sake, they would not get up and go out. The street-audience, however, is not bound by any such etiquette. If you are not interesting and tactful, you cannot hold an audience. You can *get* an audience. Yes! A fool stargazing can do that. It is one thing to get an audience, however, and it is another thing to hold it. It is still another and a greater thing to hold it and to impress it with the saving truth of the Gospel of Jesus Christ. London puts into her street-preaching such men as Spurgeon, John McNeil, and Newman Hall. America can afford to do no less. Now, do not misunderstand me on this point and infer that I mean that none but the best preachers should preach in the open air. That is not my point. I am seeking to do away with the false ideas so prevalent among mission-workers, and that is, that *any* man will do to speak in the open air.

Then, he must be a patient man. He must have the patience of Job and the hide of a rhinoceros. He must be invulnerable to attack, proof against ridicule, one that shall be able to return blessing for cursing, and a smile for a frown. In short, he must be a man who has complete control of his temper. He must keep his equilibrium. To lose that is defeat. It means a death-blow to all that he has said in the meeting. If anywhere, here more, is it true that,

> "A gentle answer turns away wrath,
> But a harsh word stirs up anger" (Proverbs 15:1).

2. *The Nature of the Meeting.*

There ought to be good singing. Song is a drawing card. There are very few people in this world who do not love singing. Music makes life worth the living. I knew an individual who did not care for music or song; he is the only man of that sort I have ever met. He was a bachelor, he always will be, and he ought to be. He was the sourest individual I ever met in my life. He was as sour as a pickle. Thank God, his number is not legion. The overwhelming majority of people love singing and will walk many a mile to hear it, too.

I was walking down a certain street the other day and I noticed, that, as person after person came to a certain house, each one stopped and, looking up to a third-story window, seemed as if they were listening to something. I followed their example, and soon found myself with the crowd listening to the words of a beautiful hymn. Brethren, music draws people. Do not forget that. Remember, it is true not only for outdoor work, but also for indoor work.

It is a good thing to have an *organ accompaniment.* I prefer a *cornet accompaniment,* however. Its tone-carrying qualities are much better. I preached on the Boston Common a few weeks ago. They had a cornet leading the singing. I was able to hear it at a very great distance from the platform. It drew a great many people. Mr. Moody recognized this fact. I remember, during the World's Fair year, when Mr. Moody was preaching in Forepaugh's mammoth tent, he wrote me a letter asking me to come and assist in the singing with my cornet. Said he, "Towner has a good strong voice, but nothing but a cornet will carry the lead in such a large tent."

Then the address – if you choose to call it such – should be interesting and picturesque. Get crammed full of good illustrations – not from books, but from life. If there is anything that is stale it is one of those illustrations culled from some encyclopedia of illustrations. The world is full of illustrations. Get them! Keep your eyes and ears open, observe the signs of the times, interpret present-day events, get illustrations from every-day life, and you will never be a dull, uninteresting speaker. That is what our Lord did. Read the sermons He delivered in the Temple and in the synagogues, and you will notice that they do not abound in illustrations, as do those delivered in the open air. There is a wonderful lesson in this thought for the street-preacher.

Do not be dogmatic.

Paul says, "Beware of the dogs" (Philippians 3:2). Someone else has added to that, "Beware of dogmatists!" If you have any hairs to split, split them before you go out into the open air to preach Christ. Do not hit at denominations, but preach Jesus Christ crucified and risen from the dead. I know an open-air worker who scarcely ever holds a meeting without pounding the Roman Catholics almost to death. Many Christian workers are themselves responsible for the trouble they have in open-air work. If a man preaches Christ and preaches Him in a loving spirit and tone, nine times out of ten he will get a quiet and respectful hearing.

Do not make long addresses. Do not preach long sermons. Rather be too short than too long. I think ten minutes should be the limit for one speaker. Have more than one speaker. Variety is the spice of life. This is especially true in open-air work. Let your talk be studied before you go to the meeting. This is not at all contrary to one's dependence upon the Holy Spirit for the message. This thing of taking a passage of Scripture which belongs to the apostles only, and under certain peculiar circumstances, applying it to ourselves is all wrong. Some men have taken that passage in the Gospel, "it will be given you in that hour what you are to say" (Matthew 10:19) as a Scripture that can be taken as a ground for no previous preparation for preaching. This is all wrong. If I have been so busy in the service of the Master that I have not had the time to prepare, or if I am called on unexpectedly to speak, then I believe that passage will be fulfilled in my experience and I can open my mouth wide and God will fill it with good words – words of power. In cases where I could have prepared, but was too indolent to do so, my mouth will be filled with wind, but surely not with good words. Inasmuch, then, as it is harder to preach to people in the open air than it is in the church, so much the more is it necessary to be well prepared for street-preaching. Do not refer to politics in your address. When you preach the Gospel, preach it in love. Do not engage in hammer-and-tongs preaching. Few men can do that successfully. Your audiences will be composed principally of men who have been abused and cuffed about all day, some who have been idle for weeks and are going home to a famished wife and starving children. They will need a clear, kind word to cheer their hearts and show them the way everlasting.

"Tell them the story of Jesus,
    Impress on their hearts every word;
Tell them the story most precious,
    Sweetest that ever was heard.
Tell how the angels in chorus
    Sang as they welcomed His birth
Glory to God in the highest!
    Peace and good tidings on earth!

Tell of the cross where they nailed Him,
    Writhing in anguish and pain;
Tell of the grave where they laid Him
    Tell that He liveth again.
Love in that story most precious
    Clearer than ever I see;
Stay, let me weep while you whisper,
    Love paid the ransom for me."

Now, just a word as to time and place. With regard to the place, let me say if you want to catch fish, go where the fish are. You will find the street-corner, the steps of some public building, the ship wharves, the racecourse on race days, the parks, especially on Sundays – these you will find to be good places to hold open-air meetings. Many preachers are in the habit of holding an open-air meeting right on the steps of their churches just before the evening service. This is a good plan, because you can immediately, on the conclusion of that meeting, invite them into the church to attend the evening service. This is the method the great preacher, Newman Hall, of London, used. He did this for many years. I think this is a good way to get a good audience on a hot night.

As to the time, that will depend altogether on circumstances.

Some people like to hold open-air meetings in the daytime. That is a good time. You can catch people then that you would not catch at any other time. Others, and this is especially true of open-air workers in England, prefer the nighttime for these meetings. They hold them after sunset. They love "the darkness rather than the Light" (John 3:19) in this respect. I think a great many of the people they preach to in these meetings do also. There are some people who would not stop to listen to an open-air address in the daylight. They naturally shrink from it. Others do not want to be seen at such a gathering. The Nicodemuses are not all dead yet. One of the common recollections of my earlier life in England is that of seeing, on each Sunday evening, groups of people at the principal street corners of the city of Liverpool, under the light of the torch lamp, listening to the story of the Cross. Men who will not patronize an open-air meeting in the daytime will steal up under cover of darkness and listen to your story, and perhaps be touched. Brethren, if the people will not come to the evening service, then take the evening service out to them.

IV. And, Finally, Results of Open-Air Work

I speak now especially of spiritual results. In the first place, open-air results cannot necessarily be counted in figures.

> "So you believe in figures. I do not.
> Where do all large ideas, all great aims,
> All schemes that uplift humanity, have birth?
> In the majority? Ah, no, my friend;
> In the minute minority of one.
> In God, Heaven, Man, one is best."

To have the privilege of leading a man like C. H. Spurgeon or D. L. Moody to Christ means to be the indirect cause of leading thousands to the foot of the Cross.

The results of open-air work are, for the most part, never known to the workers. The present Bishop of Liverpool was converted while listening to a talk given at an open-air meeting. He does not know the name of the man who spoke the word of life that night, and the man who spoke the word does not know that it touched the Bishop's heart and was the means of leading him to Christ. That man might have gone home that night and said to himself, "Well, what is the use of preaching in the open air anyway? Nobody seems to be converted. I see no results of my work." Yet how different was the case! He had that night added one more jewel to the diadem of our Lord. One man at least will meet him in the everlasting habitations and say, "It was through your instrumentality that I was led to become a Christian." Preaching in open-air work is like casting bread upon the waters (Eccl. 11:1). It is a work of faith. And that man who has not the most implicit faith in God's Word – that it will not return to Him void – had better not preach that word. Not time, but eternity alone will reveal the true results of the work.

We are allowed, however, now and then to see its results. I was at a home missionary meeting the other evening, and noticed that two churches reported that they had been holding open-air meetings right near their churches, and that in one case sixteen and in the other twenty-three members had been added to the church through these meetings held during the summer months.

Brethren, preach the Word in faith and power. That, and that alone, is our duty; leave the results with God. If it is wise to let you see them He will do it; if you do not see them as you would like to, still plod on, always remembering that,

> "He who goes to and fro weeping, carrying his bag of seed,
> Shall indeed come again with a shout of joy, bringing his
> sheaves with him" (Psalms 126:6).

Chapter 9

The Use of Tracts and Other Literature to Promote a Revival

H. W. Pope

The indiscriminate use of tracts by those whose zeal exceeds their wisdom has led many good people to have a strong prejudice against them. The character of the tracts used has also strengthened this prejudice.

Some tracts are so antiquated as to be almost useless in the present age. They were good in their day, but their day has gone by. Others are so lacking in pith, point, or power as to be of little value. To use a modern phrase, they do not "get there." Others still are so offensive in style as to defeat the very end for which they were written.

It is foolish, however, to allow prejudice against poor tracts to blind us to the value of good ones. And good ones can be had. The choicest thoughts of the best writers can now be found in leaflet form, and there is moral dynamite enough in some of them to shatter terribly the strongholds of Satan. Indeed, the Bible itself is only a collection of sixty-six little tracts bound in one volume, for, as someone has said, "holy men of God wrote small books on great subjects."

Making due allowance for unwisdom in the use of tracts and for the inferior quality of many that are used, it yet remains true that a great deal of good has been done by them. Many a soul has been awakened by one of these little "leaves of healing" which the Holy Spirit has blown into the hand at just the right moment.

A man stepped into a streetcar in New York, and before taking his seat, gave to each passenger a little card bearing the inscription: "Look to Jesus when tempted, when troubled, when dying." One of the passengers carefully read the card and put it into his pocket. As he left the car, he said to the giver, "Sir, when you gave me this card I was on my way to the ferry, intending to jump from the boat and drown myself. The death of my wife and son had robbed me of all desire to live, but this card has persuaded me to begin life anew. Good day, and God bless you!"

Doubtless many people smiled when these cards were distributed, but who will smile on the day when the Book of Life is opened?

> Though scoffers ask, "Where is your gain?"
> And mocking say, "Your work is vain,"
> These scoffers die and are forgot,
> Work done for GOD, it dieth not.
>
> Press on, press on, nor doubt nor fear,
> Through every age these words may cheer;
> Whate'er may die and be forgot,
> Work done for GOD, it dieth not.

We adore the kind Providence that led Philip to cross the path of the Ethiopian at the very moment when he was needed, but we forget that the same thing occurs every day. There is no such thing as chance in God's world, and those who seek to be led by the Spirit often find themselves messengers of mercy to some weary soul. A lady once traveled nearly two hundred miles to tell the writer personally how a little leaflet that he had given her the year before led her to conversion. By the use of a similar card, a young man was led to give his heart to the Lord, and through his influence both his father and mother were brought into the Master's service. A Christian worker in Nottingham, England, tells the following incident: "I was called to see a dying woman. I found her rejoicing in Christ, and asked her how she found the Lord. 'Reading that,' she replied, handing me a torn piece of paper. I looked at it, and found that it was a part of an American newspaper containing an extract from one of Spurgeon's sermons. 'Where did you find this newspaper?' I asked. She answered, 'It was wrapped around a parcel sent me from Australia.' Think of that! A sermon preached in London, conveyed to America, then to Australia, part of it torn off for the parcel dispatched to England, and after all its wanderings giving the message of salvation to that woman's soul! Truly God's Word shall not return unto Him void."

People Who Should Use Tracts

There are at least five classes of people who can use tracts to advantage:

First, ministers. Some ministers make constant use of them in their pastoral work. They open the way for conversation, and oftentimes they are better than words, for a soul in exercise will sometimes quarrel with the one talking to him but could hardly quarrel with a tract. A tract never gets out of patience, never answers back, and it sticks to what it has said. In many places where a Christian could not enter, a tract can slip in and speak a word for Christ. The sick, the aged, and, above all, the boys and the girls, appreciate a leaflet adapted to their condition. Other pastors use tracts to supplement their preaching. The tract recalls the sermon and deepens the impression made. A judicious use of the right kind of tracts has in some cases been a mighty factor in promoting a revival.

How Edward Judson Uses Tracts

During a ministerial experience of twenty years, this very successful pastor has made constant use of tracts. He seldom makes a pastoral call without having in his pocket an assortment of tracts adapted to almost every member of the family, and especially to the children. In this way he leaves behind him definite souvenirs of his visit and seeds of truth which will bring forth fruit later on. Then each tract generally has printed on it the notice of his services, and acts as a constant invitation to church.

At the close of the Sunday evening preaching service, he has often put some good brother in the chair, and while the meeting proceeds, he goes down into the audience and gives to each person a choice leaflet, at the same time improving the opportunity to say a timely word. In this way, he comes into personal touch with the whole audience, gives every stranger a cordial welcome, and leaves in his hand some message from God.

At least once a year, he selects one tract that has in it the very core of the Gospel. On this he prints a notice of the services and, selecting his church as a center, he has this tract put into the hands of every person living within half a mile in each direction, regardless of creed or condition. He sometimes uses ten thousand tracts at one distribution and finds it very fruitful in results.

A second class is businessmen. Some businessmen use them constantly, passing them out when the right person appears, or inclosing them in packages of goods. Ticket agents give them out with tickets. One agent says that twenty people wrote to him that they had been converted by the tracts he had given them. I remember a businessman who said to me, "I am a timid man and cannot speak in meeting, but if you will buy some good literature I will pay for it and enclose it with our packages of goods." He dealt largely with fishing-vessels, and thus he cast his bread upon the waters (Eccl. 11:1).

Recently I read of a salesman who stopped in St. Louis and called on a merchant to sell him some diamonds. The merchant said, "I do not need any more diamonds."

"Never mind," said the salesman. "I am going to show you my goods, if you have no objections." He opened his case and exhibited his wares so attractively that in a short time he sold the man a bill of goods in spite of himself. Then closing up his samples, he said, "Now I have something to show you better than all these. Here is something very choice; it is the pearl of great price." And pulling out a little pocket Bible, he said, "Are you a Christian, my friend?" And then for a few moments he told about Jesus Christ to him in the same earnest way he had talked of diamonds before. Mix religion with your business. Let the two go hand in hand.

I believe in doing as did the blacksmith in southern Vermont, who, after he was converted, was asked to shoe a horse on Sunday. "No, sir!" said he. "I am a Christian now, and I do not work on Sunday." The man met him with an oath, but he replied, "Hold on, friend! you can't swear in this place. I want you to understand that this is a Gospel shop." So should we maintain a Christian atmosphere in every place which we control, and not allow anything to be said or done there which would displease our Master.

There is no better way of rebuking profanity than by the use of little cards or leaflets prepared for this purpose. Here is one man's testimony:

"The other evening, I arrived at S. and walked over to the hotel. I entered and, after checking my things, started to mail a letter, previous to going in to supper. Between the coatroom and the mailbox stood three salesmen. Two of the number swore as they talked, imagining doubtless that they were emphasizing their point more forcibly.

"Overhearing them, and praying for guidance, I took from my pocket some attractive cards, with different colored backs, which had upon the reverse side, 'Why do you swear?' while underneath were four Scripture texts against swearing. I walked toward the group and, without uttering a word, threw the cards out between my hands, with the backs up, and offered them to the first salesman, a little fellow who had sworn the most. He looked at me curiously, reached out his hand, and drew a card. I immediately turned to the other man who had sworn, and offered him the cards, and he drew one. Then, without paying any attention to the third man, or even looking at him, I mailed my letter and started for the dining room, without having all this time spoken a word. Turning the corner, I heard a shout of laughter from the salesman who had not sworn and knew my shot had taken effect.

"I was just comfortably seated at the table, when the little salesman came to the dining-room door and, looking around, spied me at the table. He walked right in and, coming up to where I sat, said, 'Say, that is the best rebuke I ever had in my life, and I want to say I'm sorry I spoke as I did and that I had no business to do so. Could I get two or three of those cards?'

"'Yes, but be sure before you give them to anyone that you set the example yourself by not swearing again.'

"'All right, I will do so.'

"So I gave him the cards and he left. The following Saturday I found my man in Albany in a large retail grocery store. The minute he saw me he pulled out one of the cards, showed it to the buyer of the department, told him his experience, and read the upper text, "You shall not take the name of the Lord your God in vain, for the Lord will not leave him unpunished who takes His name in vain" (Ex. 20:7). God not only used His Word, as printed upon the cards, to rebuke this man, but also used him as an instrument in His hands all over the country in passing on the message to others."

I know of many businessmen who use tracts constantly, passing them out with a pleasant word to their customers, or putting them in their correspondence. One man who did the largest business of any firm in his line between New York and Chicago, always had one-half of his private desk devoted to a choice assortment of tracts. A Chicago businessman had a thousand leaflets printed and scattered them among his friends. Some time afterwards, he received a letter from another city asking him to plan to spend a Sunday there when he next passed through. He did so and was driven to a new church in the outskirts of the city. "What do you think of that?" asked his host.

"Why, that is a very pretty church, I think, but what of it?"

"That church is the result of a tract which you sent me some time ago. I read it and my soul was so aroused by it that I read it in the Endeavor Society, and it had the same effect upon them. As a result, we looked around to see what we could do for the Master, and finally started a mission in an empty store, which has grown into this church."

A businessman in Brooklyn saw a tract lying on his desk and, without much thought, put it into a letter and mailed it. No sooner had he done this than the devil whispered to him, "You have made a fool of yourself. What do you suppose that man will think of you to put a religious tract in a business letter?"

For a moment, he was ashamed and he turned to the Lord, saying, "Was it a mistake?"

Back came the answer, "Why would it not be a good idea to put a tract in every letter you send?"

"Lord, I will," was the reply. This was in 1882, and a few days ago the man told me that to the best of his knowledge he had never sent out but one letter since without enclosing some kind of Christian literature, and in that instance he was ordering some goods and forgot to put one in, and the goods proved to be the worst lot he ever received. "Presumably," he said, "because I did not enclose a tract."

A third class who can use tracts profitably is teachers. The writer owes more to a district schoolteacher than to all the professors he ever met in college or seminary. Dr. Channing used to say, "There is no office higher than that of a teacher of youth, for there is nothing on earth so precious as the mind, soul, and character of a child."

Professor Tyndall said, "If there is one profession of paramount importance, I believe it to be that of the schoolmaster."

Granted that the special work for which teachers are employed is to educate the mind; still, is it not their duty also to lead them into the realms of spiritual knowledge and, above all, to introduce them to the Great Teacher, who said, "Take My yoke upon you and learn from Me… and you will find rest for your souls" (Matthew 11:29)? We all know that young people do not like to have religion thrust upon them continually, but they do, without exception, admire a manly Christian character and they appreciate a loving interest in their welfare and an occasional earnest word upon the subject.

Those who cannot talk freely with their pupils can, at least, put into their hands the wise words of others; and who can estimate the good that would be done by occasionally giving to each pupil a choice leaflet on some vital subject? Old-fashioned tracts will not do for boys. They need something up to date, something which sets forth in a terse and manly way the attractions of the Christian life and the dangers which beset the pathway of youth.

Another class of people who ought to use tracts is housekeepers. Have them on the parlor table, so that callers may read them while waiting. There is time enough for a person to be converted while a lady is finishing her toilet, and time enough to backslide, too, before some people get down to the parlor. Place them in your guest-chamber so that your friends will have something to turn their thoughts toward the Blessed

One. White Cross tracts will do your boys and girls no harm, and even Bridget may absorb a good deal of the Gospel through an innocent little leaflet. Give them to the butcher and marketman, always accompanied with a kind word and a prayer, and God will not fail to bless them.

The last class which I wish to speak of embraces all who were not included in the other four classes. Tract work is one which everybody can engage in. Here is something which all can do – old and young, rich and poor. It is a business that does not require much time or capital, but it does require tact and prayerfulness and an earnest desire to be used of God. Timid people can in this way hold forth "the word of life" (Philippians 2:16).

How many people are mourning because they "do not know what to say"! But here is a way by which they always have something to say. Some who have begun very timidly to engage in this silent evangelization have become not only brave, but enthusiastic, and by their efforts have enlisted many others in the same work.

How to Use Leaflets

That depends upon the person you are addressing. First of all, you must know what you are using and not be giving tracts on swearing to Sunday School teachers or "Growing Old Gracefully" to little children. If you meet an acquaintance on the street, you can say to him, in a playful way, as you pass a leaflet to him, "Don't say that I never gave you anything." Or you can say, "I have something here that I think you will be interested in. Will you read it if I give it to you?" To a stranger on the cars who has no newspaper, "Would you like something to read?" Then it is an easy matter for you to inquire, "What do you think of it?"

Sometimes you can interest people in a leaflet by telling them some fact concerning it. For instance, you can say of Dr. Chickering's "What Is It to Believe on Christ?," "Here is a little book which has a remarkable record. The author, before he died, had the names of over seventeen hundred people who had written him or told him personally that they attributed their conversion to this tract."

Another way is to say, "Here is a little book that has helped me.

Perhaps you would enjoy it." Leave them in the cars when you travel, or on the parlor table in the hotel. Give one to the waiter. He will appreciate it and read it especially if you have previously shown your interest in him in some substantial way. Never use cheap-looking tracts. They belittle the cause you wish to help.

Never be ashamed of the work you are doing, but act as if you were conferring a favor upon people, which is really true if you are sowing good seed in a Christian spirit.

I am convinced that churches and Christian workers could greatly increase their influence by a more liberal use of printer's ink. The methods of using tracts are innumerable. Let each member be encouraged to keep on hand a choice supply to enclose in his letters. After a missionary sermon, let there be given to each person as he passes out a good tract bearing upon benevolence or missions. Tracts on temperance or narcotics may be wisely distributed in the Sunday School. Visit the jail, almshouse, or hospital, and give to each inmate an occasion to thank God on your behalf. It is said that there is a gentleman in France who watches the obituary column in the morning papers and sends to the bereaved ones little tracts adapted to their situation. Some railroad companies will allow a box to be kept in the station filled with good literature for the use of waiting passengers. Occasionally select a good tract and, printing upon it the name of your church, Sunday School, or Endeavor Society with an invitation to attend the services, canvass the whole neighborhood, leaving a tract at every house. Have a rubber stamp for this purpose. Accompany each tract with a silent prayer that God's blessing may attend it. Make yourself familiar with what you distribute in order that you may bestow them wisely and remember that if you trust Him, the Holy Spirit will guide you in every detail of this work.

Some tracts will doubtless be wasted, just as many a sermon fails to reach the hearts of careless hearers; but we are encouraged to "sow beside all waters" (Is. 32:20) and we never know on what soil the good seed may fall. One thing we do know, however, and that is that Jesus will appreciate the effort, for He hath said, "Truly I say to you, to the extent that you did it to one of these brothers of Mine, even the least of them, you did it to Me" (Matthew 25:40).

Useful in Opening Conversation

It is not an easy matter to open conversation on the subject of religion, especially with a stranger, but a leaflet will often open the way very happily.

I sat down beside a stranger in a railroad car. He called my attention to a fire which had occurred the night before, and then went on to speak of his own experience in having a factory burned and the difficulty which he had in collecting his insurance. When he had finished talking, I handed him a card saying, "If you insure in that company, you never have any trouble in securing your money." The card contained the question, "Are you Insured in the Everlasting Life Insurance Company?" with an attractive description of its advantages. After he had read it, I asked him if he had ever taken a policy in that company.

He said, "No, I never did, and it is a strange thing that I haven't, too. My family are all Christians, and if any man ever tried hard to get hold of it, I am the man. Perhaps you can tell me wherein I failed to grasp it." The result was a delightful talk on how to become a Christian and, as he left me, he thanked me warmly for the help I had given him. Think of it! Two entire strangers sit down together, and, in five minutes' time, each is laying bare his heart to the other on the most sacred of all subjects. Without that leaflet to open the way, it would have been well-nigh impossible.

Useful to Close Conversation

Often a conversation is interrupted by the entrance of a third party, or the lack of time and one has to leave before he has finished what he had to say. In such cases, an appropriate tract will carry on the conversation and perhaps lead the soul to Christ.

Riding on a train, I fell into conversation with a stranger. He said that he was a skeptic and was puzzled to know which of the many different religions was the best. "The Muslims say their prophet is the one to follow, and the Chinese have another, and the Mormons another. I suppose you would say that Jesus Christ is the one to worship."

I said, "My friend, did you ever embrace any of these religions?"

"No, I never did," he replied.

"Don't you think it would be better for you if you would? If you think Islam is the true religion, give your heart to Mohammed and if you can get salvation from it, well and good. If that fails, try Buddhism, or become a Mormon, and if these do not satisfy, then become a Christian." There is a fable which tells of a horse which stood between two stacks of hay, each of which was so fragrant that he could not tell which to bite from, and so he stood there and starved to death because he could not decide which to choose. This man was in precisely the same position on the subject of religion, and I tried to make him see it and realize that he was starving his soul because he could not decide which to choose.

As I urged him to embrace some religion, and that, too, without delay, he said, "My friend, there is a good deal of truth in what you say. I am sorry I have to leave you for this is my station. I hope we shall meet again." I put into his hand Dr. Chickering's tract, "What Is It to Believe on Christ," and Mr. Torrey's "Life Card," both of which make the way of life plain to any honest inquirer. The man had to leave me just as he was becoming interested, but the tracts enabled me to carry on the conversation even after he had left me.

On the same journey, I had an opportunity to talk with two other unsaved men without leaving my seat and, in each instance, just as they became really interested, they had to leave the train. In both cases, however, I gave them an appropriate leaflet which would preach to them long after I had to stop.

Useful to Counteract Infidelity

There is much infidel literature in circulation among the factory population, and thousands of pernicious books and pamphlets are scattered among the schools of the land. Unless Christians do something to counteract this influence, we are allowing the devil a very great advantage. In some cases, the young people's societies have done excellent work in the spread of good literature.

How tracts can be used to counteract error was well illustrated in

Portland. Col. Robert Ingersoll came there and lectured, it is said, to fifteen hundred people. Christians could not hinder it, but they could and did do something to counteract his influence. At the suggestion of one of the ministers, eighteen Christian Endeavor members stood at the door of the hall on the night of the lecture and gave to each person as they came out a copy of H. L. Hasting's address, "Will the Old Book Stand?" A more powerful refutation of Ingersoll's talk could hardly be found, and his attacks upon the Bible would make them all the more eager to see what could be said upon the other side. Wherever any apostle of infidelity appears, let Christian people answer his arguments in the same effective way.

Useful in Promoting a Revival

The first thing to do in promoting a revival is to awaken the spirit of prayer and expectation, and to set Christians talking about Jesus Christ and the Great Salvation. Suppose a minister, or, better still, all the ministers in the place, preach on a given Sunday on the same subject – "Prayer" – and at the close of the sermon let each minister say to his people that as they go out of the house, they will receive at the door a choice leaflet on the theme of the sermon. Let him urge them to read it and pass it on to someone else. If they wish more of the same kind, they can obtain them of such a person. In this way, the whole town will be led to talk and think about the same subject all week. The next Sunday, let the ministers all preach on "Repentance," or "Conversion," or "Sin," or "the Holy Spirit" and follow the sermon with a good tract on the same subject. In a little while, scores of people will be found using tracts to supplement their conversation and in their correspondence, and a deeper interest in spiritual work will be awakened.

Results of Tract Work

While Barnum's circus was in Brooklyn, a member of the troupe came into the prayer meeting of the Grace Baptist Church. He paid very close attention and, at the close of a hymn, he arose and said, with a voice full of emotion, "I have never heard that hymn since I heard it in Sunday School the day before I ran away with the circus. I was then nine years old; I am now fifty. During all these years, I have led a life of sin, and the only thing I had to remind me of my innocent childhood was a little tract given me in Sunday School the day before I ran away. I was led to come here tonight by seeing the light in the windows, and I want you to pray that if there is any mercy for such a sinner as I am the Lord Jesus may save me." He went home that night rejoicing in a Savior. He began at once to work among the members of his troupe, giving them tracts and inviting them to come to church. Of those who came, one professed to be saved, and another, of his own accord, asked the prayers of God's people. A good report has since been heard from the first man, who, through all those forty-one years, had treasured that little souvenir of his Sunday School days.

A pastor gave a tract to a young man who came to call on him. He was converted, and then his father and mother, and all three became active workers in the cause of Christ.

A servant girl in New York placed a searching leaflet on the dressing-case of her mistress. Her attention was arrested, her heart touched, and, though a woman of wealth and a leader in fashionable society, she became a humble Christian and devoted her splendid talents to the Lord, ever after giving much of her time to the distribution of tracts.

I know of many instances and I think it is safe to say that more than two-thirds of those who publish tracts have been led to engage in this work through some personal benefit received from tracts themselves.

A lady in Virginia writes us that in reading the *King's Business,* she came upon an article on "The Use of Tracts," and sent at once for the appended list. At first, she gave them out very timidly, but so eager were the people for them that now she can hardly keep any by her. "Last night I was talking with a poor wretched man who has hitherto evaded me, but now manifests a deep interest in his salvation, and, on inquiring the reason of the change, found that he had been reading some tracts which I gave to a neighbor of his some months ago.

"Last fall I sent out two hundred tracts to the employees on the Pulaski Division of the Norfolk & Western R. R. Returning here in

May, I was told by an engineer that the tracts had been read and passed from hand to hand until literally worn out, and there had been at least ten conversions among the trainmen.

"I am but a beginner in this work, with no training, and no methods, but I go on my knees for all I need to know, and ask God for opportunities, and for the wisdom and power of the Holy Spirit. All the time and everywhere I go I find the way opening till, in view of the great need of workers, I am constrained to cry out, 'Lord, send forth more laborers into the harvest.' All my work is by littles, so little that I cannot tell much about it, and yet I do know of quite a number who have been converted. My eyesight is so poor that I seldom can write a letter, and read no book but the Bible, but I pen a few words on the tracts which are then sent forth on the wings of prayer." If this feeble woman, an invalid in fact, can accomplish so much for Christ in this way, what could others do who have more strength?

A boy belonging to a Sunday School in Philadelphia was telling a friend of an expected visit into the country and what he was going to do there. "And what do you expect to do for your heavenly Father?" his friend asked.

"Why, nothing," said the boy. "What can such a boy as I do for God?"

"You can do much," was the reply. "Now, I will give you a bundle of tracts to take with you, and you can distribute them among your friends."

The boy had not been in the country many days when a boy in the neighborhood asked him to help drive his cows home. Here was his chance to use the tracts, so, taking out one of his silent preachers, he gave it to him, saying, "Here's something for you."

"What is it?" he asked, looking it over. "What is it?"

"It is something good to read," said the lad.

"But I cannot read. Never mind, I'll take it home; they can read it there."

Some days after, the country boy met his city friend. "Well," said he, "that little book you gave me made a great stir at our house, I tell you."

"Did it, though? How do you mean?"

"Why," he replied, "they read the tract, and then they read the Bible, and when Sunday came they made me get out the old carriage and clean it up, and then we all got in that could, and the rest got on before and behind, and rode off to church. That tract's done great things, I tell you."

Subsequently it was ascertained that this one tract was the means of converting several souls.

Chapter 10

Personal Work

R. A. Torrey

By personal work we mean hand-to-hand dealing with individual men, women, and children. This is the most effective method of winning lost souls. The apostle Peter was brought to Jesus by the hand-to-hand work of his brother Andrew. Andrew first found Christ himself, then he went to Peter quietly and told him of his great find, and thus he led Peter to the Savior he himself had found. I do not know that Andrew ever preached a sermon; if he did, it is not recorded, but he did a great day's work when he led his brother Peter to Jesus. Peter preached a sermon that led to the conversion of 3,000 people, but where would Peter's great sermon have been if Andrew had not first led him to Christ by quiet personal work?

Mr. Kimball, the Boston businessman, led D. L. Moody, the young Boston shoe clerk, to the Savior. Where would all Mr. Moody's wonderful work for Christ have been if he himself had not been led to the Savior by the faithful personal work of his Sunday School teacher? I believe in preaching. It is a great privilege to preach the Gospel, but this world can be reached and evangelized far more quickly and thoroughly by personal work than by public preaching. Indeed, it can only be reached and evangelized by personal work. When the whole church of Jesus

Christ shall rouse to its responsibility and privilege in this matter and every individual Christian become a personal worker, the evangelization of the world will be close at hand. When the membership of any local church shall rouse to its responsibility and privilege in this matter and each member become a personal worker in the power of the Holy Spirit, a great revival will be close at hand for the community in which that church is located. Personal work is a work that wins but little applause from men, but it accomplishes great things for God.

There are many who think personal work beneath their dignity and their gifts. A blind woman once came to me and said, "Do you think that my blindness will hinder me from working for the Master?"

"Not at all. It may be a great help to you, for others seeing your blindness will come and speak to you, and then you will have an opportunity of giving your testimony for Christ, and of leading them to the Savior."

"Oh, that is not what I want," she replied. "It seems to me a waste of time when one might be speaking to five or six hundred at once, just to be speaking to an individual." I answered that the Lord and Savior Jesus Christ was able to speak to more than five thousand at once, and yet He never thought personal work beneath His dignity or His gifts. Indeed, it was the work the Savior loved to do. We have more instances of our Savior's personal work recorded in the Gospels than of His preaching. The one who is above personal work thinks himself above his Master.

I. Its Advantages

Let us look at the advantages of personal work.

1. All can do it. In an average congregation, there are not more than four or five who can preach to edification. It would be a great pity, too, should all attempt to become preachers; it would be a great blessing if all would become personal workers. Any child of God can do personal work, and all can learn to do effective personal work. The mother who is confined at home by multiplicity of home duties can still do personal work, first of all with her own children, and then with the servants in the home, with the butcher, the grocer, the tramp who calls at the door, in fact, with everybody who comes within reach. I once knew a mother very gifted in the matter of bringing her own children up in the nurture and admonition of the Lord, who lamented that she could not do some work for Christ. I watched this woman carefully and found that almost everyone who came to the house in any capacity was spoken to about the Savior, and she was, in point of fact, doing more for Christ in the way of direct evangelistic work than most pastors.

Even the one shut up at home by sickness can do personal work. As friends come to the sick bed, a word of testimony can be given for Christ, or even an extended conversation can be held. A little child of twelve who was dying in the city of Minneapolis let her light shine for the Master and spoke among others to a Godless physician, to whom, perhaps, no one else had spoken about Christ. A poor girl in New York City, who was rescued from the slums and died a year or two afterwards, was used of God to lead about one hundred men and women to Christ, while lying upon her dying bed.

The servant girl can do effective and personal work. Lord Shaftsbury, the great English evangelist, was won to Christ in a Godless home by the effective work of the nurse girl.

Traveling men have unusually good opportunities for doing personal work, as they travel on the trains from town to town, as they stop in one hotel after another, and go from store to store. A professional nurse once came into my Bible class in Chicago, and at the close of the meeting approached me and said, "I was led to Christ by Mr. [a traveling man connected with a large wholesale house]. I was in a hotel parlor, and this gentleman saw me and walked across the parlor and asked me if I was a Christian, and when I told him I was not, he proceeded at once to show me the way of life. I was so startled and impressed to find a traveling man leading others to Christ that I accepted Him as my Savior then and there. He told me if I ever came to Chicago to come to your Bible class." I have watched this woman for years since, and she herself is a most devoted Christian and effective worker.

How wonderful would be the results if all Christians should begin to be active personal workers to the extent of their ability! Nothing else would do so much to promote a revival in any community, and in the land at large. Every pastor should urge this duty upon his people, train them for it, and see that they do it.

2. It can be done anywhere. There are but few places where one can preach. There is no place where one cannot do personal work. How often – as we pass factories, engine houses, lodging houses and other places where crowds are gathered – do we wish that we might get into them and preach the Gospel, but generally this is impossible, though it is altogether possible to go in and do personal work. Furthermore, we can do personal work on the street, whether street meetings are allowed or not. We can do personal work in the homes of the poor and in the homes of the rich, in hospitals, workhouses, jails, station houses, and all sorts of institutions – in a word, everywhere.

3. It can be done at any time. The times when we can have preaching services and Sunday Schools are quite limited. As a rule, in most communities, we cannot have services more than two or three days in the week, and only three or four hours in the day, but personal work can be done seven days in the week, and any time of day or night. Some of the best personal work done in this country in the last twenty years has been done on the streets at midnight and after midnight. Those who love souls have walked the streets looking for wanderers and have gone into dens of vice seeking the lost sheep, and hundreds upon hundreds of them have thus been found.

4. It reaches all classes. There are large classes of men that no other method will reach. There are the shut-ins who cannot get out to church, the streetcar men, the policemen, railroad conductors, sleeping-car men, firemen, the very poor and the very rich. Some cannot and others will not attend church, or cottage meetings, or mission meetings, but personal work reaches them all.

5. It hits the mark. Preaching is necessarily general; personal work is direct and personal. There is no mistaking who is meant, there is no dodging the arrow, there is no possibility of giving away what is said to someone else. Many whom even so expert a Gospel preacher as Mr. Moody has missed have been afterwards reached by personal work.

6. It meets the definite need, and every need of the person dealt with. Even when men are aroused and convicted, and perhaps converted by a sermon, personal work is necessary to bring out into a clear light and into a satisfactory experience one whom the sermon has thus aroused, convicted, and converted.

7. *It avails where other methods fail.* One of my best workers told me a few weeks ago that she had attended church for years and had wanted to become a Christian. She had listened to some of the best-known preachers and still was unsaved, but the very first inquiry meeting she went into, she was saved because someone came and dealt with her personally.

8. *It produces very large results.* There is no comparison whatever between what will be effected by good preaching and what will be effected by constant personal work. Take a church of one hundred members; such a church under an excellent pastor would be considered as doing an exceptionally good work if on an average fifty were added annually to this membership. But suppose that that church was trained to do personal work, and that fifty of the one hundred members actually went at it. Certainly one a month won to Christ by each one would not be a large average. That would be six hundred a year instead of the fifty mentioned above. A church of many members, with the most powerful preaching possible, that depends upon the minister alone to win men to Christ by his preaching, would not accomplish anything like what would be accomplished by a church with a comparatively poor preacher, where the membership generally were personal workers.

II. How to Succeed

Certain things are necessary to do effective personal work, but these things which are necessary are within the reach of every Christian.

1. The first is a *clear knowledge of Christ as a personal Savior.* Paul was an effective worker because he himself knew Christ as his own Savior. He could effectively bring others to Christ because he could say, "It is a trustworthy statement, deserving full acceptance, that Christ Jesus came into the world to save sinners, *among whom I am foremost of all*" (1 Timothy 1:15).

A clear knowledge of Jesus as a personal Savior includes three things:

first, a knowledge of pardon through the atoning blood of Christ; second, victory over sin through the risen Christ; third, absolute surrender to Christ as Lord.

2. A clear and firm conviction that any man who has not accepted Christ is lost. Jesus said He had "come to seek and to save that which was lost" (Luke 19:10). It was this clear apprehension and deep conviction that men were lost that drove Him to work day and night to seek and to save them. In like manner, Paul tells us that he ceased not to admonish men night and day with tears (Acts 20:31). It was doubtless the conviction that men were lost that drove him to those earnest efforts, and brought from him those tears of compassion. The conviction that men are lost will fill us with a desire for their salvation, will make us tireless in our efforts to save them, and will give pathos and power to our words as we speak with them.

But how can we get this conviction? By the study of the Word and faith in the Word. Deep convictions come through knowledge of the truth. If one would have a deep conviction that men are lost, he should dwell upon this truth as set forth in the Word of God and ask God by His Holy Spirit to give this Word truth and power in his heart and life. The conviction that all men out of Christ are lost is largely missing in professing Christians and even in ministers today, and this goes far toward accounting for the powerlessness of the average church-member and average minister as a soul winner.

3. A practical knowledge of the Bible. The Bible is the one instrument that God has appointed to produce conviction of sin, to bring men to faith in Jesus Christ, and to regenerate. In order to be used of God to produce conviction of sin, to lead men to faith in Christ, and to bring about the new birth in their experience, we must know how to use our Bible so as to produce these results. One may have a wide and profound general knowledge of the Bible, and yet be absolutely at sea in its practical use. In an after-meeting, I once asked one of the best-known and most useful teachers of the Word of God in America to speak with a woman and show her how to be saved, and he replied, "I do not know how to do that." This is something that every child of God ought to know, and it is something that every child of God may know, because there are books that tell very plainly just how to do it.

4. Love. Nothing wins like love. It is the Savior lifted up on the Cross, thus revealing His infinite love, who draws men unto Him, and we, by our love to men, can win them to the Savior. At the close of a meeting in one of the suburbs of Chicago, the first person that rose was a very large man. I was attracted by his appearance, and afterwards spoke to him. He told me that he had attended church and prayer meeting for years, but had only gone to criticize, that when men would get up and speak in prayer meeting he would take out his note book and "keep tab on them," writing down what they said, and then comparing it during the week with the way they lived. At last he was taken very sick and was supposed to be dying. A minister of the town called upon him and asked the privilege of praying with him. He replied, "You can pray if you want to."

"As the minister knelt to pray," he said to me, "I kept tab on him, too. I thought I was dying, but I lay there with my eyes open watching the preacher to see if he was real, thinking nothing about my own soul, but about him. As I watched, I saw a tear stealing down his face, and I said, 'This man is real, he loves me, though I am nothing to him,' and that broke my heart." This man recovered, and has become an untiring worker for Christ, but he was not won by my sermon, or by my dealing with him, but by the other minister's love, and that minister did not know that he had accomplished anything by his prayer.

5. Self-renunciation. Jesus said to His disciples, "Follow Me, and I will make you become fishers of men" (Mark 1:17). It is only by coming after Him that we can become successful fishers of men, but He says, "If anyone wishes to come after Me, he must deny himself, and take up his cross daily and follow Me" (Luke 8:23). If we are to be largely used in personal work, or any kind of work for the Master, there must be an utter putting away of personal interest, our own comfort, our ease, our pride, our feelings. Pride is one of the greatest hindrances to effective personal work. Oftentimes it keeps us from attempting work for fear of rebuff. It makes us unwilling to seem beaten in an argument, and so we keep on arguing, when it would be far better for the disputant to leave him alone. It leads us to get angry when the one with whom we are working seems to get the best of us, and nothing is more unfortunate than when the worker loses his temper. A cowardly worldling once spit in the face of a converted prize-fighter. He knew that the prize-fighter could whip him very easily, and the prize-fighter felt tempted to do it. The hot blood rushed to his face, but he simply took out his handkerchief and wiped the spit from his face and said, "The blood of Jesus Christ could wipe away all your sins as easily as I have wiped this spit from my face." That conquered.

6. *Prayer.* "The effective prayer of a righteous man can accomplish much" (James 5:16), but there is no line in which prayer avails more than in the line of personal work. The worker must pray for wisdom. God has promised to give it to us when we ask Him for it (James 1:5). We need it with every case with which we deal. No matter how thorough our knowledge may be of the Word of God and of men, each case presents its own peculiarities, and only the wisdom which God gives is sufficient.

We should pray for power. Yes, "...power belongs to God" (Psalms 62:11), but the power that belongs unto God is at our disposal in answer to prayer.

We should pray for those with whom we are dealing that God will open their eyes to see the truth and move their hearts to obey it. When the work is done, we should pray for God's blessing upon the seed sown, and oftentimes the work that has appeared fruitless will become fruitful by the blessing of God.

We should pray for the definite anointing of the Holy Spirit that we may become effective workers. Many a man has tried ineffectively for years to be a successful personal worker, but by coming to know the privilege of being filled with the Holy Spirit has stepped out of a place of powerlessness into a place of power. The prayer must be real, earnest, persistent.

7. *Perseverance.* There is one text that a personal worker needs to let sink deep into his heart: "Let us not lose heart in doing good, for in due time we will reap if we do not grow weary" (Galatians 6:9) No work requires as much patience and perseverance as soul-winning. No work is more worthy of it. We should show our patience by the way we deal with each case. Many say a few words to one, and then a few words to

another, and then to another. They keep flitting here and there; they are not the successful workers. Others, when they once begin to deal with a man hold on to that man until, if it is in any wise possible, he has been led to Christ. I have workers in my church who if they get hold of a person in an inquiry meeting, I feel reasonably confident will lead that person to Christ. If one attempt fails with a man, we should show our perseverance by making another and another and another. We should study how to get at men who are unreachable. There is an avenue of approach to every soul if we can only find it. It is worth much time and thought and study to find it. It took me fifteen years to win one man, but when that man, after several years of effective ministry, lay silent in death, as I stood beside his coffin, I was glad that God gave me the perseverance to work fifteen years for his conversion.

We should show our perseverance by seeking another person when we have apparently failed with one, and if we fail again, seek still another, and if again, still another.

8. Constant activity. "Sow your seed in the morning and do not be idle in the evening, for you do not know whether morning or evening sowing will succeed, or whether both of them alike will be good" (Eccl. 11:6). The personal worker's motto should be, "At it, and always at it" – by day and by night, in the home, in the place of business, on the street, in hotels, in the cars, everywhere. Nothing was more characteristic of Mr. Moody, and nothing went further to make him the mighty man of God that he was, than the fact that he was always on the watch for souls, and always sowing the seed which is the Word of God. He would speak to the conductor who took up his ticket on the car, to the reporter who came to interview him, to the servant in the home, to the man he met in business. He was at it and always at it, and so God gave him blessing and victory.

God is calling all Christians to rouse up and go to work, witnessing for Christ and striving by personal effort to bring all within their reach to Christ. Who will hear the call? A glorious reward awaits all who do. They shall shine "like the stars forever and ever" (Daniel 12:3).

Chapter 11

Drawing the Net

R. A. Torrey

M any a mighty preacher fails to get the results he might from his preaching because he does not know how to draw the net. He is skillful at hooking fish but does not know how to land them.

A friend told me three days ago that he heard a man that evening preach to a large congregation of men one of the best sermons he ever heard, and, continued my friend, "I believe there would have been fifty decisions right then, but just at the critical moment the evangelist did not know what to do, and he let the meeting slip through his fingers. He asked them all to stand up and sing some hymns. The men began to go out in crowds. Then he tried to get hold of things again, but it was too late. Though there were some inquirers, there was nothing like the result there ought to have been."

The moment the last word of the sermon is uttered, there should be opportunity for decisions. This opportunity may be given in a variety of ways. You may ask the audience to bow a few moments in silent prayer, insisting courteously but firmly that no one go out for a few moments. If the interest is deep enough, you may then ask "all who wish to be saved," or "all who have made up their minds here and now to accept Christ as their personal Savior, to surrender to Him as their Lord and

Master, and to begin to confess Him as such before the world," to rise (or come forward and give me your hand, or come kneel at the altar). If you think the interest hardly warrants that, you can ask "all in the audience who are burdened for unsaved friends," or "all who are anxious for the salvation of some friends in this audience," to rise. When they have risen, invite all who wish to be saved right now to rise. It is not well usually in the general meeting to ask all Christians to rise, as this makes it awkward for the unsaved, and they may not come back again.

Another good way is to say, "We are going to sing a hymn and I don't want anyone to go out until it is finished. The Holy Spirit is working in this meeting (don't say that unless He is), and anyone moving about may disturb someone just on the verge of a decision for Christ. Now, while we sing the second verse, all who will accept Christ (don't say, "if anyone will") arise. Stop when the second verse is sung and call for decisions. Then sing the third, and the fourth, etc., in a similar way. If you are fortunate enough to have an altar in the church where you are preaching, it is often better to have them come to the altar. If you have no altar, you can have the front seats emptied and use them for an altar. A solo may be used in place of a congregational hymn.

Still another way is to say, as you close your sermon, "We are going to have a second meeting to give those who have been converted here tonight and all who are interested an opportunity to accept Christ now and enter at once into the joy of the Christian life. We want every man who is interested in his soul's salvation and all Christians to stay to that second meeting. You can't afford to go away." It is usually better to have the second meeting in another room, if there is one, that the people have to pass as they go out. Have *wise* workers posted at every door of this room to invite and urge the people to come in as they pass. When the interest is very deep, you can have the second meeting in another building. Have the singing in the second meeting begin at once as the people come in.

When all are in, have absolute silence, and then silent prayer. Perhaps two or three audible prayers *by men and women whom you can trust as really knowing* God may follow. (Don't take any chances at this point and let some crank spoil your meeting.) The next thing to do varies with circumstances. You may call for an expression at once. If the interest is very deep, call at once for those who wish to accept Christ to rise or come forward. On other occasions ask "all who have accepted Christ and know that they are saved and are walking in fellowship with Christ" to arise. Now you and your workers see who the persons to deal with are. Next ask those who wish to become Christians to arise. It may be well to sing one or several verses as this is done. One and another and another and then many will arise.

Wherever it is possible, it is well to have now still a third room into which those who have risen as desiring to become Christians shall go. Have a wise man in charge of this room until you get there yourself. Have him put one worker, and only one, with each inquirer. These workers should be trained for the work. Every church should have a training class for this purpose. When you have gotten all you can into the inside room, turn the outside meeting into a meeting for testimony and prayer, which either you or some wise worker manages. It is a great advantage to have a choir leader who can do that. The unconverted ones who have not gone into the inside room can be gotten hold of personally in this testimony meeting or afterward. Don't have any holes in your net anywhere if you can avoid it.

Sometimes, in the second meeting, it is well to ask all who were converted after they were fifty to rise, then those who were converted after they were forty, thirty, twenty, ten, before they were ten. Then ask all who will accept Jesus tonight to rise, then all who really desire to know the way of life. A good method to use occasionally in the second meeting is to ask all who were converted after they were fifty to come forward and gather about the platform, then those who were converted after they were forty, etc. This will gradually thin out those who are seated, and the unconverted will find themselves being left behind, and it will set some of them to thinking. Especially will this be true if a man sees his wife leaving him, or a son sees a mother.

Some may think that there is too much method and maneuvering in all this, but it wins souls, and that is worth maneuvering for. Jesus Himself told us to be "shrewd as serpents," (Matthew 10:16) and also said that "the sons of this age are more shrewd in relation to their own kind than the sons of light" (Luke 16:8). Evidently Jesus would have us exercise all honest ingenuity in accomplishing His work, especially the work of soul winning. It is lawful, as Paul's example shows, to catch them "by deceit" (2 Corinthians 12:16). The methods suggested will suggest still others. The great purpose of all these methods is to get many to commit themselves and to bring them to a decision to accept Christ. Much good preaching comes to nothing because it is not driven home to the individual and the individual brought then and there to an acceptance and confession of Jesus as Savior and as Lord. When one has been led to accept Jesus, an immediate public confession – then and there – should be insisted upon (Romans 10:9-10).

The After-Meeting

The owners of mill ponds have a way of drawing off the water now and then for the purpose of catching the fish. If the pond covers ten acres of land and the fish are distributed all through its waters, it is difficult to find them and impossible to catch them without stealthy approach and enticing bait. But after the bulk of the water has been drawn off and the area reduced to half an acre, the fisherman casts in his net and draws the fish ashore with ease. Such is the object of the after-meeting. It gets rid of the elements in a crowd which are not a help, but rather a hindrance, to the work of soul-winning. It enables us to come nearer to the inquirer, and to point him to Jesus in face to face conversation. It reduces the size of the pond so that the Gospel hand-net may be used with good results. This reducing process may continue even in the after-meeting. If you have a man or a woman whom you know has grace for soul-winning, get together a group of inquirers and put him or her in the midst of them. The whole group may be rejoicing in Christ before the meeting closes. If you have small separate rooms to which you can invite these groups, all the better.

The Bible is the textbook for an after-meeting, as it ought to be for every religious service. The leader may take a few minutes to make plain the way of life from some text or paragraph of the Book. But let him remember that the purpose of the meeting is not edification, but salvation. An address to Christians, unless it be a few words at the close urging them to go out and seek the lost, is out of place in the after-meeting. If no unsaved person remains, it would be well for the Christians to have a season of humiliation and prayer. There should be earnest heart-searching while they ask God and each other, "Am I an Achan in the camp hindering the work of the Lord?"

The testimony of Christians as to the Scriptures which led them to Christ, or into larger faith and brighter hope, is a most important part of the after-meeting. Let me give, as nearly as I can remember, what was done and said in an after-meeting which I attended a few weeks ago. As soon as quiet was restored, there was an earnest prayer for guidance. The leader then arose and said, "We will now hear from as many as can speak in five minutes the Scriptures which God used in showing them the way of life. We want simply the Word of God without comment. Rise and speak distinctly, with a prayer that God will bless others through the truth as He has blessed you." The first one to respond was a young woman who quoted with a clear voice, "...the one who comes to Me I will certainly not cast out (John 6:37).

The leader said, "That invitation is also a promise; it implies that all who come to Christ He will receive, but it says very much more. He will receive and never cast out. There is in it saving and keeping power. It is the Scripture for those of you who are afraid that you may not hold out."

The next witness was a man of middle age, who said, "He is able also to save forever those who draw near to God through Him" (Hebrews 7:25).

The leader: "God is all-powerful, but you make Him able by accepting the Lord Jesus Christ, and this ability is based upon the fact that He ever liveth to make intercessions for us."

Third witness: "Come to Me, all who are weary and heavy-laden, and I will give you rest' (Matthew 11:28).

Leader: "Do you want rest of heart? Come to Jesus for it now."

Fourth witness: "Turn to Me and be saved, all the ends of the earth; For I am God, and there is no other (Is. 45:22).

Leader: "Looking is not a long process. You can look as quick as a lightning flash; look this moment and live."

Fifth witness: "Therefore there is now no condemnation for those who are in Christ Jesus" (Romans 8:1).

Leader: "We who have accepted Christ need not fear the judgment day. Our case has been settled in the court of mercy where Jesus Christ is the Advocate."

Sixth witness: "But as many as received Him, to them He gave the right to become children of God" (John 1:12).

Leader: "And if sons, then heirs; heirs of God and joint heirs with Christ. Will you not accept this rich inheritance through Christ this evening?"

Seventh witness: "...the blood of Jesus His Son cleanses us from all sin" (1 John 1:7).

Leader: "Then do not try to cleanse yourself, and do not divide your trust between the blood and ordinances. The Blood is all-sufficient; accept Jesus Christ and the Blood cleanses at once.

> "There is a fountain filled with blood,
>   Drawn from Immanuel's veins,
> And sinners plunged beneath that flood,
>   Lose all their guilty stains."

Eighth witness: "Believe on the Lord Jesus Christ, and thou shalt be saved" (Acts 16:31, KJV).

Leader: "It does not say 'believe on Jesus', nor 'believe on Christ', nor 'believe on the Lord.' Jesus means Savior, and a Savior from sin we need. Christ means the anointed one, the high priest and an intercessor, an advocate we need. Lord means Master, and the Master we need to rule our lives. You cannot accept Him as Savior while you reject Him as Lord, nor can you follow Him as Lord while you reject Him as Savior. His intercession is for those who accept Him as both Savior and Lord. So you see, Paul preached to the jailer the full Gospel when he said, 'Believe on the Lord Jesus Christ and thou shalt be saved.' The little word *on* is very important; it does not say believe *about* the Lord Jesus Christ; you may believe all *about* Him without believing *on* Him. I believe much about Washington, Lincoln, and Grant, but I am not conscious of believing on either of them in the sense that I am depending upon them for anything. When your faith *about* Christ has been translated into faith *on* Christ, you are saved."

The invitation was then given, and a number came forward and gave the leader their hands, confessing Christ as their Savior and Lord, the leader remarking that it was well to begin the Christian life with a handshake and pass it on to others.

This all took seven or eight minutes, and I do not say that it is a model method, but it has the advantage of being full of God's Word.

I would not, however, always wait till the close of the after-meeting before asking converts to confess Christ. We ought to expect God to save people while we are preaching, and Jesus Christ is worthy of the most public confession. If the purpose of the after-meeting is to make it easy for people to confess Christ because the unsympathetic crowd who might scoff are gone, it had better be abandoned. That scene on Calvary was not in a corner. Our Lord's shameful death on the cross was public, and it is fitting that our confession of Him should be "before men" (Matthew 10:32), not before Christians only, if we would have Him confess us before the Father and the holy angels.

It is well to have it understood that it is in order for the new convert to confess Christ at any time. There might be a little confusion now and then, but a glorious confusion it would be if caused by the confession of new-born faith in the Savior. While I was preaching to the unsaved, urging an immediate decision, about the middle of the sermon I saw a tall young man near the door rise up, step into the aisle, and come walking toward the pulpit. He stood just in front of me for a moment looking up into my face as if he wanted to say something. My first thought was that he was a little "off," and might create a disturbance; so I paused for an explanation, when he reached out his hand and said, with a voice full of genuine emotion: "Excuse me, sir, but I have just accepted the Lord Jesus Christ as my Savior, and I felt I could not wait for you to get through before I told you." There was no need of any more sermon. The Spirit of God fell upon the audience. Oh, that our praying and preaching may be with such power that men and women will not wait for us to ask them to request us to pray for them, nor to confess Christ, but under the conviction of the Spirit will cry out as at Pentecost, "What must we do?" And when they have accepted Christ, so full of faith and joy that they will not wait for formal invitations, but at once "make known to all around what a dear Savior they have found."

The praying in an after-meeting should be brief, and for but one thing – the salvation of the lost. Long general prayers that take in everything and everybody are apt to be powerless anywhere, but they are especially out of place in a meeting that has a definite object.

In dealing with an inquirer, when you see that he has come to the point of accepting Christ, it is well to ask him to kneel with you and pray aloud. His prayer will be an index to his heart. If he begins with confessing sin and thanking God for the gift of Christ, you may be sure that he is saved. If he apologizes for sin and fails to make a full confession, he needs further instruction.

The workers in an after-meeting should be aglow with love to Christ and souls. If they are mature Christians with large experience, all the better, provided they do not tell their experiences to inquirers and thus put them to seeking a similar experience rather than Christ. Young, intelligent Christians with a great Savior and a little experience make very effective workers. Preach Jesus in the after-meeting and spend no time in answering curious questions. A young college student rose for prayer in one of my meetings and made an engagement to see me in my study next morning at ten o'clock. When alone with him, I asked him, "What is it that troubles you?"

"Well, sir," he replied, "I have been greatly troubled for some time over the question as to where Cain got his wife, and I think, if I could settle that, I could take a step further."

I answered the question as best I could, and it seemed satisfactory to him. But with the next breath, he asked another question just as frivolous. I answered that, and he asked another. I saw he was a sort of jack-in-the-box of questions, and that it was wasting time, so I said, "My friend, answering these questions is profitless; if we could answer them all and a thousand more like them, neither you nor I would be any nearer heaven. Will you kneel with me and ask God to save you from sin?" He consented, and while we prayed, he surrendered to Christ. I might have spent the whole day in answering his questions without leading him to Christ.

A man came to Mr. Moody in an after-meeting with a long list of hard questions. Mr. Moody said, "I will answer your questions if you will promise me to do one thing."

"What is it?"

"Promise me you will do it before I tell you."

"No sensible man does a thing like that."

"Will you promise me, then, that you will try to do it?"

"Yes, I can make that promise."

"Well, give your heart to Jesus Christ and then come to me with your questions."

The man went away disappointed, but two nights afterwards he returned with a radiant face and told Mr. Moody that he had done what he asked him to do and that, for twenty-four hours, he had been one of the happiest men on earth. "Where are your questions?" asked Mr. Moody.

"I haven't any," he said. "The moment I accepted Jesus Christ they were all answered or appeared so insignificant that they were not worth answering."

Philip might have spent hours answering the eunuch's questions about Isaiah, but he began at the same Scripture and preached unto him Jesus. Let us follow his example.

The open Bible in face-to-face work is indispensable. Turn to the Scripture that suits the case and let the inquirer look at it while you read. The truth may enter through eye-gate more readily than through ear gate. A handbook for soul-winners may be useful in the worker's study, but do not take it into the after-meeting. Let the inquirer read directly from the Bible. The little New Testament which has about one hundred texts marked with red ink may do good service, and, if you can afford to give every inquirer or convert the copy from which you have read, it will be highly prized. God may continue in the home the work which began in the after-meeting.

After dealing with a poor drunkard in two after-meetings and becoming a little discouraged because of the fact that in the second the fumes of drink remained upon his breath, I gave him a little Testament and asked him to go to his room and read John 3:16 while on his knees. The next week, I met him on the street sober and rejoicing in the Lord. He told me that he went at once to his garret-room, knelt down before the only chair in it, with the little book open before him, read aloud the verse I had marked, and while he read, light came into his soul. Since that hour, God had given him strength to pass saloons without entering, and though the thirst for drink was not gone, he was trusting God for grace to overcome.

As to the length of the after-meeting, that should depend upon the work to be done. If there are earnest souls seeking Christ, and loath to leave without comfort, we should remain with them as long as we think they need our services. The Holy Spirit may not watch the clock as we do, and the nervous haste that some Christians manifest to get away at a certain time may not be pleasing to Him.

As I was about to begin an evening service in a New York church, the pastor whispered, "You must be careful to get through the whole service by nine o'clock."

"But," I replied, "suppose the Spirit should indicate we ought to remain later?"

"Oh, well, if you keep the people later than nine, they will not come back tomorrow evening." We remained until 9:45, and the next evening the audience was twice as large. To have sent the people home at nine would have been to miss the greatest blessing of the evening.

An after-meeting should be entered with the utmost reliance upon the Holy Spirit. It is to be a time of decision. There will be battles fought, and the power of the Spirit is needed to give the victory. Keep the upward look. If the Spirit seems to indicate that the program you have formed should be laid aside, let it go. Be willing that God should have the right of way. Rejoice if He burns up all red tape and makes the meeting thoroughly unconventional. "...where the Spirit of the Lord is, there is liberty" (2 Corinthians 3:17). If, as leader, you are under the complete control of the Holy Spirit, you will be able to decide at once what ought to be done or said. You will see at a glance that a brother is talking from force of habit, or for the purpose of airing a fad, and not with an earnest desire to lead souls to Christ, and you will be able to stop him with the right words and in the right tone. In an after-meeting a few evenings ago, just as the leader was giving an invitation for inquirers to accept Christ, a brother rose and began to make a speech on prayer. The leader was a stranger and had never seen the brother before, but it was evident to him that if the Holy Spirit to whom the meeting had been committed was leading it, the brother's message was not of the Spirit. He therefore quietly suggested that the time would not admit of an address. The brother left the room at once indicating by his manner that he was angry, but the meeting, which would have been killed by his long speech, went smoothly on with good results. There are a class of Christians, especially in great cities, who attend all meetings – not for the good they can do or receive, but for the purpose of finding an opportunity to speak on some favorite theme. When they rise the meeting falls, and the leader needs the wisdom that God alone can give in dealing with this class of good but rather useless people.

A whispered word, or even an elbow-touch from a friend may do more than twenty sermons in leading to a decision. An earnest businessman in New York City told me it was not the sermon, nor a word, but just a touch on the shoulder which led him to confess Christ before men. He had already accepted Him as Savior, and just needed this little encouragement. He said: "While the evangelist was inviting all who loved Christ to confess Him by going forward and giving him the hand, I felt a gentle touch on my shoulder. I looked around and saw the face of an old friend looking wistfully at me. He did not utter a word, but I knew what he meant, and I went right up and gave him my hand." This was the beginning of a businessman's Christian life.

For efficient work in the after-meeting our greatest need is that we be endued with the Holy Spirit. And this endowment comes in answer to prayer and a complete surrender of the will to God. Then the right word will be said to the right person, at the right time, in the right way.

Chapter 12

How to Make the Work Permanent

E. P. Goodwin, D.D.

A ll ministers and Christian workers who have to do with evangelistic efforts find great difficulty in securing permanent results. I
desire to name two or three methods, tested by much experience, which
have proved of great value. Take first the common experience in nearly
all revival meetings. People come from everywhere. If the meetings
are marked with unusual power and are continued for some length of
time, there is sure to be a considerable class of persons interested not
identified with any church and not under the eye or personal care of
any pastor. Then, especially in the great meetings conducted by noted
revival leaders, multitudes of such are sure to be gathered in. In Mr.
Moody's meetings, it was no uncommon thing to find scores of people
night after night in an inquiry-room, and that in my own church, not
one of whom had I ever seen, and most of whom were never met again
after the meetings ceased. But more or less the same is true of all revival
services in our city missions and in all such Christian work. Therefore,
the name and address of everyone rising for prayer or dealt with in the
inquiry-room should be secured. Every such person should then be
visited at his home or place of business as soon as possible, and again,
and again, until fully established.

In all dealing with souls, every Christian worker will find it, I am sure, of prime importance that there should be secured in some way a following up of the work by systematic Scripture teaching. People need something more than impressions to hold them fast. Not everyone is brought down by a single arrow shot at a venture. Some people have to be shot full of arrows before they surrender. Impressions, impulses, half-formed choices, and purposes often fade and lose their grip after the music and prayers are over. Men need the Master of the assembly with His nails to fasten things and make them stay. And this is what regular meetings for instruction do. Then, besides, there are difficulties to be met, doubts to be removed, truths and duties to be emphasized and pressed home, and all this takes time. Few people see and grasp truth clearly and fully at a single glance, or in an hour. Certainly, if people are to be rooted and grounded so as to stand fast, there must be time. The gourd that shoots up in a day is like to wither in a night. Most converts – yes, and most believers as well – need line upon line, precept upon precept, here a little and there a little, to make them able to give a reason for the hope that is in them.

It is a great thing to be established and stand fast in the faith, and, in order to do this, nothing, it is safe to say, is so essential as the organizing of young converts into classes for stated and continuous instruction in the Word. It is not too much to say that, without this, it is impossible to secure satisfactory results in evangelistic work, or growth and power in Christian life. In my judgment, the chief reason for the failure of most whom I have known who have dropped away from their professions and fallen back into the world, lies in their having no subsequent systematic training. They accepted the truth, had good impulses, sincere purposes, and meant to be true followers of Christ, but they were chiefly ruled by impulses (had little knowledge of truth, had no sufficient instruction as to the meaning of the life they had accepted, no adequate knowledge of the temptations of the world, the wiles of the adversary, the deceitfulness of the heart, or the secret of success in standing fast), and so, having no root, they withered away. If all such sincere inquirers after salvation could be organized into classes for Bible study, even for a few weeks, I believe but very few would abandon their hope. The very agreeing to meet for such instruction sifts out those who are only transiently impressed. I should say unhesitatingly that where such systematic teaching is secured, permanency of Christian life is almost certain, while, where it fails, permanency rarely results.

I have in mind one series of revival meetings, with which I had personally to do, where there was a very large number of professed acceptances of Christ. Very little thorough inquiry work was done, and, so far as my knowledge goes, no organized effort at instruction was attempted. Out of nearly three thousand cards signed by those expressing a purpose to lead a Christian life, I doubt if a hundred ever took any step further. In two of the most earnestly engaged churches but one person ever came forward upon profession of faith. For myself I long since ceased to expect results of any value except in connection with such training.

I do not mean to discredit all such decisions reached in inquiry-meetings or elsewhere, as transient. Let us hope that many are truly turned then and there from darkness into light, and from the power of Satan unto God. But commonly only a small percentage of such prove effective in the Master's service. Our churches are full of those who are like Gideon's army – only a handful are in dead earnest and to be counted on when the battle is joined. Bible-trained workers, inspired with the Master's love and equipped with knowledge as well as zeal, are pitifully few in all our churches, but wherever one finds even a few such, they are worth a host of others, for with them victory is sure.

What has been said implies another condition of great importance in making evangelistic work permanent. I mean the importance of making public confession of faith and becoming members of the visible church of Jesus Christ. Observe, I do not say that believers, those who truly accept Jesus Christ as Savior and Lord, are to join this or that particular church organization, but *the church* which the Holy Spirit meant when under His guidance and control the church of Christ was organized, and believers were by the Lord daily added thereto. What I say now is this: that it is not possible to fully meet the Lord's wish and realize the larger measure of grace which He desires to bestow, whether in the development of individual Christian life or in power to witness and work in His behalf, without public and continuous church membership. I do not say that such persons cannot be true believers. Unquestionably they can be. The test of salvation is not the test of visible church membership. He that truly believes on the Lord Jesus Christ is unquestionably saved. The Scripture plainly declares that the thief on the cross was saved that way, without any baptism and without joining the church. So was the woman at the well, and so of the multitudes of others. But that is not the question. The question is this: Is such a standing aloof from the visible church, as so many do, while yet in a way performing Christian duty, meeting the wish of the Lord Jesus, and doing the work He wants believers to do in the world? I say no, it is not. If anything is plain in connection with the resurrection of the Lord Jesus and the gift of the Holy Spirit, it is that our Lord established his church, a body of believers united to Him by the Holy Spirit and made thereby His Body, the body of which He is to be everlastingly the Head, and in whom and with whom all true believers are to be finally associated with Him in glory.

The Lord Jesus was obviously not using words lightly when He commanded His disciples to observe the Last Supper, nor when, by the light of the Spirit He organized the church and sent out His disciples to be His witnesses and go everywhere preaching His Gospel and calling upon men to believe and be baptized. The Lord's ideal of the believer, in other words, was of a believer led by the Spirit and seeking always and with earnest and absorbing purpose to carry out his Lord's wish and do His will. In the very nature of the case, therefore, all who desire to honor Him and secure the fullest measure of His favor and power will do as His disciples did – openly and gladly identify themselves with His church. In no other way can they secure the closest union with their Lord, and in no other way secure the fullest measure of the energy of the Holy Spirit. He cannot so fully impart Himself to believers who stand aloof from what Jesus Christ Himself appointed. There are objections and so-called reasons for holding other views, but in my judgment, they are without Scriptural warrant. One Scripture truth runs through all these teachings of the book of Acts and the Epistles – records and teachings which are divinely and infallibly inspired: one body of believers united by the indwelling of the Holy Spirit in Jesus Christ, and that one body manifesting Him before all the world, witnessing His Gospel, and seeking to win men to believe on Him unto salvation. So far as these Scriptures go, there is, in my judgment, no scrap of authority or permission to stand aloof from public avowal of Jesus Christ and meanwhile claim to be doing His will as much as in him lies.

What, then, it may be asked, as to those who, like Muslims, may incur the penalty of death by being baptized? It is enough to say that the Lord made no exceptions, and that so far as we know the apostles made none. Nor in general have true believers ever shrunk from open avowals of their faith, as the massacres of Christians all through the centuries, and these so striking examples of believers in China just now, show. The Lord has always put high honor upon those who have stood fast in the faith and have counted it a joy to bear a witness that cost even life itself.

But, in our country, none are called to endure such a test, and no such reasons can be alleged for not making open confession. I give it as my deliberate judgment that all such standing aloof is nothing other than a subtle device of the great adversary. Largely the reasons given when thoroughly analyzed prove to be excuses for worldly aims and practices, beliefs, habits, or fellowship condemned by the Word of God. I have never known such a case where I could not detect in my own mind either a plain worldly reason, or an unscriptural belief, as the underlying cause of refusal to make open confession of faith. And I go further. It is a somewhat popular idea that there are those who can accomplish more in serving the Master by staying outside the church, and sometimes examples are pointed out of those who are shining illustrations of what Christian life can be without church profession or obligation. By all means, let us recognize and rejoice in all true believing in Jesus Christ, whenever it can be found, and let us not deny that there are such genuine disciples whose names are not upon any roll of the church. But, admitting this, I deny that such are helping the Master whose names they refuse publicly to own or to wear. His own word is decisive: "Therefore everyone who confesses Me before men, I will also confess him before My Father who is in heaven" (Matthew 10:32).

He organized His church for all believers, and gave His Holy Spirit to dwell in that church as His publicly owned and recognized body. Into that fellowship He calls all true believers to come and ally themselves by being baptized and by participating in the Lord's Supper. Whoever fails to do either, fails therefore to fulfill to the letter our Lord's own appointment. He may nevertheless be a sharer in salvation, as has been already shown, but he cannot be an example of what Jesus Christ wants a believer both to be and to do, for he has never met and is not meeting, day by day, Christ's plain requirements. More than that, so long as he stands aloof from the church, he is dishonoring the very name of Him to whom he looks for salvation, and, practically, invites others to disobey His commands. Such an example of disobedience to the Lord and to the Holy Spirit would be a poor way to win men to the Master's service.

More than that, as a matter of fact, there is no greater hindrance in persuading people to rank themselves upon the Lord's side than this very attitude of non-professing believers. Those cherishing secret hopes naturally say, "If such non-church members are sure of salvation and are examples of Christian living, we are as sure of salvation as they, and there is no need of our joining the church." Every pastor in his work has this argument to meet.

Then, besides this, such non-church members almost universally stand away from all the activity of the churches. They take no part in prayer-meetings, rarely engage in Sunday School work, and never, of course, attempt to reach and bring in the unconverted or in anywise bring them to decisions for Christ. In the nature of the case, they can have no ardor for revivals, no longing for souls. As a matter of fact, they are hindrances instead of helps to all aggressive Christian work. A community of such non-confessing believers would never see a revival, and I doubt very much whether it would ever win a soul. Jesus Christ wants His sheep brought into the fold. That is the only place where they can find safety and go in and out and find pasture, and this fold is His church. To stay out is to be puny and stunted and dwarfed.

Another thing that needs to be mentioned and emphasized as a condition of securing permanency in evangelistic work, is the necessity of setting young converts at work and keeping them at it. Indeed, that is an absolute necessity for all Christians, old and young, if they are to thrive and grow. Weeds will flourish of themselves, but not flowers. They must have care and painstaking, and this must be followed up.

We seem often to forget that in dealing with newborn souls we are dealing with children. Too often, after such have reached a decision, they are left to care for themselves. Sometimes they are regarded as too weak and immature to be leaders of others. It is of course possible that such may be overzealous and unwise, but, on the whole, there is no better way of developing young Christians than to set them at work reaching and bringing in others. The early disciples may have made mistakes in going forth as witnesses after Pentecost, but, if they did, we have no record of it. The Holy Spirit, who took possession of that whole company of believers, doubtless qualified them for their work, and those whom the Lord added daily were worthy of being received. No doubt there is need of wisdom and judgment in seeking souls, but where harm is done by one who is overzealous and injudicious, it is quite safe to say that far more harm results from keeping the arms folded and the lips shut. A fervent "Amen," or a "Glory to God," or "Hallelujah" from a new-born soul would not hurt a prayer-meeting, nor would a misapplication of Scripture, or a prayer full of bad grammar. When a devout brother with a remarkable history thanked the Lord in my prayer-meeting one night, that "He and I had put up a big job on him in getting him converted," there were some smiles, but many hearts beat warmer and many "Amens" followed the prayer. We have little need to fear an excess of zeal in most churches. If four-fifths of our church members could be sent out and kept out doing some form of Christian work a part of every week, they would grow faster and become more aggressive and stable and efficient as believers than they now are, and our weekly meetings would be less like refrigerators than they often are. The best school for training Christians is trying to help others by telling them what Christ has done for us. Paul kept repeating the story of his own conversion, and that won others and helped him. There is nothing safer or wiser for a new convert than telling others how he found salvation. The less he tries to explain, philosophically, how men are saved, how the Spirit moves upon the heart, how a divine will gets a human will to decide and surrender, and the more he just sticks to what the Word says and what he has found there, the better. I believe that was what our Lord meant to have His disciples do when He said they were to go forth to the ends of the earth as His "witnesses" (Acts 1:8). They were not to argue, or make speeches, or persuade men by their eloquence, or logic, or learning. They were only to be witnesses and tell to men everywhere what Jesus Christ had done for them. And today this is, above everything else, what the world needs.

Then, as the new converts go forth, they will of course find many forms of Christian activity in which they are needed and can be made most helpful. So, some may become Sunday School teachers, Bible-class teachers, visitors among the sick and poor and unfortunate, workers in missions, and helpers in many other ways. Such work is self-developing and increases potential. The Holy Spirit delights to find such pupils and very quickly turns them into helpers. He opens the truth to others, clears their minds of misapprehensions, strengthens their faith, reinforces their zeal with knowledge, gives them fervency and power in prayer, and in every way increases their ability and efficiency. This is clearly the way the early disciples were developed. Their School of Training, which, for example, Paul so lovingly and gratefully commends in the last chapter of Romans, was the school of Christian work in which they had been mainly self-taught, or, more strictly, Paul was head master, and Phoebe and Priscilla and Aquila his chief helpers. They and their beloved associates, observe, were all pronounced and active church members, and as such they all gave themselves to individual Christian work in winning and then helping to build up believers. What is the ideal way of developing the church? Our Lord described Himself as a man taking a far journey, giving authority to his servants, and *"to each one his task"* (Mark 13:34). There was to be no one left idle, or without some specific duty assigned. Paul says the same thing when, in describing the gift of the Spirit, which, it is to be remembered, was a gift intended, as at Pentecost, for *all,* he says, "But one and the same Spirit works all these things [divine operations], distributing to each one individually just as He wills" (1 Corinthians 12:11). No one is left out, or, in other words, no one who is a true believer is to be without work. Only get all true converts, and all true church members engaged in such a fellowship with the Holy Spirit interpenetrating, energizing, empowering all, and the mystery of revivals and adding daily to the church and hastening the Kingdom, will be solved.

Every new convert should be set immediately at the daily study of the Bible. He should be given instructions in how to study the Bible. Perhaps the best book in the Bible for a young convert to begin with is the Gospel of John. It is true that this is one of the most profound books in the Bible. But John says that he wrote it "that you may believe that Jesus is the Christ, the Son of God; and that believing you may have life in His name" (John 20:31). Now, this is just what the beginner needs. The Gospel of John may well be followed by the Acts of the Apostles. Then let the young convert study the Epistle to the Romans, and then Ephesians. Each of these books should be read again and again. Topical study is also good for the young convert, taking up such great subjects as Sin, Grace, the Blood, Justification, Prayer, the Holy Spirit, etc. The New Topical Textbook (F. H. Revell) is inexpensive and useful for this purpose.

While the young convert should study chiefly the Bible, there are other books that are very helpful – the writings of Dwight L. Moody, Charles H. Spurgeon, Andrew Murray, F. B. Meyer, G. Campbell Morgan, G. H. C. MacGregor and R. A. Torrey being specially commended.

In the pages immediately following is reprinted "How to Make a Success of the Christian Life," which fittingly concludes "How to Make the Work Permanent." These pages are published separately as a tract for circulation among new converts.

Chapter 13

How to Make a Success of the Christian Life

R. A. Torrey

There are two classes of persons who start out in the Christian life: those who make a complete or partial failure of it and those who make a complete success of it. The question at once suggests itself: "Is it possible to point out a plain pathway, in which anyone who will can walk, and following which will make success *absolutely sure?*" I believe it is. I believe that God's Word gives a few simple instructions which, if followed, will make success in the Christian life a certainty.

There are seven steps in the path marked out in the Bible.

1. *Begin right.* What a right beginning is we see in John 1:12: "But as many as received Him, to them He gave the right to become children of God, even to those who believe in His name." Receive Christ. *Take Him as your Savior* who died for your sin. Trust the whole matter of your forgiveness to Him. Rest upon the fact that he has paid the full penalty of your sin. "He made Him who knew no sin to be sin on our behalf, so that we might become the righteousness of God in Him" (2 Corinthians 5:21). "Christ redeemed us from the curse of the Law,

having become a curse for us – for it is written, 'Cursed is everyone who hangs on a tree" (Galatians 3:13). It is in this first step that many make a mistake. They try to mix in their good works as a ground of salvation. They think if they are good God will forgive them, because of Christ's death and their goodness. *Take Him as your Deliverer*, the one who will save you from the power of sin, who will quicken you when dead in trespasses and sins. Don't try to save yourself from the power of sin. Trust Him to do it. *Take Him as your Master.* Don't seek to guide your own life. Surrender unconditionally to His lordship over you. Say, *"All* for Jesus." Many fail, because they shrink back from this entire surrender. They wish to serve Jesus with half their heart, and part of themselves, and part of their possessions. It is a wretched life of stumbling and failure, this life of half-hearted surrender. It is a joyous life all along the way, the life of entire surrender. If you have never done it before and wish "to make a success of the Christian life," go alone with God, get down on your knees, and say, *"All* for Jesus." Say it very earnestly; say it from the bottom of your heart. Stay there until you realize what it means and what you are doing. It is a wondrous step forward when one really takes it. If you have taken it already, take it again. Take it often. It always has fresh meaning and brings fresh blessedness.

Taking Christ as your Master involves obedience to His will, as far as you know it in each smallest detail of life. This is one of the most essential conditions of receiving "the Holy Spirit, whom God has given to those who obey Him" (Acts 5:32).

2. *Confess Christ openly before men.* "Therefore everyone who confesses Me before men, I will also confess him before My Father who is in heaven." (Matthew 10:32). "For with the heart a person believes, resulting in righteousness, and with the mouth he confesses, resulting in salvation" (Romans 10:10). The life of confession is the life of full salvation. It is when we confess Christ before men that He confesses us before His Father in heaven, and that the fullness of His blessing comes. It does not mean that we are to confess Christ just once, as for example, when we unite with the Church, but constantly. The one who would make the largest success of the Christian life should seize every

opportunity of confessing Christ before men – in the home, in shopping, at work, in the church, everywhere. I once heard a wise old preacher say, "If we make a good deal of Christ, He will make a great deal of us." How many backsliders fell away from Christ at this point! They went to a new city, or a new place to work, and neglected to confess Christ, and now they are back in the world.

3. *Study the Word.* "Like newborn babies, long for the pure milk of the word, so that by it you may grow in respect to salvation" (1 Peter 2:2). The Word of God is the soul's food. It is the nourishment of the new life. One who neglects the Word cannot make much of a success of the Christian life. All who get on in the Christian life are great feeders on the Word of God. Here many fail. Ask any backslider, "Have you fed on the Word daily?" I never have found one that could say that he had.

Two points on Bible reading are: first, read for food for your own soul; second, read a great deal on your knees. The Bible has become in some measure a new book to me since I have taken to reading it on my knees.

4 *"Pray without ceasing"* (1 Thessalonians 5:17). The one who would succeed in the Christian life must lead a life of prayer. That is easy enough if you only set about it. Have set times for prayer. The rule of David and Daniel, three times a day, is a good rule. "Evening and morning and at noon, I will complain and murmur, And He will hear my voice" (Psalms 55:17). "Now when Daniel knew that the document was signed, he entered his house (now in his roof chamber he had windows open toward Jerusalem); and he continued kneeling on his knees three times a day, praying and giving thanks before his God, as he had been doing previously" (Daniel 6:10). Begin the day with thanksgiving and prayer – thanksgiving for the definite mercies of the past, prayer for the definite needs of the present day. Stop in the midst of the bustle, worry, and temptation of the day for thanksgiving and prayer. Close the day with thanksgiving and prayer.

Then there should be the special prayer in special temptation – when we see the temptation approaching. Keep looking to God. Pray without ceasing. It is not needful to be on our knees all the time. But the *heart* should be on its knees all the time. If "Satan trembles when he sees the weakest saint upon his knees," let us keep him trembling all the time. We should be often on our knees, or on our faces literally. This is a joyous life, free from worry and care. Here is the point (neglect of prayer) where many fail.

There are three things for which the one who would make a success of the Christian life must especially pray: first, for wisdom, "if any of you lacks wisdom, let him ask of God," (James 1:5); second, for strength, "Yet those who wait for the Lord Will gain new strength" (Is. 40:31); third, for the Holy Spirit, "your heavenly Father [will] give the Holy Spirit to those who ask Him" (Luke 11:13). If you have not yet received the baptism of the Holy Spirit, you should offer definite prayer for this definite blessing and definitely expect to receive it. If you have already received the baptism of the Holy Spirit, you should with each new emergency of Christian work pray to God for a new filling with the Holy Spirit (Acts 4:31).

5. *Go to work for Christ.* "For to everyone who has, more shall be given, and he will have an abundance; but from the one who does not have, even what he does have shall be taken away" (Matthew 25:29). Note the context, and you will see that this means those who use what they have will get more, and those who let what they have lie idle will lose even that. The working Christian, the one who uses his talents, whether few or many, in Christ's service, is the one who gets on in the Christian life here, and who will hereafter hear the "Well done, good and faithful slave...enter into the joy of your master" (Matthew 25:21). Find some work to do for Christ and do it. Seek for work. If it is nothing more than distributing tracts or invitations to meetings, do it. Always be looking for something more to do *for* Christ, and you will always be receiving something more *from* Christ.

6. *Give largely.* "The generous man will be prosperous" (Proverbs 11:25). "Now this I say, he who sows sparingly will also reap sparingly, and he who sows bountifully will also reap bountifully... God is able to make all grace abound to you, so that always having all sufficiency in everything, you may have an abundance for every good deed" (2 Corinthians 9:6, 8). Success and growth in Christian life depends on few things more than

upon liberal giving. A stingy Christian cannot be a growing Christian. It is wonderful how a Christian man begins to grow when he begins to give. Give systematically. Set aside for Christ a fixed proportion of all the money or goods you get. Be exact and honest about it. Don't use it for yourself under any circumstances. A tenth is a good proportion to begin with. Don't let it be less than that. After you have given your tenth you will probably soon learn the joy of giving free-will offerings in addition to the tenth.

7. *Keep pushing on.* "Brethren, I do not regard myself as having laid hold of it yet; but one thing I do: forgetting what lies behind and reaching forward to what lies ahead, I press on toward the goal for the prize of the upward call of God in Christ Jesus" (Philippians 3:13-14). Forget that which lies behind; press on to the better things that lie before. Forget the sins which lie behind. If you fail anywhere, if you fall, don't be discouraged, don't give up, don't brood over the sin. Confess it instantly. Believe God's Word. "If we confess our sins, He is faithful and righteous to forgive us our sins and to cleanse us from all unrighteousness" (1 John 1:9). Believe the sin is forgiven, forget it, press on. Satan beguiles many a poor soul here. He keeps us brooding over our failures and sins. He even makes us think this is humility, as if it were humility to doubt God's Word and make Him a liar by not believing the sin is forgiven and put away, when He says it is.

Forget the achievements and victories of the past and press on to greater. Here Satan cheats many of us out of the larger life. He keeps us thinking so much of what we have already obtained and makes us so contented with it and so puffed up over it, that we come to a standstill, or even backslide. I have seen this in many individuals and many churches. "How well we have done!" they think. Our only safety is in forgetting those things which are behind and pressing on. "Excelsior!" ("Higher!") should be the soul's persistent cry. Press on! There is always something better ahead. You may have received a second blessing, or a twenty-second, but there is still something better until we "attain . . . to a mature man, to the measure of the stature which belongs to the fullness of Christ" (Ephesians 4:13).

Young Christian friends and older Christians, the road to certain success in the Christian life is plain enough. Shall we take it? The truths presented herein are familiar, but are you practicing them? Read them over frequently and see if there is not some point at which you fail. If you find there is, correct your mistake AT ONCE.

Chapter 14

Music in a Revival

D. B. Towner

The day is past when any intelligent person doubts for a moment the helpfulness of singing in revival services. The time was, when some very zealous people objected to singing in church services, and who even now do not encourage it to any great extent, and yet these same people make the best use of singing that they know how in revival meetings. Therefore, no matter what the objection may be to singing in the regular church services, all are agreed that for mission and revival meetings, singing is helpful. It would be a very easy matter to prove by the Scripture that the early Christians believed in singing, and that even our Lord Himself approved of it and engaged in it, but that is not the object at this time. The Wesleys certainly were heartily in favor of it and made much of it – and so have all the successful evangelists from their day down to the present time. It is very generally conceded, we think, that Mr. Moody was the prince of evangelists, and he perhaps made more of singing than any other man of his time, or before him, and if any one doubts the wisdom of his course in this direction, they have only to listen to the testimony of men and women from every country where the Gospel has been sung, to be convinced that the Gospel when sung is as powerful to convert men and women as it is when preached.

One who was an actress, but is now an evangelist, says that the singing of a Gospel song by a company of Christian Endeavor members in a public park of Chicago convicted her of her sin and turned her heart to God, and that she was saved on the spot. A pastor in a large city of this country says that the singing of a man and his wife brought him to Christ, and these are only two of a great multitude who have come under our personal knowledge, who have been led to Christ through song. But one says, "These are isolated cases, and since so much singing is done that seemingly does not produce conviction of sin, does it not follow that singing is not of much importance in revival services?" Not at all, no more than the fact that many sermons do not convict of sin is proof that there is no power in preaching to convert men.

Singing, like preaching, must be of the right sort to be helpful in bringing souls to Christ. Many who are disposed to use singing to promote evangelistic work have erroneous ideas about it. They think that the principal thing is a fine solo singer, and it does not matter very much how the people sing, or whether they sing at all. But quite the reverse is the correct idea. While solos, duets, quartets, etc., are excellent, the greater power lies in the singing of the people. Therefore, to get the greatest help from the singing in a revival meeting, the people must be made to sing. Hence it is necessary that there be a good leader, and by a good leader we mean a man skilled in music, filled with the Holy Spirit and a love for souls, a good organizer and choir conductor, a good solo singer, and a man with a fine sense of the fitness of things. Such a man will be a channel through which the Spirit can work and will under God be a power in a revival. A man may be a splendid musician and have a magnificent voice, and yet be of absolutely no use in revival work because he is not a spiritual man and does not sing for the definite purpose of winning men to Christ.

Having the right sort of a leader of the singing, you still must have a suitable collection of hymns and tunes. I say hymns and tunes, because we so often see a good hymn coupled with a poor tune, or a good tune coupled with a weak hymn. In either case, the result will not be satisfactory. Because of this, many are opposed to the introduction of new books and songs in a revival. But this should not be the case, for if you have such a leader as has been described, and give him the selection of the book, you have no more to fear than you have in giving to the Spirit-filled preacher the choice of subjects he should speak upon, or the methods he should employ. But so long as the selection of a book is left to a committee who either are not at all musical, or else are not in sympathy with revival work, or want to get the book that costs the least money, or are prompted by any other motive than to obtain the book best adapted for the work of winning souls, you will be crippled in the music. A poor book is dear at any price and does incalculable harm to the meetings. For we say frankly, that many of the so-called Gospel hymns have not a particle of the Gospel of Christ in them, and many of the tunes are such an abomination to every person with a knowledge of or taste for music, that even if there is much blessed and converting truth in the hymn it is lost sight of in the dislike awakened by the bad tune.

There are two extremes which should be avoided in choosing music for evangelistic meetings: first, the frivolous light songs, and, secondly, the too staid and grave ones. I do not say classical, for the term classical as generally applied to music is misleading. It is a prevalent opinion that classical music is difficult, which is as great a mistake as it would be to measure hymns by their length, or a picture by its size. Many of the very simple tunes are truly classical, while much of the difficult music is anything but classical. It often requires time to determine whether a tune is a classic. I venture that very few, if any, would have pronounced *"Old Hundred"* classic in the year it was written, and yet, today, no man of any caliber would pronounce it otherwise.

While great care should be exercised in the selection of music for revival meetings, yet one must not be hypercritical about new songs. About twenty years ago, a committee of literary men and musicians were compiling a denominational hymnbook, and certain hymns and tunes were rejected as not being of a high enough order. But today those same tunes and hymns are being used in all denominational books as they are revised and compiled, and have proven by their vitality that they belong among the classics. If a tune is well written, no matter how simple, don't be afraid to try it. If a hymn does not teach error, direct or implied, don't be afraid to give it a trial, but if it does, no matter what its literary merit may be, let it alone. Let it be distinctly understood that we are not opposed to the use of old hymns, not by any means, for quite the contrary is the case. We believe that the good old hymns are the heritage of the church, and should be regarded as such, that they should be sacredly kept and perpetuated, and that each successive generation should be taught to sing them well, but to hold on to these to the exclusion of the new ones would be a calamity. As new men come on the scene, they embody the truth into new hymns, and it gives it a freshness just the same as is the case with a new sermon, and new tunes awaken new interest in these themes, such as the old ones do not. As we become familiar with a tune, it gradually loses its power with us, even though we never become tired of it. But the new tune arrests the attention and gives the truth it carries a chance to enter the heart. Some people seem to outlive their usefulness, while others never do. It is just so with songs. There are those that should be in every selection, and there are others that seem to have been embalmed, as it were, and laid away in the denominational books which are never used. We do not object – they have served well no doubt, now let them rest in peace – while others come on and do service in their turn.

Then we believe there is a place for sentimental songs in evangelistic meetings. By this we mean songs with a good religious flavor, on topics calling to mind home and dear ones, for through these songs the emotions are stirred, and men are frequently made to think and finally to repent. Of course, these songs must be of a high order, and judiciously used.

In short, what is needed in revival or evangelistic meetings is hymns that contain a message for the sinner, founded on the Word of God, worshipful hymns for believers, and hymns of thanksgiving and praise, written by men and women whose hearts are aglow with the love of God, presented by a leader who is a musician anointed by the Holy Spirit for such service. When these conditions obtain, the music in evangelistic meetings will be a mighty power, and no one will doubt but that it has the approval of Almighty God.

When the soloist sings, he should do it with just as definite a purpose of leading someone to Christ as the preacher has when he preaches. He is not there to entertain people, but to save people, and he needs the baptism with the Holy Spirit for this work just as much as the one who preaches the Word. The same is true of the chorus. They should be trained to realize that the salvation of some in the audience hangs upon the way they sing and the way in which they conduct themselves. Both the soloist and the choir should come to the meeting after very much and very definite prayer to God for His blessing upon their work.

Mr. Moody made very much of solos, quartets, choir singing, and congregational singing to get the audience into a receptive mood, so that when he preached, his word dropped into prepared soil. He would have them sing and sing until he saw just the favorable moment had come, and then he would arise and deliver his message. He attributed much of the wonderful effects of that message to this fact – that the singing got the people ready for it.

A suitable solo or duet or even chorus often serves to clinch the message and bring people to immediate decision. It is well for the preacher, oftentimes, to say, "Now I am going to ask Mr. to sing, and while he sings, I want to ask the Christians to bow their heads and pray God to bless the song to someone's conversion and let the unsaved think, and when the song is ended I will give all who wish to accept Christ an opportunity to arise (or, come forward) and say so in that way."

Music can also be used very effectively while all the Christians are standing, by asking all those who wish to be saved to come forward while we sing *"Just as I Am,"* or some similar hymn of invitation. People should be so familiarized with a few choice hymns that they can sing them without a book while kneeling at the altar or bowing in prayer. Many a successful revival campaign has been signalized by one or more hymns that have been the keynote of the whole movement and were not only sung again and again at the meetings, but on the streets, on the cars, in the home, and everywhere.

In the great reformation under Martin Luther in Germany, the historic Huguenot movement in France, and the Methodist revival in England and America, hymns were one of the mightiest instruments used of God to spread and perpetuate the work. If we are wise, we shall make much of holy song in the great revival upon which we are now entering.

Chapter 15

Advertising the Meetings

A. F. Gaylord

This subject is of far more importance than the average minister or the average church realizes. One great reason why so many of our churches have such a small attendance is because the people are not made to know what is going on, or that the meetings are important, by frequent and judicious advertising. By wise and persistent advertising, the vacant seats in most of our churches could be filled. Many churches do not give this subject a second thought, but up-to-date business men are saying constantly, "This advertising pays," or, "That advertising doesn't pay." The church of Jesus Christ would do well to adopt many ideas from the commercial world relative to making important work known. The old saying, "The best tie to connect businessmen with the public is to advertise," is as true today as when first uttered.

In announcements for the Lord's Day and other meetings of the church, too great emphasis is laid upon reaching the churchgoers. One of the chief purposes, if not the paramount purpose, of the church is to reach the unsaved. The unsaved, as a rule, are within hearing of the Gospel, but the majority of them are not in attendance at our churches. C. H. Spurgeon used to say that if you could get people to thinking you could get results. Just so; if we can get people to thinking of the church and of their own responsibility thereto, we can get results.

The writer was much struck recently by an illustration in a leading paper. The saloon, brilliantly lighted within, the sidewalk in front clean, and everything bright and attractive, holding out every inducement to the young man from the country who has just reached the city, was illustrated in one cartoon. In another cartoon was represented the church with this announcement: "Open Sunday and Wednesday evenings." The sidewalk in front was covered with snow and not a single light was to be seen. This is a true picture of many of our well-equipped metropolitan churches. Statistics show that every year thousands of young men from the rural sections flock to the cities. Many of them, while in the country, have the advantages of church life, and are brought up under the influences of Christian homes; but, when they reach the city, they fall among less godly companions and forget their early training. It is the business of the church to reach these young men. Just how to reach them, every church and every organization must decide for itself, with a due regard to its environment.

The little weekly bulletin announcing the church, its services, and its church motto, together with when and where the pastor may be seen, is a very attractive way of reaching many. At all times, and on all occasions, a large bulletin-board close to the church, announcing in an attractive way the speaker and his subjects, has proved a great help, as all who have tried the bulletin know.

It is also well to place permanent bulletin-boards where a great many people pass on foot or in the cars. The bulletins should be large enough to be read from the cars, and there should be frequent changes of matter, so that people will learn to watch to see what is going on.

One of the best ways of advertising is by the use of large billboards. They are expensive, but experience demonstrates that, when they have been used to advertise evangelistic and other special meetings, they have accomplished great results. All the billboards of a large city were utilized recently for notices of special revival services. These notices were found in every part of the city. The newspaper people noticed them, felt that something important was going on, and reported the meetings daily.

A church may be well known in its own locality and city, but the pastor may be more widely known and his name, appearing in a striking way on the bulletin board, often attracts people who do not care for the church, but who wish to hear him speak.

There is perhaps no better plan for the bulletin than that followed by Mr. Moody in his wide evangelistic work. He always used a white background with plain black letters – letters that could be read a block away. As an auxiliary to the large bulletin, Mr. Moody made use very frequently of the free-admission ticket – thus creating a personal tie between the meeting and the recipient.

At the weekly prayer-meeting and other meetings, the cooperation of each individual member of the church should be obtained. They should be handed all the tickets that they will take and judiciously distribute. These tickets should have printed upon them the name and location of the church, the name of the pastor, and also the subjects for the morning and evening services. It is well to have some striking text printed upon the back of the ticket. Distributing these tickets is work that any Christian can do. What matter if many tickets *are* wasted? Many bullets are wasted in a war.

A very useful form of advertisement is an attractive card about the size of the regulation visiting-card, neatly printed, inviting people to the church service, and reading, in the corner, "Presented by" with a blank space for the name of the person immediately responsible for the invitation. Members of the church should be encouraged to carry these cards in their pockets, signed by their own hand, and to give them out to people whom they meet in business, socially, on the train, or in any other way.

In villages and cities where members of the church have stores and businesses, a plain window bulletin-board, from twenty-four to thirty inches wide, with black letters announcing the church, its pastor, and when the services are held, keeps before the eyes of the passers-by the fact that the church is at least wide-awake and has something to offer. Experience has shown that passers-by are attracted by these things and remark upon the activity of the church and are drawn to attend it. Why should not the church be as zealous and wide-awake in the business for which it stands as is the businessman for the dollars and cents that he may make while here? In one case it is things temporal; in the other, things eternal.

Small window-cards, twelve by eighteen inches, printed so that they can be read from the street, are very useful for special meetings – not only in revival services, but at Easter, Christmas, Thanksgiving, or other special occasions. These should be handed around among the members of the church and their friends to hang up in their windows. During a presidential campaign, the majority of us are quite willing to wear the emblem of the party with which we intend to cast our vote, or to hang our candidate's picture in the front window, or some other conspicuous place, and politicians say that much good is accomplished in this way.

We know that much good is accomplished by these window-cards in advertising religious meetings. A man who had placed one of these cards in his window sat behind the curtain at another window and watched the people passing by. Men, women, and children of all classes stopped and read the sign through. Much good is accomplished by placing a pointed text in the window where people may read it. Many have been blessed by these texts. A recent appeal from the pastor of the church with which I am connected brought the hearty cooperation of the members to put these cards in their windows, and this one church gave out several hundred of them. When a large number of these cards are noticed on different streets, they at once awaken comment on the part of the passers-by. They wonder what is going on and go to the church to find out. The great object is to set the people to thinking about the meetings and about Christ.

In cities, the advertisements in our surface and elevated cars, and on the platforms of elevated lines, are read by thousands of persons.

We have found transparencies very useful. They consist of a wooden frame from eighteen to twenty-four inches in length and about twelve inches high, with white linen around the four sides, on which are printed in black letters the announcements of the meetings. To the wooden bottom tallow candles are secured. When these are carried about in the evening, they do more to attract people than the most artistic printed matter. Perhaps the novelty of the thing is the strongest point in its favor. As many as possible of these transparencies should be sent out every evening. Sometimes it is well to organize the whole corps of transparency-bearers into a procession and send it through the more thickly populated part of the city.

In connection with special evangelistic meetings recently held in the city of Chicago, a van eighteen feet long and ten feet high was covered with black cloth, on which was painted in white letters the announcement of the meetings and speaker. This was driven up and down the main thoroughfares of the city and was read by thousands. Many say these things are undignified, but they fill the churches and result in bringing men to Christ. Not a few churches are dying from dignity. The up-to-date business sacrifices dignity in order to achieve results. The writer has been greatly impressed with the fact that the average church or religious institution falls far below the high standard established and maintained by successful businesses.

A thorough canvass of the locality where a church is located is very effective. The names of all non-churchgoers should be secured. There should be a well-organized corps from some of the organizations of the church to do the work, and it should be done in as short a time as possible. An invitation should be left at every house and, later, after all the names are secured, a postcard announcing the services of the church, with a kind invitation from the executive committee or the pastor, should be sent to each person. These should be followed up by a personal letter. What fails to reach one will reach another. Here again a lesson may well be drawn from the business man, who is all the time gathering the names of prospective customers and, if he or his agent is unable to call in person, he sends a letter soliciting an order, or in some way puts his work before the desired customer. Certainly a church should be as zealous and aggressive in winning men to Christ as a business is in winning customers. I have recently sent out many letters of this kind and not one has been rejected.

The great question is: How can an interest be aroused in the church? Every possibility of reaching those who do not want to be reached should be "pushed for all there is in it. " A wise advertising committee of not more than two – better still, one – which prayerfully considers each and every step to be taken before any printed matter is issued, and the hearty cooperation of those who assist in getting out such printed matter, is certain to accomplish large results in reaching those for whom the church of Christ was established.

In all our advertising, we should not forget nor neglect the newspapers. Most newspapers are willing to assist to the utmost of their ability in pushing the work of any church that shows itself alive and aggressive. If notices and descriptions of meetings, and outlines of sermons and other interesting matter is sent to them, they will publish it. They will even send reporters to the meetings if there is anything worth reporting, but it is not fair to leave it to the papers to find out what is going on, when it is our interest more than theirs that is in hand. Many ministers and churches complain of not getting satisfactory reports in the newspapers, but they are more to blame than the newspapers. They think that the newspapers ought to know that they are alive and important, but newspaper men are very busy men and, though quite pervasive, they are not omnipresent. Not a few abuse the newspapers and then wonder why the newspapers do not support them.

It is well sometimes to utilize the advertising columns of the newspapers. If this is done, an attractive advertisement should be put in the amusement column, for that is the column of advertisements read by people looking for some place to go, by travelers and commercial men, the very class which the church wishes to reach and oftentimes fails to reach. A very large church that we know, whose audiences usually filled the lower floor only, advertised a special evening service, with the subject, in the amusement columns of the papers. The next Sunday evening the church was filled upstairs and downstairs. Perhaps 800 or 1,000 additional people were present. The church did not keep up this special advertising for more than a week or so, but it has kept full from that day to this, though five years have passed.

The best kind of advertising of all is done by getting individuals to go after individuals. They should be encouraged to be persistent, going after the same people time and time again, at least until they come.

Of course, no kind of advertising, no matter how expensive or thorough, will do permanent good unless there is something in the meeting to which people are invited that is worth going for. Furthermore, the people who are brought in by the advertising should be given a hearty welcome by the church. This is a matter that needs constant watchfulness, care, and prayer.

Chapter 16

How to Win Souls for Christ

C. H. Spurgeon

I consider it a great privilege to speak to groups of preachers and teachers. Truthfully, I wish I were more fit for the task. Even as my words are captured in the pages of this book, silver of eloquent speech and gold of deep thought have I none, but such as I have, I give unto you.

What Is It to Win a Soul?

What is it to win a soul? When it comes to the winning of souls, I hope you believe in the old-fashioned way. Everything seems to be shaken and shifted from the old foundations nowadays. Today, it seems we are expected to draw out or evolve the good from men and bring it to the surface – good that is already in them. You can find much good if you make the attempt, but I'm afraid in the process of this type of evolution you will develop devils. I don't know what else you can expect out of human nature, though, because humankind is as full of sin as an egg is full of meat, and the unfolding progress of sin must be everlasting harm.

We all believe we must approach soul winning with a desire in God's name to see all things made new. This old creature is dead and corrupt and must be buried, and the sooner the better. Jesus has come so there

163

can be a passing away of the old things and a making of all things new. In the process of our work, we endeavor to bless men by trying to make them moderate – not excessive, *Let your moderation be known unto all men* (Philippians 4:5a). May God bless all work of that sort.

However, if we produce a world of total abstainers and leave them all unbelievers, we have failed. We must drive at something more than temperance, because we believe men must be born again. It's good that even a corpse should be clean. Therefore, the unregenerate should be moral. It would be a great blessing if they were cleansed of the vices which make this world reek in the nostrils of God and good men. But that's not the focus of our work, which is to see the dead in sin live, that they be made alive with spiritual life, and that Christ would reign in lives where the prince of the power of the air now has sway.

Preach with this objective: that men quit sinning and flee to Christ for pardon. So by His Spirit, they may be made new and become as much in love with everything that is holy as they are now with everything sinful. Aim at a radical cure. The axe is laid at the root of the trees. Just changing the old nature isn't satisfactory for those who gather around you in the streets. You seek the imparting of a new nature, by a divine power, so they may live unto God.

Our objective is to turn the world upside down, or, in other words, that where sin abounded grace may much more abound (Romans 5:20). We aim at a miracle. It's good to determine that objective at the start. Some think they ought to lower their note to the spiritual ability of the hearer, but that's a mistake. According to those who think this way, you ought not to urge a man to repent and believe unless you believe that he can, of himself, repent and believe.

My reply is a declaration. I command men in the name of Jesus to repent and believe the gospel, though I know they can do nothing of the kind apart from the grace of God. I'm not sent to work according to what my own reason might suggest but according to the orders of my Lord and Master. Ours is the miraculous method which comes from the endowment of the Spirit of God who asks His ministers to perform wonders in the name of the holy child Jesus. We are sent to say to blind eyes, "See," to deaf ears, "Hear," to dead hearts, "Live," and even to Lazarus rotting in that grave and stinking – "Lazarus, come forth." Dare we do this?

It is wise for us to begin with the conviction that we are utterly powerless unless our Master has sent us and is with us. But if He who sent us is with us, all things are possible to him who believes (Mark 9:23). Preachers, if you are about to stand up to see what *you* can do, it is wise for you to hurry up and sit down. However, if you stand up to prove what your almighty Lord and Master can do through you, then infinite possibilities lie before you. There is no limit to what God can accomplish if He works via your heart and voice.

The other Sunday morning, before I entered the pulpit, when my dear brothers, the deacons and elders of my church, gathered around me for prayer as is their custom, one of them said, "Lord, take him as a man takes a tool in his hand when he gets a firm hold of it, and then uses it to work his own will with it." That's what all workers need, that God may be the Worker through them. You are to be instruments in the hands of God, and you are to actively put forth all your faculties and forces which the Lord has given to you. But never depend upon your personal power. Instead, rest only upon that sacred, mysterious, divine energy which works in us, through us, and with us, upon the hearts and minds of men.

At times, we've all been greatly disappointed with some of our converts, haven't we? The fact is, if they are *our* converts, we will always be disappointed with them. But when they prove to be the Lord's work, we shall greatly rejoice over them. When the power of grace works in them, "Glory to God!" It will be for God's glory and nothing else but glory, because grace brings glory. However, mere oratory only creates sham and shame in the long run.

When we preach and think of a pretty, flowery passage or a neat poetic paragraph, I wish we could be restrained from using them by that same fear which acted upon Paul when he said he wouldn't use the wisdom of words, *lest the cross of Christ should be made void* (1 Corinthians 1:17). The gospel preacher must rethink his own ways and say, "I can say that very prettily, but then they might notice *how* I said it. Therefore, I will say it in such a way that they will only notice the fundamental value of the truth which I teach them." It's not the way we deliver the gospel, nor our method of illustrating it, which wins souls. The gospel itself does the work in the hands of the Holy Spirit. It is to Him we must look for the thorough conversion of men.

A miracle is to be performed. By which, our hearers shall become the products of that mighty power which God wrought in Christ when He raised Him from the dead and set Him at His own right hand in the heavenly place far above all principality and power. For this to happen, we must look outside of ourselves to the living God. We must go in for thorough, downright conversion and fall back upon the power of the Holy Spirit. If it is to be a miracle, it is clear God must work it. It isn't to be accomplished by our reasoning, persuasion, or threatening. It can only come from the Lord.

How Can We Expect to Be Endowed with the Spirit of God to Go Forth in His Power?

Since the winning of souls lies here, in what way can we hopefully expect to be endowed with the Spirit of God and to go forth in His power? The answer to this isn't one-size fits all. A great deal depends upon the condition of the man himself. I believe we have never laid enough stress on the work of God within our own selves in its relation to our service of God. A man dedicated to the service and worship of God may be charged with divine energy to the full, so that everybody around him can't help but see it. They can't tell what it is, where it comes from, or where it goes, but they perceive something about that man which is far beyond the common order of things.

At another time, that same person may come across as ineffective and dull, and even be conscious of it himself. Like Samson, he shakes himself as at other times but can't muster the command to do a mighty deed. It's clear that Samson himself had to be in a right condition in order to win victories. With the champion's locks clipped, the Philistines would laugh at him. If the Lord's power is gone from a man, he has no power left for useful service.

Look carefully to your own condition before God. Take care of the home farm and look after your own flocks and herds. Unless your walk is close with God, unless you dwell in that clear light which surrounds the throne of God and which is only known to those who are in fellowship with the Eternal, you will go forth from your chamber and hurry to your work, but nothing will come of it. It is true the vessel is but an earthen one. Yet, it has its place in the divine order of things. However, it won't be filled with the divine treasure unless it is a clean vessel, and unless in other respects it is a vessel fit for the Master's use. Let me show you ways in which much in soul winning depends upon the man himself.

Acting as Witnesses

We win some souls to Christ by acting as witnesses. We stand up and testify for the Lord Jesus Christ concerning certain truths. I have never had the great privilege of being bamboozled by a lawyer, but I've sometimes wondered what I would do if I were put into the witness box to be examined and cross examined. I think I would simply stand up and tell the truth as far as I knew it and wouldn't make an attempt to display my wit, language, or judgment. If I simply gave straightforward answers to his questions, I should be able to beat any lawyer under heaven. But the difficulty is, that so often when a witness is put into the box, he is more conscious of himself than of what he has to say. Consequently, he is soon worried, annoyed, and bored, and, by losing his temper, he fails to be a good witness for the cause. In the same way, open-air preachers are often bamboozled. The Devil's advocates are sure to come against you, and he has a great number of them constantly retained in his service. If you ask yourself, "How shall I answer this man cleverly, so as to get a victory over him?" you will be foolish.

The one thing you have to do is to bear witness to the truth. A witty answer is often a very proper thing. But at the same time, a gracious answer is better, *Let your word be always with grace, seasoned with salt, that ye may know how ye ought to answer each one* (Colossians 4:6). Try to remind yourself: It doesn't matter whether the man proves me to be a fool or not. Because I know I'm already content to be thought a fool for Christ's sake and not to care about my reputation. I have to bear witness to what I know, and with the help of God I will do so boldly. If the interrupter questions me about other things, I shall tell him that I do not come to bear witness about other matters, but this one thing I do. To one point I will speak and to no other.

The witnessing man must himself be saved and be sure of it. Perhaps you once enjoyed full assurance, and now you have to sorrowfully confess, "Sadly, I don't feel the full power of the gospel on my own heart." However, you can still truly add, "I still know that it is true, because I've seen it save others, and I know no other power can save *me*."

Perhaps, even that faltering testimony, so truly honest, might bring a tear into your opponent's eye and make him feel sympathy for you. John Bunyan said, "I preached sometimes without hope, like a man in chains to men in chains, and when I heard my own fetters rattle, still I told others that there was deliverance for them, and I invited them to look to the great Deliverer." I wouldn't have stopped Mr. Bunyan in preaching in this way. At the same time, it's a great thing to be able to declare from your own personal experience that the Lord has broken the gates of brass and cut the bars of iron in two.

Those who hear our witness ask, "Are you sure of it?"

Sure of it? I'm as sure of it as I'm sure that I'm a living man. They call this *dogmatism*. Never mind about that. A man ought to know what he is preaching about or let him sit down. If I had any doubt about the matters I preach from this pulpit, I would be ashamed to remain the pastor of my church. But I preach what I know and testify what I have seen. If I am mistaken, I am heartily and intensely mistaken, and I risk my soul and all its eternal interests upon the truth of what I preach. If the gospel which I preach does not save me, I shall never be saved, for what I proclaim to others is my own personal ground of trust. I have no private lifeboat. The ark to which I invite others holds myself and all I have.

A good witness ought to know all that he is going to say. He should feel himself at home and familiar with his subject. Say he's called as a witness in a certain case of robbery. He knows what he saw and has to make a declaration regarding that only. They begin to question him about a picture in the house, or the color of a dress which was hanging in the wardrobe. He answers, "You are going beyond my recollection. I can only bear witness to what I saw." What we do know and what we don't know would make two very large books, and we may safely ask to be let alone as to the second volume.

Say what you know and sit down, but stay calm and composed while speaking about what you personally know. You will never feel at home with the people or properly indulge your emotions in preaching until you are at home with your subject. When you know your purpose, your mind will be free to stay focused with an intense desire. For those open-air preachers reading this, I say, know the gospel from beginning to end and know where you are in preaching it. You can't preach with appropriate emotion unless you feel at home with your doctrine. When you do stand up to preach, be as bold, earnest, and persistent as you please.

Face the people feeling you are going to tell them something worth hearing, about which you are quite sure, which to you is your very life. In every outdoor assembly, honest hearts are present – at every indoor assembly too. They hunger to hear honest beliefs, will accept them, and be led to believe in the Lord Jesus Christ.

Pleaders for Jesus Christ

But you are not only witnesses. You are also pleaders for the Lord Jesus Christ. In a pleader, much depends upon the man. It seems as if the sign or indicator of Christianity in some preachers wasn't a tongue of fire but a block of ice. You wouldn't want to have a lawyer stand up and plead your cause in a cool, deliberate way, never showing the slightest care about whether you were found guilty of murder or acquitted. Could you endure his indifference when you were likely to be hanged? No. You'd wish to silence such a false advocate. In the same way, when a man has to speak for Christ and isn't sincere, let him go to bed. You smile, but isn't it better that he go to bed than send a whole congregation to sleep without their going to bed?

If we are to prevail with men, we must love them. We must be downright intense and heartfelt. Some have a genuine love for people, while others have a genuine dislike for people. I know gentlemen, whom I admire in a way, who seem to think the working classes are a shockingly bad segment of society to be kept in check and strictly governed. With such views, they will never convert the workingmen. To win men, you must feel that you are one of them. If they are a sad lot, you are one of them. If they are lost sinners, you are one of them. If they need a Savior, you are one of them (1 Corinthians 9:19-23). To the very chief of sinners, you should preach with this text before you, *Such were some of you* (1 Corinthians 6:11). Grace alone makes us differ from them, and that grace is what we preach. Genuine love to God and fervent love to man make up the great qualification for a pleader.

I further believe, although certain people deny it, that the influence of fear is to be exercised over the minds of men. I also believe it ought to operate upon the mind of the preacher himself. *By faith Noah, having received revelation of things not seen as yet, with great care prepared an ark to the saving of his house* (Hebrews 11:7). Noah feared for the salvation of this world from perishing in the flood. When a man gets to fear for others so that his heart cries out, "They will perish, they will perish, they will sink to hell, they will be forever banished from the presence of the Lord," and when this fear oppresses his soul, and weighs him down, and drives him to go out and preach with tears – he will plead with men to gain the victory.

To know the dread of the Lord is the means of teaching us to *persuade* and not to speak harshly. Some have used dread of the Lord to terrify, but Paul used it to persuade. Let us copy him. Say, "We have come out to tell you that the world is on fire, and you must flee for your lives and escape to the mountain, or you will be consumed." We must warn with the full conviction that it is true, or we shall be looked at as the boy who in foolishness cried, "Wolf!"

Something of the shadow of the last dreadful day must fall upon our spirit to accent the conviction of our message of mercy, or we will miss the pleader's true power. We must tell people of their pressing need of a Savior and show them we perceive their need and feel for them, or else we aren't likely to turn them to the Savior.

He who pleads for Christ should be moved himself with the prospect of judgment day. When I come in at the door behind the pulpit and catch sight of the vast crowd before me, I frequently feel depressed and disheartened. Think of these thousands of immortal souls gazing through the lenses of those wistful eyes. I am to preach to them all and will be responsible for their blood if I'm not faithful to them. I tell you, there are times it makes me feel ready to turn around and go back. But fear isn't all I feel. I am carried by the hope and belief that God intends to bless these people through the Word which He enables me to deliver. I believe everybody in that crowd is sent there by God for some purpose, and I'm sent to achieve that purpose.

Often when I am preaching, I think to myself, "Who is being converted right now?" It never occurs to me that the Word of the Lord will fail. That can never be. I often feel sure people are being converted, and that at all times God is glorified by the testimony of His truth. As you share God's good news, you can count on your hopeful conviction that God's Word can't return to Him void (Isaiah 55:11), as a great encouragement to your hearers as well as to yourself. Your enthusiastic confidence that they will be converted may be like the little finger of a mother held out to her baby to help it make its way to her. The fire within your hearts may dart a spark into their souls by which the flame of spiritual life will be kindled in them. As soul winners, let us all learn the art of pleading with the souls of men.

Be Examples

To open-air preachers, preachers, and all other Christian people, I say *we have not only to be witnesses and pleaders, but we must also be examples.* One of the most successful ways of taking wild ducks is the use of the decoy bird. The decoy duck enters the net, and the others follow it. In the Christian church, we need to use more of the holy art of decoy. By this I mean, our example in regards to our own account of coming to Christ, in living godly lives in the midst of a perverse generation, along with examples of our joy and sorrow, our holy submission to the divine will in the time of trouble, our example in all manner of gracious ways. Our daily examples will be the means of persuading others to enter the way of life. You can't, of course, stand up in the street and tell of your example, but street preachers are known better than they think. Someone in that crowd may be an unknown part of the speaker's private life. I once heard of an open-air preacher, to whom a hearer cried out, "Ah, Jack, you dare not preach like that at your own door!" It so happened, unfortunately, that Mr. John had offered to fight one of his neighbors a little while before, and consequently it wasn't likely he would have done much preaching close to home. This made the interruption an awkward one.

If any man's life at home is unworthy, he should travel several miles away before he stands to preach. Then, when he stands up, he should say nothing. The public knows us. They know far more about us than we imagine, and what they don't know they make up. At the same time, our walk and conversation should be the most powerful part of our ministry. This is what's called being *consistent,* when lips and life agree.

People Surrounding the Preacher

I have said the working of the Holy Spirit depends largely upon the man himself, but I must add that *much also depends on the kind of people surrounding the preacher.* An open-air preacher who goes out more or less alone is in a rather unfortunate position, because it's extremely helpful to be connected with a vibrant, living church which will pray for you. If you can't find such a church in the area where you labor to serve the Lord, the next best thing is to get half-a-dozen brothers or sisters who will back you up. This group would go out with you and, especially, will pray with you. I understand some preachers are so independent they think they can do without helpers, but they will be wise if they don't adopt solitude. They can look at the matter in this way: By bringing in half-a-dozen men with me, I'll be doing these young men good and will be training them to be workers. If you can partner with half-a-dozen men who aren't all very young but somewhat advanced in their knowledge of divine truth, the association will work to your mutual advantage. I admit that, although God has largely blessed me in His work, none of the credit is due to me at all. The credit goes to those dear friends at the Tabernacle and all over the world, who make me the special subject of their prayers. A man ought to do well with such people around him as I have. My dear friend and deacon, Mr. William Olney, once said, "So far, our minister has led us forward, and we have followed heartily. Everything has been a success. Don't you believe in his leadership?"

The people cried, "Yes."

My dear friend said, "If our pastor leads us to a ditch which looks as if it couldn't be crossed, let's fill it up with our bodies and carry him across." This was impressive talk and the ditch filled itself almost at once. If you have a true friend, your strength is more than doubled.

And what a blessing a good wife is. Women wouldn't be in their right place if they began to preach in the streets, but they can make their husbands happy and comfortable when they come home, and that will encourage *them* to preach all the better. Some can even help in another way if they are prudent and gentle. They can tenderly hint that their spouse was a little out of line in certain small matters, and he may take your hint and put himself right.

A good brother once asked me to give him some instruction. He put it to me like this, "The only instructor I've had is my wife, who had a better education than I was able to have. I used to say, 'We was,' and 'Us did it,' and she quietly hinted that people might laugh at me if I didn't attend to grammar." In this way, his wife became a professor of the English language to him. She was worth her weight in gold to him, and he knew it. Those who have such helpers ought to thank God daily for them.

Along with this, it's very helpful to join in a brotherly association or group with warmhearted Christians who know more than we do and who will benefit us by prudent hints. God may bless us for the sake of others when He might not bless us for our own sake. You have probably heard the story of the man who had preached and won many souls to Christ. He congratulated himself for the outcome. One night, an angel revealed to him that at the last great day he would have none of the honor for it. He asked the angel in his dream, "Who then will get the credit for it?" The angel replied, "That deaf old man who sits on the pulpit stairs and prays for you was the means of the blessing."

Let's be thankful for that deaf man, that old woman, or those praying friends who bring down a blessing on us by their intercessions. The Spirit of God will bless two when He might not bless one. Abraham didn't get one of the five cities saved all on his own even though he offered a weighty prayer. Beyond this, his nephew Lot was about the poorest sort that could be found. He didn't have more than half-an-ounce of prayer in him, but that tiny fragment turned the scale and Zoar was preserved. Therefore, add your odd half-ounce of prayer to the mightier weight of the pleadings of eminent saints, because they might need it.

To those of you called to be open-air preachers, I am not trying to instruct you. Some of you could better instruct me. Yet, from what I hear, I must be getting rather old. A woman, at the beginning of this year (1887), was trying to get something out of me. She said, "I remember hearing your dear voice more than forty years ago."

"Heard my voice forty years ago! where was that?"

She said, "You were preaching at the bottom of Pentonville Hill, near where Mr. Sawday's chapel is."

"Well, wasn't it more than forty years ago?"

"Yes," she said, "It might be fifty."

"I suppose I was quite young then?"

"Oh, yes!" she said, "you were such a dear young man."

That, of course, was a needless assurance. I don't think she thought I was quite so dear when I told her I never preached at the bottom of Pentonville Hill. And fifty years ago, I was only three years old. I also went on to tell her that I thought it shameful for her to suppose I would give her money for telling falsehoods. However, I shall postulate upon the woman's statement and suppose myself to be that venerable person she described and assert that *if we are going to win souls, we must go all in with downright labor and hard work.*

Commit to Hard Work

If we are going to win souls, first, we must work *at our preaching.* You're not growing distrustful of the use of preaching, are you? I hope you don't grow weary of it, though you certainly sometimes must weary in it. Go on with your preaching and stick with it. In the great day, when the official list of names of all who are converted through fine music, church decoration, religious exhibitions, and entertainment is read, they will amount to the tenth part of nothing. But the foolishness of preaching to save those who believe will always please God. Keep to your preaching, and if you do anything besides preaching, don't let it throw your preaching into the background. In the first place preach, and in the second place preach, and in the third place preach.

Believe in preaching the love of Christ. Believe in preaching the atoning sacrifice. Believe in preaching the new birth, and believe in preaching the whole counsel of God, *Therefore I take you to record this day that I am pure from the blood of everyone. For I have not refrained from declaring unto you the full counsel of God* (Acts 20:26-27). The old hammer of the gospel will still break the rock in pieces. The ancient fire of Pentecost will still burn among the multitude. Try nothing new but go on preaching. If we all preach with the Holy Spirit sent down from heaven, the results will astound us. Because the power of the tongue has no end.

Consider the power of a bad tongue, what great harm it can do. Won't God put more power into a good tongue if we just use it correctly? Look at the power of fire. A single spark can set an entire city ablaze. In the same way, the Spirit of God is with us, and we don't need to calculate how much or what we can do. You can't calculate the ability of a flame to develop, and there is no end to the possibilities of divine truth spoken with enthusiasm born of the Spirit of God. Have great hope despite those shameless midnight streets, despite lavish bars at the corner of every street, despite the wickedness of the rich, despite the ignorance of the poor. Go on. Go on in God's name. Because if the preaching of the gospel doesn't save men, nothing will. If the Lord's own way of mercy fails, then hang the skies in mourning and blot out the sun in everlasting midnight, because we race toward nothing but the black of darkness. Salvation by the sacrifice of Jesus is the ultimatum of God. So rejoice that it can't fail. Believe without reserve and go straight ahead with the preaching of the Word.

Private Conversation

True-hearted, open-air preachers will also join sincere private conversation to their preaching. In the Tabernacle, we've seen many people converted by the personal conversation of certain brothers. These men are all around while I'm preaching. I remember one Monday night when a brother was speaking to me, and suddenly he vanished before he finished his whispered sentence. I never learned what he was going to say, but I quickly spotted him in the left-hand gallery, sitting in the pew with a lady I didn't know. After the service, I asked him, "Where did you go?"

He said, "A gleam of sunlight came in at the window. It made me see a face which looked so sad that I hurried upstairs and took my seat in the pew close to the woman with the sorrowful countenance."

"Did you cheer her?"

"Oh, yes! She readily received the Lord Jesus. And just as she did so, I noticed another eager face – a young man. I asked the woman to wait in the pew until after the service and went after the young man."

He prayed with both of these people and would not be satisfied until they gave their hearts to the Lord. That is the way to be on the alert. As I've mention before, we need a body of sharpshooters to pick out their men one by one. When we fire great guns from the pulpit, execution is accomplished but many are missed. We want loving spirits to go around and deal with individual cases one-on-one with pointed personal warnings and encouragements. Open-air preachers shouldn't only address the hundreds but should be ready to pounce upon the individuals. He should have others with him who possess the same successful art. How much more effective could preaching in the streets be if every open-air preacher were accompanied by a group of people ready to drive his nails home for him by personal conversation.

Last Sunday night, a dear brother told us a short story I'll never forget. He was at Croydon Hospital one night, on one of those appointed visits. All the door-keepers had gone home. It was time to close for the night. He was the only person left in the hospital, except for the physician, when a boy came running in shouting that there had been a railway accident. He said, "Someone must go to the station with a stretcher."

The doctor asked my brother, "Will you take one end of the stretcher if I take the other?"

"Oh, yes!" He was happy to help, and so away went the doctor and the pastor with the stretcher. They brought a sick man back to the hospital. As my brother told the story, he said, "I visited the hospital often during the next week or two, because I was very interested in the man whom I had helped carry."

I believe he will always take an interest in that man, because he once felt the weight of him. When you know how to carry a man on your heart and have felt the burden of his situation, you will have his name engraved upon your soul. So you who privately talk to people, as you do, you are feeling the weight of souls. I believe this is what many regular preachers need to know better. If they do, they will preach better.

Have a Tract Ready

When the opportunities to preach or talk privately are not available, *have a tract ready.* This is often an effectual tool. However, some tracts wouldn't convert a beetle, because there isn't enough in them to interest a fly. Get good striking tracts or none at all. A telling, touching gospel tract can often be the seed of eternal life so don't go out without your tracts.

Visit the People

Besides giving a tract, if you can, try and find out where a person lives who frequently hears you, *so you can visit him.* What a fine thing is to receive a visit from an open-air preacher. "Why," the woman, says, "Bill, that man has come to see you. The gentleman who preaches at the corner of the street. Shall I tell him to come in?"

"Oh, yes! I've heard him many times. He's a good fellow." Visit as much as you can, for it will be a benefit to you as well as to the people.

Send a Letter

There is also power in *a letter to an individual*. Some people still have a kind of superstitious reverence for a letter, and when they get a sincere letter from a respected person such as yourself, they think a great deal of it. And who knows? Perhaps, a note received by post can hit the man your sermon missed. Young people who aren't able to preach might do much good if they write letters to their young friends about their souls. They can speak quite plainly with their pens, though they might be shy when speaking with their tongues. Let us save men by all the means under heaven.

Let's prevent men from going down to hell by any means. The fact is, we aren't half as earnest as we ought to be. Remember the dying young man who said to his brother, "My brother, how could you have been so indifferent to my soul as you have been?"

He answered, "I have not been indifferent to your soul. Indeed, I frequently spoke to you about it."

"Oh, yes!" the dying man said. "You spoke, but somehow I think if you had remembered that I was going down to hell, you would have been more sincere with me. You would have wept over me, and, as my brother, you wouldn't have allowed me to be lost." Let no one say this of you.

I hear most people notice that when they become zealous they do such odd things and say such strange things. Let them say strange things. Let them do strange things. They result from genuine earnestness. We don't want gimmicky tricks and performances that are nothing more than a mere sham of sincerity. What we want is times of real white-heat earnestness. Where you see *that,* it's a shame to be too critical. You must let a great storm rage in its own way and let a living heart speak as it can. If you are zealous but can't speak, your earnestness will invent its own method of working out its purpose. It is said that Hannibal melted the rocks with vinegar. In the same way, earnestness will dissolve the rocky hearts of men one way or another. May the Spirit of God rest upon you, one and all, for Jesus Christ's sake.

Chapter 17

The Great Revival

C. H. Spurgeon

"The Lord hath made bare his holy arm in the eyes of all the nations; and all the ends of the earth shall see the salvation of our God." (Isaiah 52:10).

When the heroes of old prepared for the fight they put on their armor, but when God prepares for battle, He makes bare His arm. Man has to look two ways – to his own defense, as well as to the offense of his enemy. God hath but one direction in which to cast His eye – the overthrow of His foeman, and He disregards all measures of defense and scorns all armor. He *makes bare* His arm in the sight of all the people. When men would do their work in earnest, too, they sometimes strip themselves, like that warrior of old, who, when he went to battle with the Turks, would never fight them except with the bare arm. "Such things as they," said he, "I need not fear; they have more reason to fear my bare arm than I their scimitar." Men feel that they are prepared for a work when they have cast away their cumbrous garments. And so the prophet represents the Lord as laying aside for a while the garments of His dignity and making bare His arm, that

He may do His work in earnest and accomplish His purpose for the establishment of His church.

Now, leaving the figure, which is a very great one, I would remind you that its meaning is fully carried out whenever God is pleased to send a great revival of religion. My heart is glad within me this day, for I am the bearer of good tidings. My soul has been made exceedingly full of happiness by the tidings of a great revival of religion throughout the United States. Some hundred years, or more, ago, it pleased the Lord to send one of the most marvelous religious awakenings that was ever known. The whole of the United States seemed shaken from end to end with enthusiasm for hearing the Word of God, and now, after the lapse of a century, the like has occurred again. The monetary pressure has at length departed, but it has left behind it the wreck of many mighty fortunes.

Many men, who were once princes, have now become beggars, and in America, more than in England, men have learned the instability of all human things. The minds of men, thus weaned from the earth by terrible and unexpected panic, seem prepared to receive tidings from a better land and to turn their exertions in a heavenly direction. You will be told by anyone who is conversant with the present state of America, that wherever you go there are the most remarkable signs that religion is progressing with majestic strides. The great revival, as it is now called, has become the common market-talk of merchants; it is the theme of every newspaper; even the secular press remarks it, for it has become so astonishing that all ranks and classes of men seem to have been affected by it.

Apparently, without any cause whatever, fear has taken hold of the hearts of men, a thrill seems to be shot through every breast at once, and it is affirmed by men of good repute that there are, at this time, towns in New England where you could not, even if you searched, find one solitary unconverted person. So marvelous – I had almost said, so miraculous – has been the sudden and instantaneous spread of religion throughout the great empire, that it is scarcely possible for us to believe the half of it, even though it should be told us.

Now, as you are aware, I have at all times been peculiarly jealous and suspicious of revivals. Whenever I see a man who is called a revivalist, I always set him down for a cipher. I would scorn the taking of such a title as that to myself. If God pleases to make use of a man for the promoting of a revival, well and good; but for any man to assume the title and office of a revivalist, and go about the country, believing that wherever *he* goes he is the vessel of mercy appointed to convey a revival of religion, is, I think, an assumption far too arrogant for any man who has the slightest degree of modesty. And again, there are a large number of revivals, which occur every now and then in our towns, and sometimes in our city, which I believe to be spurious and worthless.

I have heard of the people crowding in the morning, the afternoon, and the evening to hear some noted "revivalist" and under his preaching some have screamed, have shrieked, have fallen down on the floor, have rolled themselves in convulsions, and afterwards, when he has set a form for penitents, employing one or two decoy ducks to run out from the rest and make a confession of sin, hundreds have come forward, impressed by that one sermon, and declared that they were, there and then, turned from the error of their ways.

It was only last week I saw a record of a certain place, in our own country, giving an account, that on such a day, under the preaching of a man I chose not to name, seventeen persons were thoroughly sanctified, twenty-eight were convinced of sin, and twenty-nine received the blessing of justification. Then comes the next day, so many more; the following day, so many more; and afterwards they are all cast up together, making a grand total of some hundreds who have been blessed during three services, under the ministry of the Rev. Mr. So-and-so. All that I call farce! There may be something very good in it; but the outside looks to me to be so rotten that I should scarcely trust myself to think that the good within comes to any very great amount. When people go to work to calculate so exactly by arithmetic, it always strikes me they have mistaken what they are at.

We may easily say that so many were added to the church on a certain occasion, but to take a separate census of the convinced, the justified, and the sanctified, is absurd. You will, therefore, be surprised at finding me speaking of revival, but you will, perhaps, not be quite so surprised when I endeavor to explain what I mean by an earnest and intense desire which I feel in my heart, that God would be pleased to send throughout this country a revival like that which has just commenced in America, and which, we trust, will long continue there.

I should endeavor to mark, in the first place, *the cause of every revival of true religion;* secondly, *the consequences of such revival;* then, thirdly, I shall *give a caution or two,* that we make not mistakes in this matter, and conceive *that* to be God's work which is only man's; and then I shall conclude by making *an exhortation* to all my brethren in the faith of Christ, to labor and pray for a revival of religion in the midst of our churches.

1. *First, then, the cause of a true revival.* The mere worldly man does not understand a revival; he cannot make it out. Why is it that a sudden fit of godliness, as he would call it, a kind of sacred epidemic, should seize upon a mass of people all at once? What can be the cause of it? It frequently occurs in the absence of all great evangelists; it cannot be traced to any particular means. There have been no special agencies used in order to bring it about – no machinery supplied, no societies established – and yet it has come, just like a heavenly hurricane, sweeping everything before it. It has rushed across the land, and of it men have said, "The wind blows where it wishes and you hear the sound of it, but do not know where it comes from and where it is going" (John 3:8). What is, then, the cause? Our answer is: If a revival be true and real, it is caused by the Holy Spirit, and by Him alone.

When Peter stood up on the day of Pentecost, and preached that memorable sermon by which three thousand persons were converted, can we attribute the remarkable success of his ministry to anything else but the ministry of the Holy Spirit? I read the notes of Peter's discourse – it was certainly very simple, it was a plain narration of facts, it was certainly very bold, very cutting and pointed and personal for he did not blush to tell them that *they* had put to death the Lord of life and of glory and were guilty of His blood – but on the mere surface of the thing, I should be apt to say that I had read many a sermon far more likely to be effective than Peter's. I believe there have been many preachers who have lived, whose sermons, when read, would have been far more notable and far more regarded, at least by the critic, than the sermon of Peter. It seems to have been exceedingly simple and suitable and extremely earnest, but none of these things are so eminently remarkable as to be the cause of such extraordinary success.

What, then, was the reason? And we reply, once more, the same word which the Holy Spirit blesses to the conversion of one, He might, if He pleased, bless to the conversion of a thousand; and I am persuaded that the lowest preacher in Christendom might come into this pulpit this morning and preach the most simple sermon, in the most uneducated style, and the Holy Spirit, if He so willed it, might bless that sermon to the conversion of every man, woman, and child within this place, for His arm is not shortened, His power is not straitened, and, as long as He is Omnipotent, it is ours to believe that He can do whatsoever seemeth Him good.

Do not imagine, when you hear of a sermon being made useful, that it was the sermon itself that did the work. Conceive not, because a certain preacher may have been greatly blessed in the conversion of souls, that there is anything in the preacher. God forbid that any preacher should arrogate such a thing to himself. Any other preacher, blessed in the same manner, would be as useful, and any other sermon, provided it be truthful and earnest, might be as much blessed as that particular sermon which has become notable by reason of the multitudes who by it have been brought to Christ. The Spirit of God, when He pleaseth, blows upon the sons of men. He finds a people hard and careless, and He casts a desire into their minds, He sows it broadcast in their spirits – a thought towards the house of the Lord – and straightway, they know not why, they flock in multitudes to hear the Word preached.

He casts the seed, the same seed, into the preacher's mind, and he knows not how, but he feels more earnest than he did before. When he goes to his pulpit, he goes to it as to a solemn sacrifice, and there he preaches, believing that great things will be the effect of his ministry. The time of prayer cometh round and Christians are found meeting together in large numbers; they cannot tell what it is that influences them, but they feel they must go up to the house of the Lord to pray. There are earnest prayers lifted up, there are earnest sermons preached, and there are earnest hearers. Then God, the Almighty One, is pleased to soften hard hearts, subdue the stout-hearted, and bring them to know the truth. The only real cause is His Spirit working in the minds of men.

But while this is the only actual cause, yet there are instrumental causes, and the main instrumental cause of a great revival must be the bold, faithful, fearless preaching of the truth as it is in Jesus. Why, brethren, we want every now and then to have a reformation. One reformation will never serve the church; she needs continually to be wound up and set a-going afresh, for her works run down and she does not act as she used to do. The bold, bald doctrines that Luther brought out began to be a little modified, until layer after layer was deposited upon them, and at last the old rocky truth was covered up, and there grew upon the superficial subsoil an abundance of green and flowery errors, that looked fair and beautiful, but were in no way whatever related to the truth, except as they were the products of its decay. Then there came bold men who brought the truth out again and said, "Clear away this rubbish. Let the blast light upon these deceitful beauties; we want them not. Bring out the old truth once more!" And it came out. But the tendency of the church perpetually is, to be covering up its own naked simplicity, forgetting that the truth is never so beautiful as when it stands in its own unadorned, God-given glory. And now, at this time, we want to have the old truths restored to their places. The subtleties and the refinements of the preacher must be laid aside. We must give up the grand distinctions of the school-men, and all the lettered tech-nicalities of men who have studied theology as a system, but have not felt the power of it in their hearts, and when the good old truth is once more preached by men whose lips are touched as with a live coal from off the altar, this shall be the instrument, in the hand of the Spirit, for bringing about a great and thorough revival of religion in the land.

But added to this, there must be the earnest prayers of the church. The most indefatigable ministry is all in vain, unless the church waters the seed sown with her abundant tears. Every revival has been com-menced and attended by a large amount of prayer. In the city of New York, at the present moment, there is not, I believe, one single hour of the day wherein Christians are not gathered together for prayer. One church opens its doors from five o'clock till six for prayer; another church opens from six to seven and summons its praying men to offer the sacrifice of supplication. Six o'clock is past, and men are gone to their labor. Another class finds it then convenient – such as those, perhaps, who go to business at eight or nine – and from seven to eight there is another prayer meeting. From eight to nine, there is another, in another part of the city, and what is most marvelous, at high noon, from twelve to one, in the midst of the city of New York, there is held a prayer meeting in a large room, which is crammed to the doors every day, with hundreds standing outside. This prayer meeting is made up of merchants of the city, who can spare a quarter of an hour to go in and say a word of prayer and then leave again, and then a fresh company come in to fill up the ranks, so that it is supposed that many hundreds assemble in that one place for prayer during the appointed hour. This is the explanation of the revival. If this were done in London – if we for once would out-vie old Rome, who kept her monks in her sanctuaries, always at prayer, both by night and by day, if we together could keep up one golden chain of prayer, link after link of holy brotherhood being joined together in supplication – then might we expect an abundant outpouring of the Divine Spirit from the Lord our God. With the Holy Spirit as the actual agent, and the Word preached and the prayers of the people as the instruments, we have thus explained the cause of a true revival of religion.

2. *But now what are the consequences of a revival of religion?* Why, the consequences are everything that our hearts could desire for the church's good. When the revival of religion comes into a nation, the minister begins to be warmed. It is said that in America the sleepiest preachers have begun to wake up; they have warmed themselves at the general fire, and men who could not preach without notes, and could not preach with them to any purpose at all, have found it in their hearts to speak right out, and speak with all their might to the people. When there comes a revival, the minister all of a sudden finds that the usual forms and conventionalities of the pulpit are not exactly suitable to the times. He breaks through one hedge; then he finds himself in an awkward position, and he has to break through another. He finds himself,

perhaps, on a Sunday morning, though a Doctor of Divinity, actually telling an anecdote – lowering the dignity of the pulpit by actually using a simile or metaphor – sometimes perhaps accidentally making his people smile and, what is also a great sin in these solid theologians, now and then dropping a tear. He does not exactly know how it is, but the people catch up his words. "I must have something good for them," he says. He just burns that old lot of sermons, or he puts them under the bed and gets some new ones, or gets none at all, but just gets his text, and begins to cry, "Men and brethren, believe on the Lord Jesus Christ and you shall be saved." The old deacons say, "What is the matter with our minister?" The old ladies, who have heard him for many years, and slept in the front of the gallery so regularly, begin to rouse, and say, "I wonder what has happened to him? How can it be? Why, he preaches like a man on fire! The tear runs over at his eye; his soul is full of love for souls." They cannot make it out; they have often said he was dull and dreary and drowsy. How is it that all this is changed? Why, it is the revival. The revival has touched the minister; the sun, shining so brightly, has melted some of the snow on the mountain-top, and it is running down in fertilizing streams to bless the valleys; and the people down below are refreshed by the ministrations of the man of God who has awakened himself up from his sleep and finds himself, like another Elijah, made strong for forty days of labor. Well, then, directly after that, the revival begins to touch the people at large. The congregation was once numbered by the empty seats, rather than by the full ones. But on a sudden – the minister does not understand it – he finds the people coming to hear him. He never was popular, never hoped to be. All at once he wakes up and finds himself famous, so far as a large congregation can make him so. There are the people, and how they listen! They are all awake, all in earnest, they lean their heads forward, they put their hands to their ears. His voice is feeble, they try to help him, they are doing anything so that they may hear the Word of Life. And then the members of the church open their eyes and see the chapel full, and they say, "How has this come about? We ought to pray." A prayer meeting is summoned. There had been five or six in the vestry; now there are five or six hundred and they turn into the chapel. And oh! how they pray! That old stager, who used to pray for twenty minutes, finds it now convenient to confine himself to five, and that good old man, who always used to repeat the same form of prayer when he stood up and talked about the horse that rushed into the battle, and the oil from vessel to vessel, and all that, leaves all these things at home, and just prays, "O Lord, save sinners, for Jesus Christ's sake." And there are sobs and groans heard in the prayer meetings. It is evident that not one, but all, are praying; the whole mass seems moved to supplication. How is this again? Why, it is just the effect of the revival, for when the revival truly comes, the minister and the congregation and the church will receive good by it.

But it does not end here. The members of the church grow more solemn, more serious. Family duties are better attended to; the home circle is brought under better culture. Those who could not spare time for family prayer, find they can do so now; those who had no opportunity for teaching their children, now dare not go a day without doing it for they hear that there are children converted in the Sunday School. There are twice as many in the Sunday School now as there used to be, and, what is wonderful, the little children meet together to pray. Their little hearts are touched and many of them show signs of a work of grace begun, and fathers and mothers think they must try what they can do for their families: If God is blessing little children, why should He not bless theirs?

And then, when you see the members of the church going up to the house of God, you mark with what a steady and sober air they go. Perhaps they talk on the way, but they talk of Jesus; and if they whisper together at the gates of the sanctuary, it is no longer idle gossip, it is no remark about, "How do you like the preacher? What did you think of him? Did you notice So-and-so?" Oh, no! "I pray the Lord that He might bless the word of His servant, that He might send an unction from on high, that the dying flame may be kindled, and that where there is life, it may be promoted, and strengthened, and receive fresh vigor." This is their whole conversation.

And then comes the great result. There is an inquirers' meeting held. The good brother who presides over it is astonished; he never saw so many coming in his life before. "Why," says he, "there are a hundred, at least, come to confess what the Lord has done for their souls! Here are fifty come all at once to say that under such a sermon they were brought to the knowledge of the truth. Who hath begotten me these? How hath it come about? How can it be? Is not the Lord a great God that hath wrought such a work as this?" And then the converts who are thus brought into the church, if the revival continues, are very earnest ones. You never saw such a people. The outsiders call them fanatics. It is a blessed fanaticism. Others say, they are nothing but enthusiasts. It is a heavenly enthusiasm. Everything that is done is done with such spirit. If they sing, it is like the crashing thunder; if they pray, it is like the swift, sharp flash of lightning, lighting up the darkness of the cold-hearted, and making them for a moment feel that there is something in prayer. When the minister preaches, he preaches like a Boanerges (Mark 3:17), and when the church is gathered together, it is with a hearty good will. When they give, they give with enlarged liberality, and when they visit the sick, they do it with gentleness, meekness, and love. Everything is done with a single eye to God's glory – not of men, but by the power of God. Oh! that we might see such a revival as this!

But, blessed be God, it does not end here. The revival of the church then touches the rest of society. Men who do not come forward and profess religion, are more punctual in attending the means of grace. Men that used to swear, give it up; they find it is not suitable for the times. Men that profaned the Sabbath and that despised God, find it will not do; they give it all up. Times get changed; morality prevails; the lower ranks are affected. They buy a sermon where they used to buy some comic book of nonsense. The higher orders are also touched; they, too, are brought to hear the Word. Her ladyship, in her carriage, who never would have thought of going to so low a place as a conventicle, does not now care where she goes so long as she is blessed. She wants to hear the truth, and a drayman pulls his horses up by the side of her ladyship's pair of grays, and they both go in and bend together before the throne of sovereign grace. All classes are affected. Even the senate feels it; the statesman himself is surprised at it and wonders what all these things mean. Even the monarch on the throne feels she has become the monarch of a people better than she knew before, and that God is doing something in her realms past all her thought – that a great King is swaying a better scepter and exerting a better influence than even her excellent example. Nor does it even end there. Heaven is filled. One by one the converts die and heaven gets fuller, the harps of heaven are louder, and the songs of angels are inspired with new melody, for they rejoice to see the sons of men prostrate before the throne. The universe is made glad; it is God's own summer; it is the universal spring. The time of the singing of birds is come; the voice of the turtle is heard in our land. Oh! that God might send us such a revival of religion as this!

3. *Now we shall have to turn to the third point, which was a caution.* When Christmas Evans preached in Wales, during a time of revival, he used to make the people dance; the congregation were so excited under his ministry that they positively danced. Now, I do not believe that dancing was the work of the Spirit. Their being stirred in their hearts might be the Holy Spirit's work, but the Holy Spirit does not care to make people dance under sermons; no good comes of it. Now and then among some of our friends there is a great break-out, and we hear of a young woman in the middle of a sermon getting on top of a form and turning round and round in ecstasy, till she falls in a fainting fit, and they cry, "Glory be to God!" Now, we do not believe that that is the work of the Spirit; we believe it is ridiculous nonsense, and nothing more.

In the old revivals in America, a hundred years ago, commonly called "the great awakening," there were many strange things, such as continual shrieks and screams and knockings and twitchings, under the services. We cannot call that the work of the Spirit. Even the great Whitefield's revival at Cambuslang, one of the greatest and most remarkable revivals that was ever known, was attended by some things that we cannot but regard as superstitious wonders. People were so excited that they did not know what they did. Now, if in any revival you see any of these strange contortions of the body, always distinguish between things that differ. The Holy Spirit's work is with the mind and heart, not with the body in that way. It is not the will of God that such things should disgrace the proceedings. I believe that such things are the result of Satanic malice. The devil sees that there is a great deal of good doing. "Now," says he,

"I'll spoil it all. I'll put my hoof in there and do a world of mischief. There are souls being converted; I will let them get so excited that they will do ludicrous things and then it will all be brought into contempt." Now, if you see any of these strange things arising, look out. There is that old Apollyon busy, trying to mar the work. Put such notions down as soon as you can, for where the Spirit works, He never works against His own precept, and His precept is, "Let all things be done decently and in order." (1 Corinthians 14:40). It is neither decent nor orderly for people to dance under the sermon nor howl nor scream while the Gospel is being preached to them; therefore it is not the Spirit's work at all, but mere human excitement.

And again, remember that you must always distinguish between man and man in the work of revival. While, during a revival of religion, a very large number of people will be really converted and there will be a very considerable portion who will be merely excited with animal excitement whose conversion will not be genuine. Always expect that and do not be surprised if you see it.[3] It is but a law of the mind that men should imitate one another, and it seems but reasonable, that when one person is truly converted, there should be a kind of desire to imitate it in another who yet is not a possessor of true and sovereign grace. Be not discouraged, then, if you should meet with this in the midst of a revival. It is no proof that it is not a true revival; it is only a proof that it is not true in that particular case.

I must say, once more, that if God should send us a great revival of religion, it will be our duty not to relax the bonds of discipline. Some churches, when they increase very largely, are apt to take people into their number by wholesale, without due and proper examination. We ought to be just as strict in the paroxysms of a revival as in the cooler times of a gradual increase, and if the Lord sends His Spirit like a hurricane, it is ours to deal skillfully with the sails, lest the hurricane should wreck us by driving us upon some rock that may do us serious injury. Take

---

3   Behold, the sower went forth to sow; and as he sowed, some *seeds* fell by the way side, and the birds came and devoured them: and others fell upon the rocky places, where they had not much earth: and straightway they sprang up, because they had no deepness of earth: and when the sun was risen, they were scorched; and because they had no root, they withered away. And others fell upon the thorns; and the thorns grew up, and choked them: and others fell upon the good ground, and yielded fruit, some a hundredfold, some sixty, some thirty. He that hath ears, let him hear. (Matthew 13:3-9 RV)

care, ye that are officers in the church, when ye see the people stirred up, that ye exercise still a holy caution, lest the church become lowered in its standard of piety by the admission of persons not truly saved.

4. With these words of caution, I shall now gather up my strength, and with all my might labor to stir you up to seek of God a great revival of religion throughout the length and breadth of this land.

Men, brethren, and fathers, the Lord God hath sent us a blessing. One blessing is the earnest of many. Drops precede the April showers. The mercies which He has already bestowed upon us are but the forerunners and the preludes of something greater and better yet to come. He has given us the former, let us seek of Him the latter rain, that His grace may be multiplied among us and His glory may be increased. There are some of you to whom I address myself this morning who stand in the way of any revival of religion. I would affectionately admonish you and beseech you not to impede the Lord's own work. There be some of you, perhaps, here present today who are not consistent in your living. And yet you are professors of religion, you take the sacramental cup into your hand and drink its sacred wine, but still you live as worldlings live, and are as carnal and as covetous as they. Oh, my brother, you are a serious drawback to the church's increase.

God will never bless an unholy people, and in proportion to our unholiness, He will withhold the blessing from us. Tell me of a church that is inconsistent, and you shall tell me of a church that is unblessed. God will first sweep the house before He will come to dwell in it. He will have His church pure before He will bless it with all the blessings of His grace. Remember that, ye inconsistent ones, and turn unto God, and ask to be rendered holy. There are others of you that are so cold-hearted that you stand in the way of all progress. You are a skid upon the wheels of the church. It cannot move for you. If we would be earnest, you put your cold hand on everything that is bold and daring. You are not prudent and zealous; if you were so, we would bless God for giving you that prudence which is a jewel for which we ought ever to thank God, if we have a prudent man among us. But there are some of you to whom I allude who are prudent, but you are cold. You have no earnestness, you do not labor for Christ, you do not serve Him with all your strength. And there are others of you who are imprudent enough to push others on, but never go forward yourselves. O ye Laodiceans, ye that are neither hot nor cold, remember what the Lord hath said of you – "So because you are lukewarm, and neither hot nor cold, I will spit you out of My mouth" (Revelation 3:16). And so will He do with you. Take heed, take heed! You are not only hurting yourselves, but you are injuring the church.

And then there are others of you who are such sticklers for order, so given to everything that has been, that you do not care for any revival, for fear we should hurt you. You would not have the church repaired, lest we should touch one piece of the venerable moss that coats it. You will not cleanse your own garment, because there is ancient dirt upon it. You think that because a thing is ancient, therefore it must be venerable. You are lovers of the antique. You would not have a road mended, because your grandfather drove his wagon along the rut that is there. "Let it always be there," you say. "Let it always be knee-deep." Did not your grandfather go through it when it was knee-deep with mud? Why should not you do the same? It was good enough for him, and it is good enough for you. You always have taken an easy seat in the chapel. You never saw a revival; you do not want to see it. You believe it is all nonsense and that it is not to be desired. You look back; you find no precedent for it. Doctor So-and-so did not talk about it. Your venerable minister who is dead did not talk so, you say; therefore it is not needed. We need not tell you it is scriptural – that you do not care for. It is not orderly, you say. We need not tell you the thing is right; you care more about things being ancient than being good. Ah, you will have to get out of the way now; it isn't any good. You may try to stop us, but we will run over you if you do not get out of the way. With a little warning, we shall have to run over your prejudices and incur your anger. But your prejudices must not, cannot, restrain us. The chain may be ever so rusty with age and ever so stamped with authority, but the prisoner is always happy to break it and, however your fetters may shackle us, we will dash them in pieces if they stand in the way of the progress of the kingdom of Christ.

Having thus spoken to those who hinder, I want to speak to you who love Jesus with all your hearts and want to promote it. Dear friends, I beseech you remember that men are dying around you by thousands. Will you let your eye follow them into the world of shades? Myriads of them die without God, without Christ, without hope. My brother, does not their fearful fate awaken your sympathy? You believe, from Scriptural warrant, that those who die without faith go to that place where "their worm does not die, and the fire is not quenched" (Mark 9:44). Believing this, is not your soul stirred within you in pity for their fate? Look around you today. You see a vast host gathered together, professedly for the service of God. You know also how many there are here who fear Him not but are strangers to themselves and strangers to the cross. What! Do you know yourself what a solemn thing it is to be under the curse, and will you not pray and labor for those around you that are under the curse today? Remember your Master's cross. He died for sinners; will not you weep for them?

> "Did Christ o'er sinners weep;
> And shall your cheek be dry?"

Did He give His whole life for them, and will not you stir up your life to wrestle with God, that His purposes may be accomplished on their behalf? You have unconverted children – do you not want them saved? You have brothers, husbands, wives, fathers, that are this day in the gall of bitterness, and in the bonds of iniquity (Acts 8:23) – do you not want a revival, even if it were only for their sakes? Behold, how much of robbery, of murder, of crime, stains this poor land. Do you not want a revival of religion, if it were merely for quenching the flames of crime? See how God's name every day is blasphemed. Mark how, this day, trades are carried on, as if it were man's day, and not God's. Mark how multitudes are going the downward course, merry on their way to destruction. Do you not feel for them? Are your hearts hard and stolid? Has your soul become steeled? Has it become frozen like an iceberg? O Sun of Righteousness (Malachi 4:2), arise and melt the icy heart and make us all feel how fearful it is for immortal souls to perish – for men to be hurried into eternity without God, and without hope! O, will you not now, from this time forth, begin to pray that God may send forth His Word and save them, that His own name may be glorified?

As for you that fear not God, see how much ado we are making about you. Your souls are worth more than you think for. O that ye would believe in Christ, to the salvation of your souls!

Chapter 18

Miscellaneous

We are indebted to the editor of *The Epworth Herald* for the privilege of reprinting the articles in this section. They have appeared in several of the special Revival Numbers of The Epworth Herald and are specially helpful and suggestive.

The Work of the Spirit

Joshua Stansfield

In revival work, the spirit counts for more than anything else; not the Holy Spirit alone in personal work upon the unconverted, but the spirit of Christ and of holy zeal as made known in the believer. Neither numbers nor prestige is the determining factor. "'Not by might nor by power, but by My Spirit,' says the Lord of hosts" (Zechariah 4:6). That is to say, success is not primarily nor principally brought about by either intellectual, numerical, or organized advantage, but by the spirit of God in the workers.

Numbers, caliber, and organized effort may be an advantage or a disadvantage. The brightest and brainiest of our workers may always be used to highest advantage *if their work be in the Spirit*. Otherwise, they are seeking results according to the capital invested – namely, brains, brilliance, social prestige, and systematic work. By these they may, and probably will, secure additions to the church, but *not conversions*. In our glorious twentieth-century movement, the aim is, and should be, to secure *conversions* – persons who have received Christ and thereby become the sons of God. Persons born, not of blood nor of the will of the flesh nor of the will of man, but of God (John 1:13).

Let it be clearly understood, then, that with excellent material and numbers – or without them – God can work unto salvation. He can use the many or the few; the few or the many. But success depends largely upon the spiritual character and condition of the workers.

On one of my first charges, in the earlier years of our young people's work, after diligent and careful attention to the matter, we secured a weekly attendance of seven persons. This continued for nearly eight months, during which time we had systematic and faithful work according to the organization under which we were then living. As early as possible after the organization of the Epworth League, we became a chapter of the same, and the spirituality and fidelity of these faithful few were the nucleus from which there grew one of the most vigorous chapters of the league, and has so continued to this day. Success has been not by numbers, but by the spirit *in* and *of* the membership.

Last year I conducted special revival meetings at Albion College, Michigan. Of the four hundred or more students in the college, over seventy percent were Christians; some of them were only nominally so, but a goodly number both of the young men and young women rejoiced in the indwelling of the Holy Spirit.

I found among them some of the brightest young people it has ever been my privilege to meet, using the best of their powers in the highest of all work, the salvation of souls. There were, however, on the part of about fifty persons, an intelligent consecration for spiritual power and an intense zeal in their labors such as I have not seen for many years, if indeed ever. Private prayer and group prayer meetings between class hours, personal and written invitations to the unsaved to come to Christ, deputations of two persons or more to bring certain individuals to the services, and an accurate list of the names of all the students, with the church standing and largely the present religious condition of each person.

A grand revival did not "break out." *It came.* It had to come from such conditions. On the fourth day of the meeting, seventy-five persons were at the altar at one time. The president and professors, as well as a number of the fourth-year men, were pointing the unsaved to Christ and the unsanctified to a better life.

Of all the young men who came forward, not one came alone, for some spirit-filled, earnest Christian either brought them or came with them. One hundred and two persons gave intelligent testimonies to saving grace in twenty minutes on the closing evening. But surely one of the brightest parts of that whole work was to see the president, professors, and senior men – strong, cultured men – leading souls into the kingdom.

With such conditions and such a spirit, it was not surprising that, before the brief meeting closed, it was stated that there were not twelve unconverted students who had not been to the altar in prayer.

"'Not by might nor by power, but by My Spirit,' says the Lord of hosts" (Zechariah 4:6). Let the weakest person or chapter in our league take courage. Here is our help.

Honoring the Holy Spirit

W. S. Harrington, D.D.

The place – the small village of S N, in Chenango County, N. Y. The time – 1840, or '41. The spiritual condition of the community was one of stagnation.

In this town stood a Methodist house of worship, and by its side the home of a Methodist physician. In that home was a commodious kitchen where the social meetings of the church were often held. The society was small and its members did not feel able to supply fuel and lights for special services in the church edifice. The circuit was large and the pastor unavailable at that point because employed elsewhere. A few devout souls gathered in that kitchen night after night, crying mightily to God for help. He heard and answered the cry of these hungry ones. The Spirit fell upon them. Believers were sanctified. These tidings reached the ears of those who had been uninterested and they began to come to the meetings. Sinners were converted. Night after night every unconverted person in attendance was brought to Christ. Some curious ones hardly dared enter, so they stood outside observing the course of the meeting. Some of these, while standing outside, were stricken with conviction, and came into the house crying for mercy.

One very small boy who belonged to that home can never forget those services, so Spirit-filled, so loaded with good to many people. That home belonged to the father of this writer. That small boy was myself. I do not know of any others living who had part in those wonderful meetings, but the memory thereof, after these sixty years, continues to warm my heart and has been an inspiration to me through the more than forty years of my ministry.

The conditions above named were very unfavorable, but as these devout souls pleaded for the Holy Spirit, the divine promises were to them fulfilled. Nothing is too hard for God. No place is so remote, no society is so weak, but there may be a glorious revival if the Holy Spirit is properly honored. "You will receive power when the Holy Spirit has come upon you" (Acts 1:8).

The Revival with a Plan

Isaac Crook, D.D.

It began in my study. I was a "transfer." My predecessor – a gifted, beloved man with entrancing pulpit ability – had twice served that same church. He was loved by the people.

The church was generous, magnanimous, and thrifty, but had not grown by revivals. The young, vigorous city – Winona, MN – had seen little of that sort of work. The writer was not a "revivalist."

Seated in my study one forenoon, some time after conference, prayerfully thinking over the state of the church, a plan of campaign broke in upon me. I resolved to propose it to the official board at the next meeting. When it was outlined, one of the younger men of the board promptly moved its adoption. It was done with an unanimity that brought assurance of victory. It was of the Lord. The main feature of the plan was a visit *from* the church *to* the church and congregation. A committee was selected to choose workers and assign the work. It required many a night's session and careful adjustment. No battle was ever more carefully planned. As subsidiary and essential to this was the appointment of evening meetings to which the people were to be invited. But there was no evangelist nor guest singer as an attraction.

The visit was to be more than an invitation. It was a proposal to cooperate.

Another meeting, at eight in the morning, was announced, not solely nor mainly as a prayer-meeting, but as a council of war and to plan definite work for the day. Of course, there was prayer for help to do this, but no throwing off duty on the Lord.

The arrangement was a sifting process. One of the committee members, a man of large business, said, "This is ticklish business. What if we have not treated some of these folks right to whom we are assigned?"

"Then all the more go and apologize," was the answer.

When the plan was ready and the visitors called out, there were about fifty of them. The request was made that others ready to do visiting should tarry. This was to prevent a feeling that any were slighted. None such was reported, so well had the work been done. In fact, some of the visitors' names appeared among those to be visited. There was no "nobler than thou" in the arrangement. It was a cooperation.

Soon the nightly audiences swelled to overflow. The pastor preached a short sermon. The young people sang and many of them were saved. The church members personally asked seekers to go with them to the prayer-meeting room at the rear of the pulpit. They were often almost in the kingdom before they had walked the aisle into that room, where they prayed, talked, sang, and were saved.

Mary C. Nind, then out on her missionary district, coming home after a few weeks of such work, said, "What has come to pass? I meet people on the street and find them talking religion. We never saw it in this fashion."

Families were saved. Drunkards were redeemed and some went to heaven in a year's time. Children were born again. Dance clubs were broken into. One young man gave up an inherited fortune to come with us. One young woman surrendered a marriage engagement rather than compromise with Christ. A bookkeeper in a wholesale liquor-house, who had a family dependent upon him, left his desk. He never suffered and went home in a year. Universalism was knocked out of a drunken policeman, who lost his place on the force, but he soon went to heaven. A Roman Catholic, heartbroken over the death of his wife, came in as a fruit of the revival, and said, "Had I known what I was missing, no four-horse team could have kept me from it." The work was pervasive. It extended by correspondence to distant states. Those were "days of the Son of Man" (Luke 17:26).

The revival had three essential elements in it:

It came as an answer to prayer.
It went forward by lay-workers in cooperation.
It was guided by the Holy Spirit.

These all will characterize the twentieth-century movement.

Seven Vital Paragraphs

Charles W. Baldwin

1. Make up your mind it is your work and your people's, and by God's blessing you can and will do it.

2. Get together such as are disposed to lay hold with you. Pray and plan. Pledge all you can to personal effort, immediate and continuous, and to mighty prayer.

3. Before public meetings are held, visit every house. Take with you the best man or woman you can. Talk about religion and the revival and pray, yourself and assistant, by turns. Make your visits short.

4. Preach the Word. Preach Christ: His divine and supernatural character, His human heart of love, His readiness to forgive, His vicarious death and His shameful sufferings, His resurrection, His ascension, and His heavenly intercession. Declare the judgment day, heaven and hell. Preach the necessity of being born again and invite sinners and backsliders to come to Jesus.

5. Have your best people around the altar or inside. Some time during every meeting get all the church, if possible, to come and stand around the altar. If the members come forward, a kind and urgent request to everybody who wants to see the meetings prosper to stand in the pews close behind the church members will usually be heeded. Tact and perseverance will get nearly all to move. This makes the congregation mobile and tractable, and one step may be followed by another.

6. Exhort much, not from the pulpit only, but up and down the aisles, and, kneeling with the people in the aisles, pour out your soul in prayer. Let all see that you are in earnest.

7. Do not be discouraged. Keep at it and always at it. Love the work and devote yourself to it. Believe God, and thus justify your name as a *believer.* "Therefore, knowing the fear of the Lord, we persuade men" (2 Corinthians 5:11).

Praying-Bands

B. H. Hart

One thing I never fail to do. About three months before I begin my special revival services, I begin to preach on revival themes and subjects exclusively to the church at the morning service and to the unsaved in the evening. I never permit special services of any kind to interfere with this purpose. I try to pack these sermons full of love, compassion, rewards, etc., leaving the penalty for neglect until the special meetings are well under way. Another great help to me has been the praying-band. This is nothing more than a company of young men or women who have covenanted with the pastor to go wherever he might send them for the purpose of praying with the unsaved. I am aware that other pastors, equally happy in the work of saving men, do not approve of this aid. But I am quite certain that a faithful trial will convince them of its efficiency. In what I am pleased to look upon as the greatest revival of my ministry – one in which more than four hundred souls were converted – such a band of young men did splendid service. They would go anywhere, at any hour of the day or night, and pray with anyone I might suggest.

Getting under Way

W. P. Macvey

Several specific things can be done:

1. You will be impressed that certain persons ought to be reached. Make a list of them – not indiscriminately of the unsaved, but of all for whom some godly heart is burdened. In nine cases out of ten, ninety percent of such people will be saved and ninety percent of the total converts will have been thus listed.

2. You will "feel" that certain persons are adapted to be lieutenants – not because of position, but because the Spirit points them out to you. Get in touch with them, work with them, understand them, pray together.

3. Preliminary meetings, notably cottage-meetings, are in order. Let the lieutenants have charge of them. The league can plan them. Let the people pray until they are burdened for the salvation of others. Inquiry-meetings, following the Sunday preaching service, prepare the way.

4. There is little use in trying to reach others until the heart of the church is right. When this beats responsive to the heart of God, you cannot help but save others – an irresistible spiritual law works out that result.

5. Abundant visitation, judicious advertising, inspiring music, good janitor-ship, cordial ushering, and reasonable hours (there is no need to tire the people out), all contribute to success.

But life is the gift of God and a revival is the work of the Holy Spirit.

An Important Factor in Revivals

Louis Albert Banks, D.D.

The most remarkable conversions which have occurred under my ministry in times of revival have been those which took place in the homes of people who sometimes had not been present at all in the meetings. Personal visitation by the pastor and wise Christian workers while the revival is going on is a very important factor in revival work.

Exalt Personal Effort

George B. Wight, D.D.

Be baptized by the Holy Spirit. This will give you a proper sense of the importance of the work of saving souls, a right preparation for it, and the needed enthusiasm in it, without which there can be no success. This is more important than all human helps. Evangelists, music, and methods all have their place in the work, but power and result come from the Spirit only.

Be persistent and do not be weary in well-doing (Galatians 6:9). Some meetings accomplish but little because they are discontinued too soon. I knew a meeting to be held three weeks without apparent result; at nine o'clock on the evening which began the fourth week, not a person had been forward. At quarter past nine, forty were seeking salvation and a great work followed. Results belong to God, so do not be discouraged if they are not seen at once. Work faithfully, pray earnestly, and leave the rest to Him.

Personal work is of the utmost importance. You can do much in the public meeting, but much preparatory work can be accomplished by personal interviews with the unconverted at their homes or places of business. I have often heard expressions of surprise because certain persons went to the altar when no one knew they were under concern, but I was not at all surprised, for I knew what good brother or sister had for days been quietly working up those cases. I cannot too strongly urge upon you this personal work. Persistent, intelligent, and systematic, when directed by the Holy Spirit, it will be more effective than any other agency you can employ except the direct preaching of the Word.

From a number of cases of the results of personal work which I have known, the following may be of interest: A Sunday School teacher once told me that she expected her entire class of young ladies would be converted in the meetings which were about to be held in her village. She had asked God for their souls and she knew He would answer her prayers. With this assurance, she worked judiciously and prayerfully and the result was according to her faith; every one of her class was soundly converted to God.

An Unlooked-For Revival

Robert Watt, D. D.

The subjoined incident may be of some service to the cause of Him whose we are and whom we serve (Acts 27:23). It occurred during the second year of the writer's ministry, on this wise:

The usual week-night prayer service was being held. The only unusual feature that evening was that a visiting minister made the address. His remarks were not as felicitous as could have been desired, and the devotional spirit might have been more propitious. The mention of a special service, beginning that night, would have provoked a broad smile. It seemed wise, under the circumstances, to conclude the service. With that thought in mind, the pastor rose to announce a closing hymn. At that juncture, however, an unlooked-for event happened. There came upon him an almost resistless impulse to open his heart to the people. And yet there was such an utter absence of so-called "special indications" that the impulse was about to pass unheeded. So persistent, so insistent was it that it could not be disregarded entirely. Something must be done, and quickly, too, for the burden was becoming unbearable.

Relief was at hand. Seated in that quiet room that autumnal night was a goodly company of young people whose respect and love had been gained by the pastor. Why not make use of this to win them to the Master? Surely the thought was divinely given. The fact was referred to in those closing words. Allusion was made also to the heart-hunger for souls felt by every true pastor. The words, falteringly spoken, were listened to with an interest that was surprising. Feeling deepened and intensified. Many eyes were luminous with the mist of unshed tears.

Why not open the door of opportunity at once? Without waiting to parley or debate the wisdom or un-wisdom of such a course, the suggestion was acted on. Imagine the feelings of that inexperienced pastor, when, in response to a simple invitation, twelve young people – some of whom had been conspicuously careless hitherto – rose and requested the prayers of the church! It is needless to add that the service did not close at the usual hour. The dreamed-of revival had come! The tide must be taken at its flood. Services for the rest of the week were announced, and that series of meetings continued for over six weeks. The revival in that obscure little church became the subject of general remark throughout the whole community. Its seen results were seventy souls saved, believers edified, and a discouraged, struggling church put on its feet so that it became one of the best charges in the conference.

I have called it the "unlooked-for revival," for such it was. There was no season of formal preparation, no scolding of the church. There were some hearts longing for a revival, and it came!

And what a blessed revival it was! Its memory abides and, not infrequently, has it proved a spiritual tonic when faith was languid and the "signs" lacking. How my heart glows as it all comes back again through the mist of years! And with this memory comes this passage:

> "They will be glad in Your presence
> As with the gladness of harvest,
> As men rejoice when they divide the spoil" (Is. 9:3).

Fortunate the pastor and the church who are sensitive to the presence of "the King," and whose faith is keen-visioned enough to detect the sign of the Son of man.

O for a Baptism of Prayer!

Mrs. M. N. Van Benschoten

He was the principal of the academy in the place and a member of my Bible-class. I had been told he was skeptical in his views. I found him keen, alert, and appreciative. For three months, I prepared every lesson with reference to him. When the revival services commenced I thought, "Now is the time to bring him in." For two weeks he was indifferent and at times frivolous. One afternoon, I was reading about the destruction of Sennacherib's host, when suddenly I could read no more, for a strange strength took hold of me. I said. "This mighty God is ours. He is the same yesterday, today and forever. He who answered Hezekiah's prayer can give me this soul." I arose at once and, with a commanding faith that thrilled me, I slowly ascended the stairs to my secret place of prayer. I had only uttered, "Oh, thou God of Hezekiah!" when a tidal wave of intercession was rolled upon me. An hour passed, but still I wrestled against the powers of darkness and with God, that Christ might gain that soul.

At last a great calm came over me. I heard the rush of dark wings, the morning broke, and the clear light shone. I knew I was victor.

That night I could not go to meeting and I learned he was not there. It did not disturb me for it had passed out of my hands; all anxious care was gone. The second night I was again detained, but my husband, on his return, said, "The professor was there and came forward and was gloriously saved. He said he had been under great conviction, but had resisted, for he knew if he was converted he must preach. 'But,' said he, 'I have surrendered, and Jesus is mine.'"

That young man has been preaching the Gospel for several years.

Oh, Sunday School teacher, pray mightily to God, and win that unsaved soul in your class to Jesus!

Chapter 19

Suggestive Outlines

These outlines have been very carefully selected from the published sermons of those whose preaching has been blessed to the salvation of men. The outlines are obtained by reducing to their present form many of the best sermons of such eminent evangelists as D. L. Moody, Charles G. Finney, C. H. Spurgeon, Chas. Ingles, Harry Moorehouse, R. A. Torrey, and others. The compilation and editing is by the editor of this volume.

– THE PUBLISHERS.

Regeneration

"Jesus answered and said to him, 'Truly, truly, I say to you, unless one is born again he cannot see the kingdom of God.'" – John 3:3

I.   Regeneration is an absolute necessity.

II. What regeneration is not.

   1. It is not going to church.

   2. It is not good works.

   3. It is not reformation.

4. It is not baptism.

5. It is not the Lord's Supper.

III. Necessary for everyone without regard to character or reputation.

IV. Not the work of man, but of God.

V. Wrought through faith in Jesus Christ.

VI. Accomplished by the Holy Spirit.

VII. The only way to see heaven and heavenly things.

1. Changed into a new man with a new nature.

2. With power to overcome temptation.

3. Fitness to dwell in heaven.

4. Singing a new song.

5. Seeing sainted ones in glory.

    – D. L. M.

The Gospel – I

"The Spirit of the Lord is upon Me, Because He anointed Me to preach the gospel to the poor." – Luke 4:18

I. What is the Gospel?

II. Good tidings.

1. Takes away the fear of death.

2. Tells us we shall rise again.

3. Promises the forgiveness of sins.

4. Gives assurance of everlasting life.

5. Proclaims God's love for even the chief of sinners.

    – D. L. M.

The Gospel – II

"The Spirit of the Lord is upon Me, Because He anointed Me to preach the gospel to the poor." – Luke 4:18

I. To whom shall the Gospel be preached?

 1. To every creature.

 2. To the sinning and to the unworthy.

 3. To all who take the place of guilty sinners.

II. For whom is there blessing?

 1. For all the poor and needy.

 2. For those who believe Christ died in their stead.

 3. For all who accept Him.

  – D. L. M.

Christ as a Deliverer

"'Can the prey be taken from the mighty man, Or the captives of a tyrant be rescued?' Surely, thus says the Lord, 'Even the captives of the mighty man will be taken away, And the prey of the tyrant will be rescued; For I will contend with the one who contends with you, And I will save your sons.'" – Isaiah 49:24-25

I. There are two classes of people.

 1. Those bound by Satan.

 2. Those delivered by Jesus.

II. Some do not know they are bound by Satan.

III. All are born into slavery.

IV. Christ came to deliver the captives.

V.   The proclamation of deliverance is to all.

VI.   To know the truth is to be made free.

VII. Christ delivers now from the power of every sin.

VIII. All who believe in Him are delivered.

– D. L. M.

Compassion of Christ

"When He went ashore, He saw a large crowd, and felt compassion for them and healed their sick."
– Matthew 14:14

I.   Christ knows the history of each one of us.

II.   He is moved with compassion when we tell it over to Him.

III. A sinner's confession moves Christ with compassion.

IV. Christ has compassion for all kinds of sinners.

V.   He receives all who come to Him with any distress.

VI. The sad stories of your life will move His heart with compassion.

– D. L. M.

Christ's Mission to the World

"For the Son of Man has come to seek and to save that which was lost."– Luke 19:10

I.   God sent His Son into the world to do a work.

II.   He gave Him power to do that work.

III. Ask Him to use His power in your behalf.

IV. He gives an instantaneous salvation.

V.   His salvation is genuine and thorough.

VI. Salvation is for those who are lost.

VII. Take the place of a lost sinner and be saved.

    – D. L. M.

Retribution

"Child, remember." – Luke 16. 25

I.   There is everlasting retribution, future punishment.

II. There will be a quickened memory and condemnation for all sin.

III. The Bible plainly teaches future retribution.

IV. Justice demands that there be future retribution.

V.   There is a place where Jesus will not come offering salvation.

VI. Present Christian privileges despised, will there be remembered for judgment.

VII. A reaping in kind must follow the sowing of tares.

VIII. Grace refused hardens the heart and makes future retribution more sure.

IX. Mercy spurned makes a death-bed the fearful beginning of unending punishment.

    – D. L. M.

Love

"Finally, brethren, rejoice, be made complete, be comforted, be like-minded, live in peace; and the God of love and peace will be with you." – 2 Corinthians 13:11

God is love.

I.   His love is universal.

II. His love is unchangeable.

III. His love is everlasting.

IV. His love is unfailing.

    – D. L. M.

Confessing Christ

"For with the heart a person believes, resulting in righteousness, and with the mouth he confesses, resulting in salvation." – Romans 10:10

I.   Confessing Christ must follow believing on Him.

II.   Some professed Christians are moral cowards.

III. Christians are in darkness because they do not confess Christ.

IV.   Pride is the one hindrance to their confession.

V.   Christ confesses in heaven those who confess Him on earth.

VI.   Confessing Christ brings great blessings in this life.

VII. Confession of salvation through Christ leads others to Him.

    – D. L. M.

Seeking the Lord

"Seek the Lord while He may be found; Call upon Him while He is near." – Isaiah 55:6

I.   The sinner seeking the Lord.

II.   It is a direct command.

III. With all the heart.

IV. Must be in earnest.

V.   While He is near.

VI. When He may be found.

    – D. L. M.

Grace – I

I.   What is grace?

II.   It is a free gift.

III. Unto whom is it given?

1. To those who confess they are lost.

2. To those who take the lowest place.

3. To those who know they are unworthy.

4. To those who stop working for salvation.

5. To all men.

    – D. L. M.

Grace – II

I.   Law cannot save the sinner.

II.   The distinction between law and grace.

III. What is it to be under grace?

IV. Unbelief is a hindrance to grace.

V.   How to be partakers of grace.

VI. Every necessity is provided for in grace.

    – D. L. M.

What Will You Do with Jesus?

"Pilate said to them, 'Then what shall I do with Jesus who is called Christ?"– Matt 27:22

I.   It is a direct question.

II. It is a disturbing question.

III. It is a personal question.

IV. It is an imperative question.

V.   It is a present question.

   – D. L. M.

On Trusting in the Mercy of God

"I will trust in the mercy of God forever and ever."
– Psalms 52:8 (KJV)

I.   What mercy is.

   1. Mercy is not to be confounded with mere goodness.

   2. Mercy is a disposition to pardon the guilty.

   3. Mercy is exercised only where there is guilt.

   4. Mercy can be exercised no farther than one deserves punishment.

II. What is implied in trusting in the mercy of God.

   1. A conviction of guilt.

   2. That we have no hope on the score of justice.

   3. A just apprehension of what mercy is.

   4. A belief that He is merciful.

   5. The conviction of deserving endless punishment.

   6. The cessation from all excuses and excuse-making.

III.   The conditions on which we may safely trust in God's mercy.

1.   Public justice must be appeased.

2.   We must repent.

3.   We must confess our sins.

4.   Make restitution so far as lies in our power.

5.   Must really reform.

6.   Go the whole length in justifying the law and its penalty.

7.   Must be entirely submissive to those measures of the government bringing him to conviction.

8.   Must close in cordially with the plan of salvation.

IV.   Mistakes which are made on this subject.

1.   Many really trust in justice and not in mercy.

2.   Many trust professedly in the mercy of God without fulfilling the conditions on which mercy can be shown.

3.   Sinners do not consider that God cannot dispense with their fulfilling these conditions.

4.   Many are defeating their own salvation by self-justification.

5.   Many pretend to trust in mercy who yet profess to be punished for their sins as they go along.

6.   Persons, in the letter, plead for mercy who often rely really upon justice.

7.   Some are covering up their sins, yet dream of going to heaven.

8.   We cannot ask for mercy beyond our acknowledged and felt guilt.

    a.   If we ask for little mercy, we shall get none at all.

    b.   To deny the desert of endless punishment is to render salvation impossible.

    c.   All are not saved because they defeat the efforts God makes to save them.

– C. G. F.

The Savior Lifted Up, and the Look of Faith

"As Moses lifted up the serpent in the wilderness, even so must the Son of Man be lifted up; so that whoever believes will in Him have eternal life." – John 3:14-15

"'And I, if I am lifted up from the earth, will draw all men to Myself.' But He was saying this to indicate the kind of death by which He was to die." – John 12:32-33

The object was to save men from perishing.

I.   Christ must be lifted up as the serpent was in the wilderness.

1. As a remedy for sin.

2. As a full and adequate remedy.

3. As a present remedy.

4. As a divinely certified remedy.

5. As one crucified for the sins of men.

II.   Christ must be looked at when He is lifted up.

1. Look expecting divine power to save.

2. Looking to Jesus implies that we look away from ourselves.

3. Salvation must be the object for which they look.

4. Sinners must look to Christ as a remedy for all sin.

5. Sinners may look at once without the least delay.

6. Must look, for blessings, not to works, but to faith.

Remarks

1. A great multitude will be saved.

2. Faith is here put to the test.

3. Many perish through mere unbelief.

4. Many are stumbled by the simplicity of the Gospel.

5. Natural man seeks for a way of salvation creditable to himself.

6. Many have religion, but with Christ out of view.

7. Many are looking for some wonderful sign or token.

8. Many also perish from delay.

9. Some are driven off into the wilderness through despair.

10. Others neglect to look because they think they are improving.

11. Many refuse to look because full of doubts.

12. Sinners look every other way but toward Christ.

    – C. G. F.

The Excuses of Sinners Condemn God

"Will you really annul My judgment? Will you condemn Me that you may be justified?" – Job 40:8

I.   Every excuse for sin condemns God

1. Nothing can be sin for which there is a justifiable excuse.

2. If God condemns that for which there is a good excuse, He must be wrong.

3. But God does condemn all sin.

4. Consequently every excuse for sin charges blame upon God.

II.   Consider some of these excuses in detail:

1. Inability.

2. Want of time.

3. A sinful nature.

4. Willing to be a Christian, but hindered.

5. Waiting God's time.

6. Circumstances are very peculiar.

7. Temperament is peculiar.

8. Health is too poor to go to the meetings.

9. The heart is so hard there is no feeling.

10. My heart is so wicked I can't.

11. My heart is so deceitful.

12. I have tried to become a Christian.

13. It will do no good to try.

14. I have offered to give my heart to Christ, but He won't receive me.

15. There is no salvation for me.

16. I cannot change my own heart.

17. I cannot change my heart without more conviction.

18. I must first have more of the Spirit.

19. God must change my heart.

20. I can't live a Christian life if I were to become a Christian.

21. This is a very dark and mysterious subject.

22. I can't believe.

23. I can't realize these things.

24. I can't repent.

III. All excuses for sin add insult to injury

1. A plea that reflects injuriously upon the court is an aggravation of the original crime.

2. A plea that is false, made in self-justification, is an aggravation of the crime charged.

3. It is truly abominable for the sinner to abuse God and then excuse himself for it.

Remarks

1. No sinner under the light of the Gospel lives a single hour in sin without some excuse to justify himself.

2. Excuses render repentance impossible.

3. Sinners should lay all their excuses at once before God.

4. What infinite madness to rest on excuses which you dare not bring before God now.

5. Sinners don't need their excuses. God does not ask for even one.

6. Sinners ought to be ashamed of their excuses and repent of them.

7. Admit your obligation and you are, of course, stopped from making excuses.

8. To admit the obligation and still plead excuses is to insult God to His face and charge Him with infinite tyranny.

    – C. G. F.

The Spirit Not Striving Always

"Then the Lord said, 'My Spirit shall not strive with man forever.'" – Genesis 6:3

I.   What is implied in the assertion, "My Spirit shall not strive with man forever"?

1. That the Spirit does sometimes strive with man.
2. That men resist the Spirit.

II. What is not intended by the Spirit's striving?

III. What, then, is the striving of the Spirit?

IV. How may it be known when the Spirit of God strives with an individual?

1. When one finds his attention arrested to the great concerns of his soul.

2. When a man finds himself convinced of sin.

3. When the mind is convicted of the great guilt and ill desert of sin.

4. When the soul is convicted of the guilt of unbelief.

5. When men see the danger of dying in their sins.

6. When sinners feel the danger of being given up of God.

7. When sinners are convicted of the great blindness of their minds.

8. When sinners are shown their total alienation from God.

9. When men are convinced that they are ashamed of Christ.

10. When sinners are convicted of worldly mindedness.

11. When such a personal application of the truth is made as to fasten the impression.

12. When sinners are convinced of the enmity of their hearts against God.

13. When sinners are powerfully convicted of the deceitfulness of their own hearts.

14. When, not infrequently, the sinner is stripped of his excuses, and clearly shown his great folly and absurdity.

15. When men are convicted of the folly of seeking salvation in any other way than through Christ alone.

16. When men are convinced of the great folly and madness of clinging to an unsanctifying hope.

17. When sinners are convinced that all their goodness is selfish.

18. When self-deceived men feel that they are now having their last call from the Spirit.

V.   What is intended by the Spirit's not striving forever?

VI. Why God's Spirit will not strive forever.

1. Because longer striving will do the sinner no good.

2. Because to strive longer not only does the sinner no good, but positive evil.

3. Because sinners sin willfully when they resist the Holy Spirit.

4. Because their resistance tempts the forbearance of God.

5. Because there is a point beyond which forbearance is not a virtue.

VII. Consequences of the Spirit's ceasing to strive with men.

1. A confirmed opposition to religion.

2. An opposition to revivals and to Gospel ministers.

3. Men betake themselves to some refuge of lies and will settle down in some form of fatal error.

4. Those who are left of God come to have a seared conscience.

5. This class of sinners will inevitably wax worse and worse.

6. Another consequence of being abandoned by the Spirit will be certain damnation.

7. Christians find themselves unable to pray in faith for such sinners.

8. When the Spirit has ceased to strive with sinners, no means whatever employed for the purpose can be effectual for their salvation.

Remarks

1. Christians can account for the fact why there are some for whom they cannot pray.

2. Sinners should be aware that light and guilt keep pace with each other.

   – C. G. F.

God's Love Commended to Us

"But God demonstrates His own love toward us, in that while we were yet sinners, Christ died for us."
– Romans 5:8

I.   How does God commend His love to us?

II. Why does He commend His love to us?

III. He would show that His love is unselfish.

IV. Again, God designed to reveal the moral character of His love for men, especially its justice.

V.   He sought in thus commending His love to us to subdue our slavish fear.

VI. He would lead us to serve Him in love and not in bondage.

Remarks

1. We see that saving faith must be the heart's belief of this great fact that God so loved us.

2. God would have men see His love in the gift of His own dear Son.

3. Men find it difficult to repent because they do not receive this great fact in simple faith.

4. In no other way could God so forcibly demonstrate His great love to our race.

5. If we had been His friends, there had been no need of His dying for us.

6. It is not sinless beings but sinful men that move God's heart to its very foundations.

7. Christ died for us that He might save us; not *in,* but *from* our sins.

8. You must infer that Jesus is willing to save you from wrath if you truly repent and accept Him as your Savior.

9. You may infer that God, having spared not His Son, will also with Him freely give you all things else.

– C. G. F.

Salvation of the Lord

"Salvation is from the Lord." – Jonah 2:9

Where Jonah learned this sentence of good theology!

I.   An exposition of the doctrine of salvation.

1. The plan of salvation is entirely of God.

2. It was of the Lord in execution.

3. It is of the Lord in the application of it.

4. It is the Lord who sustains the work in any man's heart.

5. The ultimate perfection of salvation is of the Lord.

II.   How God has hedged this doctrine about.

1. Salvation is not the result of natural temperament.

2. It is not the minister who converts men.

III.   What is – what should be – the influence of this doctrine of men?

1. With sinners it is a great battering-ram against their pride.

2. With saints it keeps from error and distrust.

3. It nerves one to work for God.

IV.   What is the obverse of this truth?

1. Salvation is of God: then damnation is of man.

– C. H. S.

Salvation to the Uttermost

"Therefore He is able also to save forever those who draw near to God through Him, since He always lives to make intercession for them." – Hebrews 7:25

Revelation affords us a complete history of salvation. Nowhere else can we find any trace thereof.

I.   The people who are to be saved.

  1. Where these people come to.

  2. How they come.

  3. What do they come for?

  4. In what style do these persons come?

II.   What is the measure of the Savior's ability?

  1. To the uttermost extent of the sinner's guilt.

  2. To the uttermost of the sinner's rejection of Him.

  3. To the uttermost of the sinner's despair.

  4. To the uttermost of the saint's distress.

III.   Why is Jesus Christ able to save to the uttermost?

  1. Because He died to save.

  2. Because He lives to make intercession.

      a. A warning. There is a limit to God's mercy.

      b. A question. Christ has done so much for you; what have you ever done for Him?

  – C. H. S.

The Royal Prerogative

"God is to us a God of deliverances; And to God the Lord belong escapes from death. Surely God will shatter the head of His enemies, The hairy crown of him who goes on in his guilty deeds." – Psalms 68:20-21

We gather from the text that death is in the hand of God, that escapes from death are manifestations of His divine power, and that He is to be praised for them.

I.   The sovereign prerogative of God.

    1. To God belongs the right to exercise it.

    2. The Lord has the power of this prerogative.

    3. The Lord has actually exercised this prerogative.

    4. Let Him have all the glory of it for your deliverance.

II.   The character of the Sovereign in Whom that prerogative is vested

    1. Salvation is the most glorious of all God's designs.

    2. The most delightful works which the Lord has performed have been works of salvation.

    3. To those who can call him "Our Lord," He is specially and emphatically the God of salvation.

III. Hear the solemn warning of our Sovereign Lord.

    1. He will by no means spare the guilty.

    2. He is not indifferent to human character.

    3. He has the power to smite those who rebel against Him.

    4. He will smite with a terrible, even an utter overthrow.

      – C. H. S.

Salvation by Knowing the Truth

"...God our Savior... desires all men to be saved and to come to the knowledge of the truth." – 1 Timothy 2:3-4

It is the wish of God that all men should be saved.

I.   It is by a knowledge of the truth that men are saved.

  1. It is a knowledge of *the* truth.

  2. This knowledge saves him from carelessness.

     a. This knowledge saves him from prejudice.

     b. This knowledge saves him from despair.

  3. How a saving knowledge works.

     a. Shows a man his personal need of being saved.

     b. Reveals the atonement by which we are saved.

     c. Shows us what that faith is by which the atonement becomes available for us.

  4. How we are to know the truth.

     a. By a believing knowledge.

     b. By a powerful knowledge.

     c. By an experimental knowledge.

II.   Two inferences.

  1. To you that are seeking salvation.

  2. To you who desire to save sinners.

     – C. H. S.

The Plain Man's Pathway to Peace

"As Jesus went on from there, two blind men followed Him, crying out, 'Have mercy on us, Son of David!' When He entered the house, the blind men came up to Him, and Jesus said to them, 'Do you believe that I am able to do this?' They said to Him, 'Yes, Lord.' Then He touched their eyes, saying, 'It shall be done to you according to your faith.' And their eyes were opened. And Jesus

sternly warned them: 'See that no one knows *about this!*' –
Matthew 9:27-30

The extreme simplicity of the cure! Conversion as a work of the Holy
Spirit is likewise extremely simple.

I.   Many persons are much troubled in coming to Christ.

  1. In some cases, it is ignorance.

  2. In many cases, men are hindered by prejudice.

  3. With others, the hindrance lies in downright bad teaching.

  4. Then there is the natural pride of the human heart.

  5. In some instances, the trouble arises from a singularity of
      mental conformation.

  6. Some are kept from coming to Christ through remarkable
      assaults of Satan.

II.   This is not at all essential to a real saving, to a coming to
      the Lord Jesus Christ.

  1. It is very hard to see how despairing feelings can be essen-
      tial to salvation.

  2. Much of all this struggling and tumult within, which some
      have experienced, is the work of the devil.

  3. Many instances prove that all this law, work, doubting,
      fearing, despairing and being tormented by Satan are not
      essential, because there are scores and hundreds of Christians
      who came at once to Christ, as these two blind men did,
      and to this very day know very little about these things.

  4. There are all the essentials of salvation in the simple, pleas-
      ant, happy way of coming to Jesus just as you are.

  5. The Gospel command implies in itself nothing of the kind,
      which some have experienced.

III. Those persons who are privileged to come to Jesus Christ
      softly, pleasantly, and happily, are not losers.

1. They may lose a sensational religious experience, but there is not much in that.

2. Do not suppose that persons who come thus gently lose something by way of evidence afterwards.

3. Do not think that those who come gently to Christ lose a good deal of adaptation for after usefulness because they will not be able to sympathize with those who are in deep perplexity and in awful straits when they are coming to Christ.

– C. H. S.

The Great Arbitration Case

"There is no umpire between us, Who may lay his hand upon us both." – Job 9:33

There is an old quarrel between the thrice holy God and His sinful subjects, the sons of Adam. The infinite grace of God proposes an arbitration.

I.   What are the essentials of an umpire, or an arbitrator?

1. Both parties should be agreed to accept him.

2. Both parties must be fully agreed to leave the case entirely in the arbitrator's hands.

3. To make a good arbitrator it is essential that he be a fit person.

4. He should be a person desirous to bring the case to a happy settlement.

II.   Enter into the court where the trial is going on and see the legal proceedings before the great arbitrator.

1. He opens His court by laying down the principles upon which He intends to deliver judgment.

   a. Strict justice.

     b. Fervent love.

2. Next He calls upon the plaintiff – the Great Creator – to state His case.

3. Then the defendant – the guilty sinner – is called upon by the arbitrator for his, and he pleads:

     a. I confess to the indictment, but I say I could not help it.

     b. I am no worse than other offenders.

     c. I have done a great many good things.

     d. I promise that for the future I will do better.

     e. I have with me a friend to help me out – Ritualism.

     f. I have nothing more to plead; I appeal to the mercy of the plaintiff.

4. The plaintiff declares He will not spare the guilty; he has offended and he must die.

5. The arbitrator now gives Himself for the sinner, with the pledge to suffer in His own proper person all that the weeping, trembling sinner ought to have suffered.

III. Let us now look at the arbitrator's success.

1. The case has been settled conclusively.

2. The case has been settled on the best principles.

3. The case has been so settled that both parties are well content.

4. But what is more wonderful still, both parties have gained the case.

5. Both parties have come to be united in the strongest, closest, dearest, and fondest bond of union.

    – C. H. S.

Only Trust Him! Only Trust Him!

> "As He entered a village, ten leprous men who stood at a distance met Him; and they raised their voices, saying, 'Jesus, Master, have mercy on us!' When He saw them, He said to them, 'Go and show yourselves to the priests.' And as they were going, they were cleansed." – Luke 17:12-14

It was required by the Savior to perform an act of faith in Him before there was the slightest evidence in themselves. He had wrought a good work upon them.

I.   What signs are commonly looked for by unconverted men as reasons for believing in Christ?

   1.   A consciousness of great sin and a horrible dread of divine wrath, leading to despair.

   2.   The experience of quite a blaze of joy before they can trust Christ.

   3.   Others expect a text to be impressed upon their minds.

   4.   Some expect an actual conversion to be manifest in them before they will trust the Savior.

   5.   Others have an idea that if they were to be saved they would experience some very singular sensation.

II.   What the reason is for our believing in Jesus Christ.

   1.   God's witness concerning His Son Jesus Christ.

   2.   The next warrant for our believing is Jesus Christ Himself.

   3.   Again, the warrant for believing is in the fact that God commands us to believe.

   4.   Moreover, there is the promise made to us and to every creature: "Believe in the Lord Jesus, and you will be saved." (See Acts 16:31)

   5.   These poor lepers believed because they had heard of others whom He had cleansed.

III. What is the issue of this kind of faith that I have been preaching?

1. The very existence of such a faith as that in the soul is evidence that there is already a saving.

   a. It will be an evidence also that you are humble.

   b. It will be the best evidence that you are reconciled to God.

2. Before long, sooner or later, you will become delightfully conscious of the fact that you are saved.

   a. By simply trusting Christ alone, without miracles, signs or evidences, you will have within you a power which will carry you through life and preserve you in holiness even to the end.

   b. This is faith to die with as well as to live with; it is to trust because of what *Jesus is* and not because of what *you are*.

   – C. H. S.

Jesus Only

"And when they had lifted up their eyes, they saw no man, save Jesus only." – Matthew 17:8 (KJV)

The quiet but delightful ordinary fellowship with "Jesus only," which ought to be the distinguishing mark of all Christian life, is better for every day than the excessive strain of the transfiguration glory.

I.   What might have happened to the three disciples after they had seen the Transfiguration.

1. They might have seen nobody with them on the holy mount.

2. When they lifted up their eyes, they might have seen Moses only.

3. As a third alternative, they might have seen Elijah only.

4. Or they might have seen Moses and Elias with Jesus.

II.   What really did happen.

    a. "Jesus only" was all they wanted to see for their comfort.

    b. "Jesus only" was enough as their power for future life.

    c. "Jesus only" shall be our reward – to be with Him where He is.

III.   What we anxiously desire may happen to those who hear us.

1. For ourselves and fellow Christians, that, more and more, the great object of our thoughts, motives, and acts may be "Jesus only."

2. For those who are not yet believers in Jesus our desire is that this may happen to them – that they may see "Jesus only."

– C. H. S.

Faith: What Is It? How Can It Be Obtained?

"For by grace you have been saved through faith."
– Ephesians 2:8

The fountainhead of our salvation is the grace of God. Faith is the channel along which the flood of mercy flows down to refresh the thirsty sons of men.

I.   Faith, what is it?

1. It is made up of three things: knowledge, belief, and trust.

2. It is believing that Christ is what He is said to be.

3. It is believing that Christ will do what He has promised.

4. It is expecting this of Him.

5. Sometimes it is little more than a simple clinging to Christ.

6. Another form of faith is to freely follow Christ as a leader.

7. Again, one exerts faith in Christ while learning of Him.

8. A higher form of faith is that which grows out of love.

9. Again, faith also realizes the presence of the loving God and Savior.

10. A firm form of faith arises out of assured knowledge.

11. This faith makes it easy to commit our soul and all its eternal interests into the Savior's keeping.

II. Why faith is selected as the channel of salvation.

1. Because there is a natural adaptation in faith to be used as the receiver.

2. Because it gives all the glory to God.

3. Because it is a sure method, linking man with God.

4. Because it touches the springs of action.

5. Because faith again has the power of working by love.

6. Because, moreover, faith creates peace and joy.

III. How can we obtain and increase our faith?

1. If you have a difficulty concerning faith, take it before God in prayer.

2. The Holy Spirit will enable you to believe if you hear very frequently and earnestly that which you are commanded to believe.

3. Next consider the testimony of others.

4. Note the authority upon which you are commanded to believe.

5. Think over what it is that you have to believe.

6. Think upon the person of Jesus Christ. You cannot doubt Him.

7. Submit yourself to God. Yield to Him.

    – C. H. S.

All Things Are Ready – Come

"Come; for all things are now ready." – Luke 14:17 (KJV)

The readiness of everything on God's part is the argument why men should come and partake of His grace.

I.   It is God's habit to have all things ready, whether for His guests or for His creatures.

    1. God's thoughts go before men's comings.

    2. This also proves how welcome those are who come.

II.   This readiness should be an argument that His saints should come continually to Him to find needed grace.

    1. Therefore come to the storehouse of divine promise.

    2. Come next to the mercy-seat in prayer.

    3. Christ is always ready to commune with His people.

    4. All things are ready for every daily duty.

    5. Those who aspire to a higher degree of holiness can come.

III.   The perfect readiness of the feast of divine mercy is evidently intended to be a strong argument with sinners why they should come at once.

    1. Come, for *all things* are now ready.

    2. Come, for all things are now *ready*.

    3. Come, for all things are *now* ready.

    4. *Come*, for all things are now ready.

IV.   This text disposes of a great deal of talk about the sinner's readiness or unreadiness.

    1. The unreadiness of those who were bidden arose out of their possessions and out of their abilities.

    2. Personal condition does not constitute an unfitness for coming to Christ.

3. It is a great truth that what we regard as unfitness is often our truest fitness.

– C. H. S.

Every Man's Need of a Hiding-Place

Text: "And a man shall be as an hiding-place from the wind, and a covert from the tempest; as rivers of water in a dry place, as the shadow of a great rock in a weary land."
– Is. 32:2

Introduction: The man of this text is the man Christ Jesus. Every man needs a hiding-place from five things: the displeasure of God, his own conscience, the power of sin within, the power of Satan, and the wrath of God.

I. Every man's need of a hiding-place.

1. *From the displeasure of God.* All have sinned and God is holy.

2. *From the accusations of his own conscience.* No torment like the torment of an accusing conscience. Illustrate from the Bible, literature, and experience. Conscience sometimes sleeps, never dies; the time of awakening comes. Illustrate.

3. *From the power of sin within.* No man is able in his own strength to overcome the evil within. Anyone who fancies he is, is self-deceived. Illustrate.

4. *From the power of Satan.* Some people do not believe there is a devil,

   a. The teaching of the Bible;

   b. Evidence of the devil's existence all around us; the devil is too cunning and too strong for us.

5. *From the wrath of God.* Many in this day do not believe in the wrath to come,

      a. The Bible teaches it and it is safe to depend upon the Bible;

      b. Common sense also teaches it.

II.   Christ – the refuge every man needs.

  1. Christ is a refuge from the displeasure of God (John 3:36). Experience.

  2. Christ is a refuge from the accusations of conscience.

  3. Christ is a refuge from the power of sin within (John 8:36). Illustrations from life.

  4. Christ is a refuge from the power of Satan. Satan is too strong for us; not strong enough for Christ (1 John 4:4). Illustrate from life.

  5. Christ is a refuge from the wrath to come (1 Thessalonians 1:10). Common sense teaches that the Christ who can save us from the power of sin here can save us from the consequences of sin hereafter.

Conclusion: Close with an appeal.

   – R. A. Torrey

Refuges of Lies

Text: "Then hail will sweep away the refuge of lies."
– Is. 28:17

Introduction: Every man needs a refuge from the displeasure of God, the accusations of his own conscience, the power of sin within, the power of Satan, and the wrath to come. Almost all men have something in which they are trusting. How many are trusting in a false refuge, a refuge of lies!

I.   Tests whereby a refuge of lies can be known. A true refuge must have five characteristics:

1. It must meet the highest and the fullest demands of our own conscience; if it does not it is not a refuge from the accusations of our conscience; neither is it a refuge from the displeasure of God.

2. Trust in it must make us better men. If our refuge is not making us better men, it is not a refuge from the power of sin nor the power of Satan; neither is it a refuge from the wrath of God. The refuge that does not save us from the power of sin here will not save us from the consequences of sin hereafter.

3. It must stand the test of the dying hour.

4. It must stand the test of the judgment day.

5. It must stand the test of God's Word.

II. Refuges of lies.

1. *Trusting in our own goodness.* Apply the tests given above.

2. *Other people's badness,* "I am not as bad as other men." Apply the tests given above.

3. *Hope that God is too good to let anyone go to hell.* Apply tests.

4. *Infidelity.* Apply tests.

5. *Religion.* To have religion is one thing, to have Christ is another; many trusting in their performance of religious duty. Apply tests.

III. Christ a true refuge.

1. Apply the tests.

Conclusion: Appeal to throw away all confidence in refuges of lies and flee to Christ at once.

– R. A. Torrey

A Solemn Question

"Where are you?" – Genesis 3:9

God puts to every man and woman a very solemn question.

I.   A question all ought to answer.

1.   We should want to know how we stand before God.

2.   We must answer the question someday.

II.   How to consider and answer it.

1.   Seriously.

2.   Deliberately

3.   Honestly.

4.   Prayerfully.

5.   Scripturally.

III.   The most important points to consider in regard to our standing.

1.   Are you saved or are you lost?

2.   Are you a child of God or a child of the devil?

3.   Are you for Christ or against Him?

4.   Are you an earnest, consecrated Christian or a lukewarm and worldly one!

IV.   *Conclusion:*

1.   Some know where they are – saved.

2.   Others cannot answer the question so.

3.   Answer the question definitely and at once.

– R. A. Torrey

What It Costs Not to Be a Christian

Introduction: Show the folly of making ventures in all phases of life without counting the cost.

I.   It costs the sacrifice of peace of conscience. (Isaiah 57:21)

II. It costs the sacrifice of the sense of perfect security which the Christian enjoys. (Isaiah 26:3)

III. It costs the sacrifice of the highest joy of which the human soul is capable. (1 Peter 1:18)

IV. It costs the sacrifice of the hope the Christian has. (Titus 1:2; 1 Peter 1:4; Romans 8:17)

V.   It costs the sacrifice of the highest manhood and womanhood.

VI. It costs the sacrifice of God's favor. (Hebrews 11:6)

VII. It costs the sacrifice of Christ's acknowledgment. (Matthew 10:32-33)

VIII. It costs the sacrifice of eternal life. (John 3:15-16; John 3:36)

   – R. A. Torrey

How Will We Escape?

"How will we escape if we neglect so great a salvation?"
– Hebrews 2:3

There are some things it will not do to neglect – the folly and wickedness of neglecting the salvation offered to us in Christ Jesus.

I.   Because of the greatness of that salvation.

   1. In the way in which it was given.

   2. In what it cost.

   3. In what it accomplishes.

   4. In the greatness of the opportunity.

II. Because it is the only salvation.

III.   Because we incur the just and awful displeasure of God.

1. There need be no grave offense against morality.

2. No conscious or unspoken rebellion against God.

3. No speaking against the salvation.

4. No decided refusal; simply a neglect.

5. All one needs to do in order to be lost is to do nothing.

   – R. A. Torrey

"Today"

"Therefore, just as the Holy Spirit says, 'Today…'"
– Hebrews 3:7

Men say "tomorrow"; the Holy Spirit says "today." There are many reasons why all should accept Jesus "today."

I.   Because Jesus brings peace to the tormenting conscience and a wise man will wish that peace as soon as he can get it.

II.   Because Jesus brings joy unspeakable and full of glory, and a wise man will wish that glory as soon as he can have it.

III.   Because Jesus brings deliverance from sin, and a wise man will wish for that deliverance as soon as he can get it.

IV.   Because Jesus brings beauty of character, and a wise man will desire that beauty of character as soon as he can have it.

V.   Because Jesus fills our lives with highest usefulness, and every wise man wishes to begin being useful as soon as possible.

VI.   Because the sooner we come to Christ the richer will be our eternity, and a wise man wishes to begin at once.

VII.   Because if we do not come to Jesus today we may never come at all, and a wise man will want to come at once before it is too late.

VIII. Conclusion: Many things that may make this the last opportunity and a refusal now may be fatal.

    a. Death is ever lurking at our doors.

    b. Loss of opportunity may come.

    c. A hardened heart may seal your doom.

  – R. A. Torrey

David's Sin

"But the thing that David had done was evil in the sight of the Lord." – 2 Samuel 11:27

"Why have you despised the word of the Lord by doing evil in His sight?" – 2 Samuel 12:9

The Bible is faithful to recount the sins as well as the virtues of its characters, thus teaching us good lessons, as in the case of David's sin.

I.   We are taught that a very good man, if he gets his eyes off from God and His Word may easily fall into very gross sin.

II.   We are taught that God never looks upon any man's sin with the least degree of allowance.

III. We are taught that whatsoever a man soweth he shall also reap; and, like the farmer, he will reap much more than he sows (Galatians 6:7).

IV. We are taught that the sins of God's servants give great occasion for enemies of the Lord to blaspheme (2 Samuel 12:14).

V.   We are taught that the sin of God's people is base ingratitude toward God.

VI. We are taught a brighter lesson from this dark story – that there is full, free, and abundant pardon for the vilest sinner.

VII. We are taught that God's pardon is to be found by the confession of our sin.

  – R. A. Torrey

What Shall We Do with Jesus?

"Then what shall I do with Jesus who is called Christ?"
– Matthew 27:22

The most important question one can put to himself.

I.   How much depends on doing the right thing with Christ.

   1.   Our acceptance or condemnation before God. (John 3:18)

   2.   Our peace of conscience depends solely on this. (Romans 5:1)

   3.   Our becoming sons of God. (John 1:12)

   4.   True joy. (1 Peter 1:8)

   5.   Eternal life. (John 5:24; 3:36)

II.   What we must do with Him.

   1.   Accept Him or reject Him. (John 12:44-48)

   2.   Let Him in or shut Him out. (Revelation 3:20)

   3.   Confess Him or deny Him. (Matthew 10:32-33)

   4.   Be for Him or against Him. (Matthew 12:30)

III.   Think who He was.

   1.   Your divinely anointed King. (Acts 2:36; 5:31)

   2.   The Son of God. (Mark 1:1)

   3.   Your Savior. (Is. 53:5)

IV.   *Conclusion:* Sum up and put the question: What will you do with Jesus right now? Illustrate by Pilate's awful mistake and its consequences.

   – R. A. Torrey

What Are You Waiting For?

"Now why do you delay?" – Acts 22:16

There is no reason for delay for which the Word of God has not an answer.

I.   "I am waiting until I am convinced." (John 7:17)

II. "I am waiting until I have enjoyed the world enough." (Mark 8:36)

III. "I am waiting for my friends." (Matthew 10:37)

IV. "I am waiting until Christians are more consistent." (Romans 14:12)

V.   "I am waiting until there is not so much to give up." (Philippians 3:7-8)

VI. "I am waiting for feeling." (Acts 16:31; John 1:12)

VII. "I am waiting until I am better." (Matthew 9:13)

VIII."I am waiting until I am sure I can hold out." (Jude 24)

IX. "I am waiting for God's time." (2 Corinthians 6:2)

X.   "I am waiting until I die." (Proverbs 29:1)

   – R. A. Torrey

The Price of Power

"And Stephen, full of grace and power, was performing great wonders and signs among the people." – Acts 6:8

This poor world needs men and women of power, and God has made it possible. We can become such by paying the price of power.

I.   Power costs the putting away of all sin.

II. We must set right the things we have done.

III. There must be absolute surrender to God.

IV. It costs a large expenditure of time and strength as well as time in prayer.

V. It requires a large expenditure of time in Bible study.

VI. There must be the entire renunciation of self-interest and self-sparing in all their forms.

VII. There must be humiliation of self.

    – R. A. Torrey

The Drama of Life in Three Acts

(Luke 15:11-33)

I. The first act – the wandering, going away from home; or, the nature of sin.

  1. Scene 1: The young man in his beautiful and sumptuous home. The beginning of sin, a desire to be independent of God.

  2. Scene 2: The young man with his portion of goods goes from home. The growth of sin. His heart went first, his feet afterwards.

II. The second act – the desolation in a far country; or, the fruits of sin.

  1. Scene 1: Is one of gaiety. The first fruit of sin is pleasure.

  2. Scene 2: Is one of hard times. The second fruit of sin is want.

  3. Scene 3: Is one of utter wretchedness. The third fruit of sin is degradation and abject slavery.

III. The third act – wanderer's return home again; or, the remedy for sin.

  1. Scene 1: His thoughts are turned homeward and father-ward.

Serious reflection is the first ingredient in the remedy for sin and its bitter consequences.

2. Scene 2: His threefold resolution,

    a. To go to his father;

    b. to confess his sin;

    c. to seek acceptance.

3. Scene 3: His welcome home. "So he got up and came to his father" (Luke 15:20). The father is watching for him, and seeing him coming, runs to meet him and welcomes him with the best his heart and hand have to give.

    – R. A. Torrey

Infidelity – Its Causes, Consequences, and Cure

I.   Its causes.

1. The misrepresentation of Christianity by its professed disciples,

    a. in doctrine;

    b. in life.

2. Ignorance of what the Bible contains and teaches.

3. Conceit. Men become infidels because they find things in the Bible they cannot understand.

4. Sin. This is the commonest and most fundamental cause of infidelity.

5. Resistance to the Holy Spirit.

II.   Its consequences.

1. Sin. Infidelity breeds sin.

2. Anarchy. Anarchists are almost, if not always, infidels.

3. Wretchedness and despair.

4. Suicide.

5. Hopeless graves.

6. Eternal ruin.

III. Its cure.

1. Christ-like living on the part of professed Christians.

2. A surrendered will on the part of the infidel. (John 7:17)

3. Study of the Word of God. (Psalms 119:130)

- R. A. Torrey

Eternal Life, or the Wrath of God – Which?

"He who believes in the Son has eternal life; but he who does not obey the Son will not see life, but the wrath of God abides on him." – John 3:36

The great question that confronts each of us: Eternal life or the wrath of God? Which shall it be?

I.   The things contrasted.

1. "Eternal life." What is it?

   a. It is really life.

   b. It is fullness of life.

   c. It is life of highest knowledge.

   d. It is the life of God.

   e. It is endless life.

2. "The wrath of God." What is it?

   a. It is the intense and settled displeasure of the infinitely holy Being who created us and all things, and who has the absolute control of all the powers of this universe.

II. How to decide between them.

1. God answers the question.

   a. Believe on the Son of God.

   b. Accept God's testimony concerning Jesus Christ.

   – R. A. Torrey

Broken Hearts

"The Lord is near to the brokenhearted And saves those who are crushed in spirit." – Psalms 34:18

The Lord knows the proud afar off (Psalms 138:6),

but he dwells with him that is of a contrite spirit (Is. 57:15).

When the sinner feels his distance from God, then it is that he is drawing nigh to God. He has a broken heart, and God draws nigh to him (Luke 15:18, 20).

I.   In a broken heart there is,

   1. A sense of sin. (Psalms 38:4; Luke 18:13)

   2. Self-abhorrence on account of sin. (Job 42:6; Ezek. 16:63)

   3. Justifying God's dealings. (Psalms 51:4)

   4. A view of the love of a dying Savior. (Zechariah 12:10)

   5. A confidence in returning to God. (Hosea 6:1; Luke 15:18)

II.   The Lord is nigh, and saves them.

   1. He accepts such a heart as His sacrifice. (Psalms 51:17; Is. 66:2)

   2. He makes such a heart His abode. (Is. 57:15)

   3. He speaks peace to such a heart. (Is. 57:18; Luke 7:50)

   4. He heals such a heart. (Psalms 147:3; Is. 61:1)

Let us search into the cause of hardness of heart.

Guard against the continuance of a careless spirit.

Direct the eye of faith constantly to the cross of Jesus.

Be faithful to the first convictions of the Spirit.

Cease not to pray, till such a frame of mind be obtained.

Look forward to the time when we shall no longer complain of hard hearts, and when broken hearts shall be healed forever. (Revelation 7:17; 21:4)

> – C. B.

Rest

> "Come to Me, all who are weary and heavy-laden, and I will give you rest." – Matthew 11:28

I.   What is rest?

1.   That which every human creature is seeking. (Psalms 4:6)

2.   That which the world offers. (Proverbs 9:16-17)

3.   But can never give. (Eccl. 1:13-14; 2:22-23)

II.   Where is it to be obtained?

1.   Not in sin. (Is. 57:10, 20; Jeremiah 2:36)

2.   Not in riches. (Psalms 39:6; Eccl. 5:10, 12)

3.   Not in idleness. (Proverbs 15:19)

4.   Not in pleasure. (Eccl. 2:1)

5.   Not in fame. (Eccl. 2:16)

6.   Not in knowledge. (Eccl. 1:18)

7.   Not in self-righteousness. (Hebrews 4:3, 10)

8.   But only in Christ. (Hebrews 4:3)

    a.   In His atonement. (Romans 5:10)

    b.   In His righteousness. (Psalms 32:1-2)

    c.   In His intercession. (Romans 8:34)

    d. In His glory. (Hebrews 4:9; Revelation 7:16-17)

III.   Therefore, come to Him:

1. At all events and hazards. (Matthew 15:22)
2. Guilty. (Luke 7:37, etc.)
3. Naked. (Revelation 3:18)
4. Lost. (Matthew 8:25)
5. Ignorant. (Luke 10:39)
6. Tempted. (2 Corinthians 12:7-8)
7. Backsliding. (Jeremiah 3:22)
8. Abide in Him. (John 15:9)
9. Follow Him. (Matthew 11:29)

    – C. B.

A Seeking Mind

"You will seek Me and find Me when you search for Me with all your heart." – Jeremiah 29:13

I.   What is the disposition of mind here intended?

1. It is not lip-service. (Jeremiah 3:10; Ezek. 33:31; Matthew 15:8)

    a. Indolence. (Song of Sol. 3:1)

    b. Impatience. (2 Kings 6:33)

2. But it is a heart perfect with God. (2 Chronicles16:9; 15:17)

    a. Steadily fixed on God's. (Psalms 108:1; Is. 26:8-9)

3. It is the earnestness of Jacob. (Genesis 32:24-28)

    a. The confidence of David. (Psalms 27:7-14)

    b. The perseverance of the woman of Canaan. (Matthew 15:22)

    c. The importunity of the widow. (Luke 18:3-5; See Is. 62:6-7)

II.   What is the blessing promised?

   1. "You will… find Me" (Jeremiah 29:13). (2 Chronicles 15:2, 4, 15; Is.45:19; Matthew 7:7-8)

      a. In time of contrition. (Deuteronomy 4:29; Jeremiah 3:22; Hosea 14:2, 4)

      b. In time of affliction. (Psalms 50:15)

      c. In time of perplexity. (2 Chronicles 20:12)

      d. In every time. (Hebrews 4:16)

   2. Let every sin be mortified. (Psalms 66:18)

   3. Let the heart be prepared. (2 Chronicles 19:3)

   4. Let the assistance of the Spirit be sought. (Romans 8:26; Ephesians 6:18; Jude 20)

      – C. B.

Repentance

"They went out and preached that men should repent."
– Mark 6:12

Repentance is a distinguishing grace of the man of God.

He cannot know himself to be a sinner without deep shame and humiliation of soul.

What have I done? What have I neglected to do?

The first sign of spiritual life is an awakened sense of sin.

Therefore the ministers of Christ go out and preach "that men should repent."

I.   Mark the necessity of repentance.

1. As saving from deserved punishment. (Ezek.18:28, 30; Luke 13:3-5; Revelation 2:5; 3:3)

2. As justifying God in the punishment of sin. (Joshua 7:19; Psalms 51:4)

3. As a means of forgiveness. (Job 33:27-28; Luke 24:47; Acts 2:38; 3:19; 5:31)

II.   Mark its character. It has many counterfeits.

1. Natural repentance produces

    a. Alarm. (Matthew 27:3-5; Acts 24:25)

    b. Conviction. (John 17:8)

    c. Confession. (1 Samuel 25:24, 30; Matthew 3:1, 6)

    d. Resolutions. (Ex. 9:27-28; 10:16-17)

    e. Partial amendment. (2 Kings 21:27-29)

2. Spiritual repentance has all these, but it has more.

    a. It is connected with faith. (Acts 20:21)

3. It includes a hearty sorrow for sin. (2 Corinthians7:10)

    a. An entire forsaking of all sin. (2 Chronicles 33:12, 15-16; Ezek. 18:28)

    b. An instant return to God. (Hosea 5:15; 6:1; Luke 15:18-20)

    c. An evidence in godly fruits. (Matthew 3:8; Acts 26:20; 2 Corinthians 7:11)

III. Its origin is of God.

1. The gift of Almighty God. (Ezek. 36:26; Acts 11:18; 2 Timothy 2:25)

2. The blessing of an exalted Savior. (Acts 5:31)

3. The work of the Holy Spirit. (Zechariah 12:10)

It is produced –

By a sight of our own guilt and need. (Psalms 51:4; Jeremiah 31:18-19; Luke 15:16-17)

By a sight of the love and sufferings of Christ. (Zechariah 12:10; Acts 2:36-37)

It is deepened –

By a view of the character of God. (Job 42:5-6)

By an assurance of pardon. (Ezek. 16:63)

   – C. B.

Faith

"If thou canst believe, all things are possible to him that believeth." – Mark 9:23 (KJV)

I.   The very nature of faith supposes difficulty.

  1. It is opposed to sight. (John 20:29; 2 Corinthians 5:7; Hebrews 11:27)

  2. It rises above sense and feeling. (Job 13:15)

  3. It puts reason to silence. (Luke 1:34-38; John 6:12-16)

  4. It implies a consciousness of weakness. (Mark 9:24; Matthew 15:25)

  5. It acknowledges dependence upon Almighty strength. (2 Chronicles 14:11; 20:12; Psalms 40:17; 2 Corinthians 3:5)

II. Let us mark some of the achievements of this wonderful principle: *"All things are possible with faith."*

  1. It overcomes all the temptations of time and sense. (Hebrews 11:8-10, 24-26; 1 John 5:4-5)

  2. It stands firm in the promise, notwithstanding all natural impossibilities. (Romans 4:17-21; Hebrews 11:11)

3. It is unshaken by all seeming contradiction. (Hebrews 11:17-19)

4. It obediently ventures upon present difficulty. (Exod. 14:2, 15; Hebrews 11:29)

5. It performs the greatest work by the weakest means. (Judges 7:16-22; Is. 41:14-15; 1 Corinthians 1:21; Hebrews 11:30)

6. It overcomes even the prescript of the Divine will. (Deuteronomy 23:3, with Ruth 1:16 and 4:10; Matthew 15:24-28, with 10:5-6)

7. It triumphs over the forebodings of the most frowning providences. (1 Samuel 30:6; Habakkuk 3:17-18)

8. It maintains an assured confidence under conflict and chastening. (Psalms 65:3; Micah 7:8-9)

9. It prevents hard thoughts of God under the most afflicting dispensations. (2 Kings 4:26; Job 1:21)

10. It obtains the supply of grace to the utmost of our desire. (Psalms 81:10; Matthew 21:22)

III. Be sure that faith is grounded upon the clear warrant of Scripture. (1 John 5:14)

IV. Act present faith as the way to encourage its fruitfulness. (Matthew 25:29; 2 Peter 1:5)

V. Face the most appalling difficulties in the resources of faith. (Zechariah 4:7; Mark 11:22-23; Philippians 4:13)

VI. Connect the exercise of faith with every Christian duty. (Luke 17:3-6)

VII. Let the habitual exercise of faith prepare you for every emergency. (Galatians 2:20)

– C. B.

The Water of Life

I.   Its character.

    1. Living. (John 4:10)

    2. Clear. (Revelation 22:1)

    3. Pure. (Revelation 22:1)

    4. Abundant. (Ezek. 47:1-9)

    5. Free. (Revelation 21:6)

II.   For whom provided.

    1. The thirsty. (Revelation 21:6)

    2. Whosoever. (Revelation 22:17)

III.   Way to obtain it.

    1. Come. (Revelation 22:17)

    2. Take. (Revelation 22:17)

      – C. I.

Repentance

I.   The nature of. (Matthew 21:9)

II.   The source of. (2 Timothy 2:25)

III. The necessity for. (Acts. 8:22)

IV.   The results of. (Luke 15:7; Luke 17:3)

V.   By whom commanded. (Acts 17:30)

VI.   In whose name? (Luke 24:47)

    -C. I.

Forgiveness

I. The foundation of it – His blood. (Ephesians 1:7)

II. The author of it – God. (Ephesians 4:32)

III. The completeness of it all. (Psalms 103:3)

IV. The proclamation of it is preached. (Acts 13:38)

V. The reception of it – all that believe. (Acts 13:39)

VI. The certainty of it – are forgiven. (1 John 2:12)

VII. The results of it – saved. (Luke 7:50)

VIII. The results of it – peace. (Luke 7:50)

IX. The results of it – blessed. (Psalms 32:1)

    – C. I.

A Sevenfold View of the Love of God

I. It is infinite in its character. (John 17:23)

II. It is constraining in its power. (2 Corinthians 5:14)

III. It is inseparable in its object. (Romans 8:35-37)

IV. It is individual in its choice. (Galatians 2:20)

V. It is universal in its extent. (John 3:16)

VI. It is unchanging in its purpose. (John13:1)

VII. It is everlasting in its duration. (Jeremiah 31:3)

    – C. I.

Ten Steps in the Prodigal's Life

I. His demand – "give… the share" (Luke 15:12).

II. His departure – "went on a journey" (Luke 15:13).

III. His distress – "famine" (Luke 15:14)

IV. His condition – "impoverished" (Luke 15:14)

V. His depravity – "to feed swine" (Luke 15:15)

VI. His conviction – "came to his senses" (Luke 15:17)

VII. His determination – "I will get up and go" (Luke 15:18)

VIII.His confession – "I have sinned" (Luke 15:18)

IX. His contrition – "no longer worthy" (Luke 15:19)

X. His conversion – "the best robe…" etc. (Luke 15:22)

    – C. I.

Justification

I. What is it? (Romans 4:5-8)

II. The One who justifies. (Romans 8:33)

III. Whom He justifies. (Romans 4:5)

IV. How He is justified. (Romans 3:24; 4:9)

V. From what He is justified. (Acts 13:39)

VI. Result of being justified. (Romans 5:1)

    – C. I.

Redemption

I. What I am redeemed with –

1. By blood. (1 Peter 1:19)

2. By power. (Nehemiah 1:10)

II. What I am redeemed from –

1. Bondage. (Ex. 6:6)

2. Enemy. (Psalms 106:10)

3. Iniquity. (Titus 2:14)

4. Curse of the law. (Galatians 3:13)

III. What the Lord has redeemed –

1. The soul. (Psalms 49:8)

2. The body. (Romans 8:23)

3. The life. (Psalms 103:4)

IV. The beauty of the redemption –

1. It is plenteous. (Psalms 130:7)

2. It is precious. (Psalms 49:8)

3. It is eternal. (Hebrews 9:12)

    – C. I.

Mercy

I. The author. (1 Peter 1:3)

II. The ground. (Romans 3:25)

III. The subjects. (Luke 17:13)

IV. The character. (Psalms 103:4)

V. The measure. (Psalms 103:8)

VI. The extent. (Psalms 103:11)

VII. The duration. (Psalms 103:17)

    – C. I.

Sin

I. The servants. (Romans 6:20)

II. The wages. (Romans 6:23)

III. The deceitfulness. (Hebrews 3:13)

IV. The pleasures. (Hebrews 11:25)

V. The sacrifice. (Hebrews 10:12)

VI. The eternal consequences. (Jude 7)

– C. I.

Jesus, the Friend

I. The sinner's friend. (Matthew 11:19)

II. My friend. (Song of Sol. 5:16)

III. Who satisfies. (Song of Sol. 5:1)

IV. Who sticks closer than a brother. (Proverbs 18:24)

V. The unchanging friend. (Proverbs 17:17)

VI. The surety. (Proverbs 6:1)

VII. Who dies. (John 15:13)

VIII. Who reproves. (Proverbs 27:6)

IX. Who counsels. (Proverbs 27:9-10)

X. Communion. (Proverbs 27:17)

XI. Resurrection. (John 11:25)

My Beloved is my friend. Christians need an object for their heart –
Jesus only (Matthew 17:1-8).

– H. M.

Rules for Evangelists

(Those given by Paul to Timothy)

I. "I remind you to kindle afresh the gift of God which is in
    you" (2 Timothy 1:6).

II. "Therefore do not be ashamed of the testimony of our Lord"
    (1:8).

III. "Retain the standard of sound words which you have heard from me, in the faith and love which are in Christ Jesus" (1:13); and again, in v. 14, "Guard, through the Holy Spirit who dwells in us, the treasure which has been entrusted to you."

IV. You want strength; then, "be strong in the grace that is in Christ Jesus" (2:1).

V. "Suffer hardship... as a good soldier of Christ Jesus" (2:3).

VI. Remember that Jesus Christ, of the seed of David, was raised from the dead (2:8). Evangelists, that is the doctrine for you. Christ raised from the dead is God's receipt in full for the sinner's justification.

VII. "Be diligent to present yourself approved to God as a workman who does not need to be ashamed, accurately handling the word of truth" (2:15).

VIII. "Now flee from youthful lusts and pursue righteousness, faith, love and peace, with those who call on the Lord from a pure heart" (2:22).

IX. "But refuse foolish and ignorant speculations, knowing that they produce quarrels" (2:23).

X. "You, however, continue in the things you have learned" (3:14). Not only preach to others, but live out the truth you preach.

XI. "All Scripture is inspired by God" (3:16). Be persuaded of the inspiration of the Scripture. Use it, for it is the sword of the Spirit (Ephesians 6:17).

XII. "I solemnly charge you in the presence of God and of Christ Jesus... preach the word; be ready in season and out of season;" (4:1-2).

XIII. "Do the work of an evangelist" (4:5). *Do* the work, don't merely talk about it, or be satisfied with the title of an evangelist. DO the work – it is tough work, hard work, but blessed work.

– M. R.

Conversion

"Let the wicked forsake his way And the unrighteous man his thoughts; And let him return to the Lord, And He will have compassion on him, And to our God, For He will abundantly pardon." – Is. 55:7

To be converted means to be turned about or to be turned to God. Man has turned his back upon God, but, when converted, he faces a loving and forgiving God.

I.   The first step toward conversion is an earnest desire and intention to forsake sin.

II. The second step toward conversion is a willingness to accept God's salvation, whatever it may require.

III. The third step toward conversion is making up your mind to believe what God wants you to know in order to be saved.

 1. That the race is totally depraved.

 2. That the death of the Son of God was vicarious.

 3. That the Word of God gives assurance of your salvation.

  – F. S.

He Still Waits

"Therefore the Lord longs to be gracious to you, And therefore He waits on high to have compassion on you."
– Is. 30:18

Now that God has done all He can do for our salvation, He has to stop and wait for us.

I.   The first class of people that the Lord has to wait for is the Christian.

1. There are three reasons why Christians ought to be willing to respond to God in efforts to save the lost:

    a. The honor conferred upon us in working for God.

    b. The great privilege we have to at once work for God.

    c. The great reward that comes to the faithful in God's service.

II. Another class that God has to work for is the backslider.

III. Still others God is waiting for are those who thus far have rejected God's grace.

> – F. S.

A Great Conditional Promise

"Did I not say to you that if you believe, you will see the glory of God?" – John 11:40

Something to be done in order to enjoy the accomplishment of the divine promise. Look at some of the stones to be rolled away:

I.   The awful stone of unbelief.

II. The miserable stone of prejudice.

III. We need to get rid of criticism.

IV. Another one to remove is the stone of excuse.

V.   Again is the lack of ability to do anything.

    1. We must believe that until we do our part. God will not, or, I may say, *cannot* do His part.

    2. We must also believe that when we do our part there is nothing impossible with God.

> – F. S.

Christ Our Example

"If we say that we have fellowship with Him and yet walk
in the darkness, we lie and do not practice the truth"
– 1 John 1:6

The moment we accept the Son of God as our Savior, we must take
Him as our example.

I.   In His devotion to His father.

II.   In His submission to God.

III. In His compassion.

IV.   In His humility.

V.   In His patience.

VI.   In His love for communion with the Father.

– F. S.

Christ Our Mighty One

"Therefore He is able also to save forever those who draw
near to God through Him, since He always lives to make
intercession for them." – Hebrews 7:25

I.   Look at some of the things He is able to do for us.

  1. He is able to keep us from falling. (Jude 1:24)

  2. He is able to subdue all things unto Himself. (Philippians 3:21)

  3. He is able to deliver us when tempted. (Hebrews 2:18)

  4. He is able to prepare us for every good work. (Hebrews 13:21)

      – F. S.

Christ Our Friend

"The Son of Man came eating and drinking, and they say, 'Behold, a gluttonous man and a drunkard, a friend of tax collectors and sinners!'" Yet wisdom is vindicated by her deeds." – Matthew 11:19

I.   He is the friend of sinners.

II.   He is the friend that sticketh closer than a brother.

III. He is the friend that loveth at all times.

IV.   He is the faithful friend.

V.   He is the friend that gives us hearty counsel.

VI.   He is the friend that makes us like himself.

    – F. S.

Saving the Lost

"For the Son of Man has come to seek and to save that which was lost." – Luke 19:10

A soul saved or lost – which?

I.   Lost.

   1. Every soul out of Christ is lost.

      a. In that they are all sinners. (Romans 3:22-23)

      b. In that they are all the slaves of sin. (John 8:34)

      c. In that if they do not turn to Christ they will be lost eternally. (John 3:36)

II.   Saved.

   1. Christ is seeking to save.

      a. By His providence.

      b. By His Spirit.

   c. By His Word.

 2. He can save.

   a. From the guilt of sin. (Acts 10:43)

   b. From the power of sin. (John 8:36)

   c. From hell. (1 Thessalonians 1:10)

   d. To the uttermost. (Hebrews 7:25)

 3. He came to seek the utterly lost.

 4. He is seeking to save now.

   – R. A. Torrey

God-Given Conviction

"Now when they heard this, they were pierced to the heart." – Acts 11:37

To be pricked in the heart with the conviction of sin is not a pleasant experience, but if rightly received leads to very great blessing.

I.   Why these men were pricked in their hearts.

 1. They saw the appalling enormity of the sin of rejecting Christ. (v. 36)

II.   How they were pricked in their hearts.

 1. It was by the preaching of the Word of God.

 2. It was by Peter's testimony to a risen and exalted Savior.

 3. It was by the power of the Holy Spirit.

III.   The results of their being pricked in their hearts.

 1. They turned from their awful sin. (v. 38)

 2. They publicly confessed their sin and their acceptance of Christ. (v. 41)

 3. They were saved. (v. 47)

4. They found a deep and lasting joy. (v. 46)

5. They received the Holy Spirit. (v. 38-39)

   – R. A. Torrey

Saved

"For by grace you have been saved through faith"
– Ephesians 2:8

One of the greatest words in the English language is the word "saved."

I.   Who are saved?

1. Everyone who believes in Jesus Christ.

II.   From what are we saved?

1. From all guilt.

2. From God's displeasure.

3. From the condemnation of our own conscience.

4. From the power of sin.

5. From future judgment.

III.   To what are we saved?

1. We are saved to peace and joy.

2. We are saved to a true, pure, holy, and useful life.

3. We are saved to God's favor and delight.

4. We are saved to sonship.

5. We are saved to eternal life.

6. We are saved to an inheritance incorruptible, etc.

IV.   How we are saved.

1. We are saved by grace. Salvation is a gift.

2. We are saved by grace through faith.

   – R. A. Torrey

How to Become Sons of God

"But as many as received Him, to them He gave the right to become children of God, even to those who believe in His name" – John 1:12

To be a child of God involves so much – so much in the life that now is, and so much in the life which is to come.

I.   What is involved?

    1. Our absolute security in this present life.

    2. The supply of every real need.

    3. Joy.

    4. Peace.

    5. Likeness to God.

    6. Infinite glory hereafter.

II.   How may we become sons of God?

    1. We are all God's offspring, but we are not all sons of God. (Acts 17:28; John 8:44)

    2. We are made sons of God by receiving Jesus. (John 1:12; Galatians 3:26)

    3. To receive Jesus is to receive Him as He offers Himself to us.

        a. As our atoning Savior. (Matthew 20:28)

        b. As our Deliverer from sin's power. (John 8:36)

        c. As our Rest-giver. (Matthew 11:28)

        d. As our Teacher. (John 13:13)

        e. As our Way of Access to God. (John 14:6)

        f. As our King. (1 Timothy 6:15)

        g. As our Lord and God. (John 20:28; John 5:22)

III.   Who may become sons of God in this way?

    1. Anyone. How sweeping it is! "...as many as" (John 1:12).

2. The loveliest character or the vilest sinner.

3. It is possible to anyone at this moment.

Believe and Be Saved

"Believe in the Lord Jesus, and you will be saved" – Acts 16:31

Introduction: This text makes the way of salvation as clear as day.

I. There can be no doubt that this is the true way to be saved and a sure way to be saved.

1. An inspired apostle whom God sent for this very purpose declares it.

2. Positive affirmative: "…you will be saved" (Acts 16:31).

II. What is involved in believing on the Lord Jesus?

1. Trust in Jesus for pardon for all my sin.

2. Surrender to the Lord Jesus as Lord and Master of my thoughts and acts.

3. Confession of Jesus as my Lord. (Romans 10:9-10)

4. Looking to the Lord Jesus for guidance in all I do.

5. Obedience to the will of the Lord Jesus as far as His will is known. (Luke 6:46)

6. Study of the words of Jesus in order to know His will.

7. Dependence upon Jesus and not upon self or others for strength to do His will.

"God Calling, Yet"

Then the Lord said, "My Spirit shall not strive with man

forever, because he also is flesh; nevertheless his days shall be one hundred and twenty years." – Genesis 6:3

I. God calls in many ways. (Revelation 22:17; Acts 2:21; 2 Peter 3:9)

1. Calls by pastors, Sunday School teachers, parents' prayers, Bible, songs, memories, His Spirit.

2. Unusual ways, still small voice, cyclone, lightning, death of child or loved one, loss of business, etc. (Hebrews 12:6; Eccl. 7:14)

II. God is *always* calling.

1. But man is *not* always *heeding!* The heart hardens like the hand, like the bone, like the face. "While the lamp holds out to burn, the vilest sinner may return." But will he? *May* is God's part! Will is man's part! (John 7:17; Hebrews 4:2)

III. God is *able, willing, ready* to save.

1. But man is a *free moral* agent. "Tho' God be good and free be heaven, no force divine can love compel."

2. There are two parties to every gift – the giver and the receiver. (John 1:11-13; Romans 10:13)

    – C. N. H.

"Convicted, but Not Regenerated"

But as he was discussing righteousness, self-control and the judgment to come, Felix became frightened and said, "Go away for the present, and when I find time I will summon you." – Acts 24:25

Jesus answered, "Truly, truly, I say to you, unless one is born of water and the Spirit he cannot enter into the kingdom of God. – John 3:5

I.   This was Felix's chance of heaven. He lost it; no other ever came. (Hebrews 3:15; 2 Corinthians 6:2; Hebrews 2:3; Eccl. 12:1)

    1. It is a terrible thing to be *lost*. Shut *out*; not shut *in*. (John 8:21; Revelation 21:8; 2 Thessalonians 1:7-9)

II.   Paul, a prisoner, *reasoned* before Felix, a prince in purple.

    1. Religion is the *only reasonable* thing! It is not *just* emotion, prayer, song, ceremony, creed. It is that and more; it is life – life as Christ would have us live it. (Romans 12:1-2; Isaiah 1:18)

    2. Paul reasoned of *righteousness*. Yet he talked "Christ and Him crucified." (Romans 14:17; Romans 10:4)

    3. Of *temperance* in *self-control*. (John 8:32-36)

    4. Of *judgment*. (Hebrews 9:27; Hebrews 10:27; 1 Peter 4:17; John 5:22)

III. Felix *trembled*. The devils *believed* and trembled, but were *not* saved. One must not only tremble, but *turn from* sin *to* Christ. "*Almost* persuaded," but LOST.

    – C. N. H.

Salvation: A Lawyer's View

"How will we escape if we neglect so great a salvation?"
– Hebrews 2:3

I.   The great doctrine of jurisprudence, as of grace, is *neglect*. Not reject, spurn, abuse – just *neglect*.

    1. Companion Texts:

        a. "For what does it profit a man to gain the whole world, and forfeit his soul?" (Mark 8:36).

b. "For what is the hope of the godless when he is cut off,
When God requires his life?" (Job 27:8)

II.   God's salvation is measured by His gift – His "only begotten
Son" (John 3:16). *Saved from what?* The penalty of sin! The
guilt of sin! The power of sin!

1.   To make it *practical. Saved* so you won't think only of self,
so you won't lie, cheat, drink, swear, gamble, use tobacco,
play cards, or dance.

2.   Saved *to* what? Life abundant here (John 10:10). Life eternal
hereafter (John 17:3).

III. How? By accepting Jesus Christ as Savior. When? *Now!*
(Romans 10:13; John 1:11-13; Romans 10:10)

– C. N. H.

Christ or the Robber?

Text: "Truly, truly, I say to you, everyone who commits sin
is the slave of sin." – John 8:34

"… the Holy Spirit… God has given to those who obey
Him." – Acts 5:32

One is either a child of obedience or a child of disobedience, of God
or of the devil!

I.   Man can choose Christ. If he does not choose Christ, he
has chosen the Robber. Paul, Peter, and John chose Christ;
Judas, Felix, and Pilate chose the Robber. Life is made up
of decisions; they soon become *permanent.*

1.   Pilate was influenced by his friends against Jesus. But no
one could crucify Jesus that day but Pilate. *You* alone! The
world – society, ambition, politics – says, "Crucify Him!" But

hold! Let's wait until we have a reason for it. Pilate wanted the world's friendship. He got it, but oh – the price he paid!

II.   The Robber today! Worldliness – love of money, love of ease, love of pleasure, cards, theaters, dancing, slander, liquor, tobacco, evil thinking, etc. All cry out as of old, "Crucify Him!"

III.   *I choose Christ!* "…as for me and my house, we will serve the Lord." (Joshua 24:15) "Take the world, but give me Jesus." "For a day *in* Your courts is better than a thousand *outside*" (Psalms 84:10). Good-bye, Robber! Come in, Jesus!

"God's Justice and His Mercy"

For God so loved the world, that He gave His only begotten Son, that whoever believes in Him shall not perish, but have eternal life. John 3:16

I.   Preach justice and wrath from standpoint of Love. "God is love" (1 John 4:8). "… everyone who loves is born of God" (1 John 4:7). But God is also *Justice.* "For our God is a consuming fire" (Hebrews 12:29). Wrath, justice, and judgment are mentioned more often in the Bible than love!

II.   The test of love is *something surrendered.* God gave His *"only Begotten Son"* (John 3:16).

1.   The purpose: "that whoever believes in Him shall not perish" (John 3:16).

2.   But by receiving the gift have *everlasting* life.

3.   In law it is *presumed* that a man will *not* do an *idle* thing. What an idle, absurd, foolish thing God did in giving His Son to die upon the cross – unless there was a purpose! What other purpose could there be than that stated?

III.   In law, mercy is never asked until *guilt* is admitted.

1. Sin is against God. Hence only God can *forgive* sin (Psalms 51:4). "…without shedding of blood there is no forgiveness" (Hebrews 9:22).

   – C. N. H.

Topics and Texts for Sermons and Bible Readings

Genesis 1:26 (with 1 Corinthians 15:45). The Two Adams.

5:24. Walking with God. (The Secret of Abiding Peace.)

5:24. How to move in the Best Society, or Walking with God.

7:1. Noah and the Deluge.

Exodus 8:10. The Fool's Day.

12:13. The Power of the Blood.

Numbers 13:30. Faith of Caleb and Joshua.

32:23. Found Out.

Joshua 1. Courage and Enthusiasm.

1 Samuel 8:4. Disobedience.

1 Kings 18. Elijah at Carmel.

18:21. How Long Halt Ye?

18:38. A Mighty Prayer.

Psalms 1:1-3. God's Picture of a Happy Man.

14:1. The Fool's Creed.

32:1. How to Be a Happy Christian.

51. David's Confession and Prayer.

51:10. "Create in me a clean heart, O God"

62:11. Power: Its Source and How to Obtain It.

103:3, 5. He Forgives Our Iniquities.

119:59-60. A Message for the Dying Year.

119:126. The Need of a General Revival.

139:23-24. David's Prayer: Search Me and Know Me.

Proverbs 8:36. Our Most Dangerous Enemy.

11:30. Business That Always Pays and That Is Open to All.

13:15. A Hard Road.

14:9. The Awfulness of Sin. "Fools mock at sin."

27:1. Uncertain.

Isaiah 9:6. The Wonderful Jesus.

49:24-25. Christ as a Deliverer.

53:4-5. Death of Christ.

55:6. Seek Ye the Lord While He May Be Found.

55:6 (with Hebrews 11:6; Hosea 10:12). A Wise Secret.

57:7. Seven Facts about the Way of the Wicked.

57:21. Peace.

Jeremiah 17:9. The Heart of Man.

21:8. Two Ways.

23:28. The Bible: Wherein It Differs from All Other Books.

23:29 (with Hebrews 4:12; Luke 8:11). The Power of the Word.

33:17. God's Power to Save a Drunkard.

Ezekiel 33:11. "Why then will you die…?"

33:18. A Mad Choice.

Daniel 5. A King's Folly and What It Cost: A Tragedy.

Amos 4:12. A Great Meeting for Saint and Sinner, Believer and Infidel.

Malachi 3:8. A Remarkable Robbery.

Matthew 4:19. A Sermon to Christian Workers.

5:29. Hell.

6:24. No Man Can Serve Two Masters, etc.

7:6. Hopeless Cases.

7:13. Paths to Perdition.

7:22-23. False Hopes.

10:32. The Duty of the Hour.

11:19. A Friend Worth Having.

11:19. A True Friend.

11:27-30. Coming to Christ.

11:28. "Come"

11:28. The Cure for All Our Woes.

11:28-29. Every Man's Great Need Met.

12:24-32. Sin against the Holy Spirit.

12:30. With or Against: Which?

22:14. Speechless before God.

22:42. "What do you think about the Christ?"

23:37-38. The Failure of Jesus Christ.

24:35. Certainties and Uncertainties about the Future.

24:44. "'…be ready; for the Son of Man is coming at an hour when you do not think *He will*."

27:22. The Great Question of the Day.

27:22. Decision.

27:22. The Question of Questions.

Mark 8:36. An Idiotic Bargain.

10:26. Then Who Can Be Saved?

11:22. Have Faith in God.

13:22-23. False Christs and False Prophets.

13:34. To Every Man His Work.

14:1-20. Parable of the Sower.

14:14. Compassion of Christ.

15:25-26. Who Can Be Saved?

16:16. How to Be a Daniel.

16:16. How to Be Saved and How to Be Damned.

Luke 2:7. No Room for Christ.

4:18. The Blessed Gospel.

4:18. The Gospel in the New Testament.

5:27. Sudden Conversions.

7:48. "'Your sins have been forgiven."

7:50. A Woman Who Is Sure to Be in Heaven.

9:1-62. Losing Sight of Self.

10:25-37. Christ the Good Samaritan.

12:20. God's Estimate of a Certain Rich Man

14:18. Profitless and Wicked Manufacturing.

15:4-7. The Lost Sheep.

15:11-24. Prodigal Son.

15:14-23. The Road from Starvation to Plenty.

16:25. Retribution.

17:32. A Woman Who Should Never Be Forgotten.

18:9-14. A "Good Man" Lost, and a "Bad Man" Saved.

18:22. One Thing You Lack.

18:35-43 (with Mark 10:46-52). Bartimaeus.

19:1-10. An Extraordinary Case: A Rich Man Saved.

19:10. Christ's Mission to the World.

19:10. Saved or Lost.

19:14. High Treason.

24:34. Easter Promises and Warnings.

24:49. The Christian Worker and the Holy Spirit.

John 1:38 (with Matthew 6:33). "'What do you seek?"

1:41. Working for Christ.

2:1-12. Christ's Miracle at Cana of Galilee.

3:7. You Must Be Born Again.

3:16. "For God so loved the world, that He gave His only begotten Son, that whoever believes in Him shall not perish, but have eternal life."

3:16. Amazing Love.

3:16. God is Love.

3:16. The Most Wonderful Thing in the World.

3:16. The World's Greatest Gift: Enterprise.

3:18. Condemned.

4:14. Eternal Satisfaction.

5:40. A Strange Refusal.

6:35. Christ, the Bread of Life.

6:44. God's Cables.

8:32. Freedom for All Men.

8:36. Liberty.

9:1-41. Christ Restoring the Blind.

10:1-30. Christ, the Good Shepherd.

10:1-30. The Shepherd and His Sheep.

12:42-43. Open Confession of Christ.

14:6. The Way to God.

15:9. An Open Door.

15:25. A Strange Hatred.

15:25. "They hated Me without a cause."

16:5. Where Will You Spend Eternity?

18:38. Some Absolute Certainties.

18:40. A Strange Election.

19:30. "'It is finished!"

Acts 1:8. Witnessing for Christ.

2:1-4. Pentecostal Power.

4:12. No Salvation except in Christ.

4:12. An Imperative and Immediate Need.

4:31-35. A Model Church.

6:7. Stephen.

8:4. Spreading the Gospel.

9:1 (with 22:10). A Brilliant and Bitter Infidel Converted.

11:13-14. Sincere but Not Saved.

11:13-14. What a Man Must Believe and What He Must Do to Be Saved.

13:39. Taking God at His Word.

16:25-34. In Jail at Midnight.

16:30. Genuine Salvation and How to Get It.

16:30-31. A Plain Answer to a Great Question.

16:33. All in One Hour.

17:30. "God is now declaring to men that all *people* everywhere should repent." A New Year's Call.

18:8. Family Religion.

20:31. Love for Souls.

24:25. A Fatal Mistake.

26:28. A King's Costly Folly.

Romans 1:1. A Servant of Jesus Christ.

1:16. God's Power at Man's Disposal.

1:16. Salvation for Everybody

1:22. Where Infidelity and Liberalism Fail.

3:22. Man's Great Failure.

3:22-23. The Universal Equality of Men.

5:6. God's Love for Sinners.

6:23. An Easy Question for a Wise Man to Answer.

6:23. Outrageous Wages.

6:23. Eternal Life: What It Is and How to Get It.

8:17. Joint Heirs with Christ.

9:20. Man's Right Attitude before God.

10:1. How to Get Men Saved.

10:13. Saved by a Cry.

1 Corinthians 1:18 (with v. 31). God's Instrumentalities.

1:27. Weak Things Employed to Confound the Mighty.

3:11. The Only Foundation.

5:6-7. Little Sins.

13:1-13. Love.

13:5. Self-Examination.

15:16. Some Certainties Connected with the Resurrection of Christ.

15:57. Glorious Victory.

2 Corinthians 2:11. The Devices of the Devil.

6:17-18. Separation.

11:13-15. Ministers Who Are Doing the Devil's Work.

Galatians 3:10. A Wonderful Contrast.

5:22. Fruits of the Spirit.

6:7. "Do not be deceived…"

6:9. Perseverance.

Ephesians 1:2, 12. Men Out of Christ. Their Condition Today.

2:12. No Hope.

4:30. Grieving the Spirit.

5:15. Fools in God's Sight.

5:16. Redeeming the Time.

5:25-27. Christ and the Church.

Philippians 3:7-8. A Great Sacrifice for a Greater Gain.

4:4. How to Be Always Happy.

1 Timothy 1:6. The One Thing to Get.

1:15. Why Jesus Christ Came into the World.

1:15. One Thing That Every Man Should Believe.

4:8. A Paying Investment.

2 Timothy 2. God's Pattern for a Christian Worker.

2:15. An Approved Workman.

3:14-15. Saving the Children.

Hebrews 2:3. A Startling Question.

2:3. No Escape.

3:13. Hardened.

7:25. Christ Mighty to Save.

9:27. The Judgment.

10:11 (with 13:14). Heaven: What Sort of a Place It Is and How to Get There.

12:25 (with 10:28). Three Classes.

James 4:2. The Power of Prayer.

4:3. Hindrances to Prayer.

5:16. The Prayer of the Righteous Man.

1 Peter 1:4-5. A Great Inheritance and How to Get It.

1:8. How to Be Unspeakably Happy.

1:8. Why Christians Sing.

2:21. In His Steps.

2 Peter 2:1. Infamous Ingratitude.

3:9. Not God's Fault.

1 John 3:15-17. The World.

4:8. God Is Love.

5:1-21. The Glory of the Believer as Seen.

5:15. The Prayer That God Hears, or How to Pray so as to Get What You Ask.

Jude 20. Praying in the Holy Spirit.

Revelation 3:17. Blind Eyes.

12:9. How the Devil Fools Men.

22:17. God's Last Call.

Christ's Call to Peter.

John 1:40.

Matthew 14:28.

Luke 9:28.

John 6:66.

Luke 22:45.

Christ – The Bread of Life.

Christ in the Old Testament.

"Come."

Isaiah 55:1.

Isaiah 55:3.

Mark 6:31.

Matthew 11:28.

Confession of Sin.

Divinity of Christ.

Five Things That No Man Can Do.

    Romans 5:6-8.

    Romans 3:20.

    John 14:6.

    John 6:44.

    Hebrews 12:14.

Foundations of Faith, The.

    1 Peter 3:15.

    Matthew 24:35.

    John 9:25.

    John 4:29.

Fourfold View of Christ.

    Galatians 3:13.

    Galatians 2:20.

    Romans 15:14.

    John 14:1-13.

Four Skeptics: Nathaniel, Thomas, Pilate, the King's Courtier.

God's Attitude toward the Wicked.

    Matthew 5:44.

    Hebrews 11:6.

    John 3:16.

    Romans 5:6-8.

    Psalms 7:11.

    Is. 57:21.

    Psalms 86:5.

    2 Peter 3:9.

    Hebrews 7:25.

    Hebrews 11.

Holy Spirit, The.

Holy Spirit and the Word, The.

Hope.

How to Study the Bible so as to Get the Most Good Out of It.

Mark 8:36.

1 Peter 4:17.

Matthew 27:22.

What It Is to Believe on Christ.

What Christ Is to Those Who Believe on Him

1 Peter 2:24.

2 John 2:1.

Romans 7:24-25.

Matthew 11:28.

John 10:28.

Why Jesus Christ Is Coming Again.

Why I Believe that Jesus Is the Son of God.

Why the King Came.

Matthew 5:17.

Matthew 9:13.

Luke 19:10.

John 10:10.

Mark 10:45.

John 10:28.

Reuben A. Torrey – A Short Biography

Reuben. A. Torrey was an author, conference speaker, pastor, evangelist, Bible college dean, and more. Reuben Archer Torrey was born in Hoboken, New Jersey, on January 28, 1856. He graduated from Yale University in 1875 and from Yale Divinity School in 1878, when he became the pastor of a Congregational church in Garrettsville, Ohio. Torrey married Clara Smith in 1879, with whom he had five children.

In 1882, he went to Germany, where he studied at the universities at Leipzig and Erlangen. Upon returning to the United States, R. A. Torrey pastored in Minneapolis, and was also in charge of the Congregational City Mission Society. In 1889, D. L. Moody called upon Torrey to lead his Chicago Evangelization Society, which later became the Moody Bible Institute. Beginning in 1894, Torrey was also the pastor of the Chicago Avenue Church, which was later called the Moody Memorial Church. He was a chaplain with the YMCA during the Spanish-American War, and was also a chaplain during World War I.

Torrey traveled all over the world leading evangelistic tours, preaching to the unsaved. It is believed that more than one hundred thousand were saved under his preaching. In 1908, he helped start the Montrose Bible Conference in Pennsylvania, which continues today. He became dean of the Bible Institute of Los Angeles (now Biola University) in 1912, and was the pastor of the Church of the Open Door in Los Angeles from 1915 to 1924.

Torrey continued speaking all over the world and holding Bible conferences. He died in Asheville, North Carolina, on October 26, 1928.

R. A. Torrey was a very active evangelist and soul winner, speaking to people everywhere he went, in public and in private, about their souls, seeking to lead the lost to Jesus. He authored more than forty books, including *How to Bring Men to Christ, How to Pray, How to Study the Bible for Greatest Profit, How to Obtain Fullness of Power in Christian Life and Service*, and *Why God Used D. L. Moody*, and also helped edit the twelve-volume book about the fundamentals of the faith, titled *The Fundamentals*. He was also known as a man of prayer, and his teaching, preaching, writing, and his entire life proved that he walked closely with God.

Other Similar Titles

A Word to Fellow Pastors and Other Christian Leaders,
by Charles H. Spurgeon

The objective of the Christian ministry is to convert sinners and to edify the body of Christ. No faithful minister can possibly rest short of this. Applause, fame, popularity, honor, and wealth – all these are vain. If souls are not won, and if saints are not matured, our ministry itself is futile.

Questions we have to ask ourselves: Has it been the purpose of my ministry and the desire of my heart to save the lost and guide the saved? Is this my aim in every sermon I preach and in every visit I make? Is it under the influence of this feeling that I continually live and walk and speak? Do I pray and toil and fast and weep for this? Do I spend and am I spent for this, counting it, next to the salvation of my own soul, my greatest joy to be the instrument of saving others? Is it for this that I exist? To accomplish this, would I gladly die? Have I seen the pleasure of the Lord prospering in my hand? Have I seen souls converted under my ministry? Have God's people found refreshment from my lips and gone on their way rejoicing, or have I seen no fruit of my labors? ?

Opinions are not what man needs; he needs truth. Not theology, but God. Not religion, but Christ. Not literature and science, but the knowledge of the free love of God in the gift of His only begotten Son.

Available where books are sold.

The Soul Winner, by Charles H. Spurgeon

As an individual, you may ask, *How can I, an average person, do anything to reach the lost?* Or if a pastor, you may be discouraged and feel ineffective with your congregation, much less the world. Or perhaps you don't yet have a heart for the lost. Whatever your excuse, it's time to change. Overcome yourself and learn to make a difference in your church and the world around you. It's time to become an effective soul winner for Christ.

As Christians, our main business is to win souls. But, in Spurgeon's own words, "like shoeing-smiths, we need to know a great many things. Just as the smith *must* know about horses and how to make shoes for them, so we *must* know about souls and how to win them for Christ." Learn about souls, and how to win them, from one of the most acclaimed soul winners of all time.

Available where books are sold.

Words of Counsel, by Charles H. Spurgeon

Is there any occupation as profitable or rewarding as that of winning souls for Christ? It is a desirable employment, and the threshold for entry into this profession is set at a level any Christian may achieve – you must only love the Lord God with all your heart, soul, and mind; and your fellow man as yourself. This work is for all genuine Christians, of all walks of life. This is for you, fellow Christian.

Be prepared to be inspired, challenged, and convicted. Be prepared to weep, for the Holy Spirit may touch you deeply as you consider your coworkers, your neighbors, the children you know, and how much the Lord cares for these individuals. But you will also be equipped. Charles Spurgeon knew something about winning souls, and he holds nothing back as he shares biblical wisdom and practical application regarding the incredible work the Lord wants to do through His people to reach the lost.

Available where books are sold.

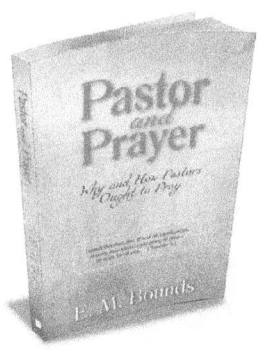

Pastor and Prayer, by E. M. Bounds

"What the church needs today is not more and better machinery, not new organizations or more innovative methods, but men whom the Holy Spirit can use – men of prayer, men mighty in prayer. The Holy Spirit does not flow through methods, but through men. He does not show up on machinery, but on men. He does not anoint plans, but men – men of prayer."

– E. M. Bounds

Available where books are sold.

The Greatest Fight, by Charles H. Spurgeon

This book examines three things that are of utmost importance in this fight of faith. The first is *our armory*, which is the inspired Word of God. The second is our army, the church of the living God, which we must lead under our Lord's command. The third is *our strength*, by which we wear the armor and use the sword.

The message in this book, when originally presented by Charles Spurgeon in his final address to his own Pastor's College, was received rapturously and enthusiastically. It was almost immediately published and distributed around the world and in several languages. After Charles Spurgeon's death in 1892, 34,000 copies were printed and distributed to pastors and leaders in England through Mrs. Spurgeon's book fund. It is with great pleasure that we present this updated and very relevant book to the Lord's army of today.

Available where books are sold.

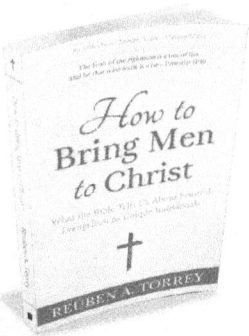

How to Bring Men to Christ, by Reuben A. Torrey

How to Bring Men to Christ sheds light on how to reach the lost with the gospel – not new light, but tested and true light. Reuben A. Torrey will show you how to use appropriate, applicable Bible passages to reach every kind of lost individual. Regardless of the angle the lost may use to try to justify why they remain in their sad condition, Torrey offers Scripture passages and biblical principles that have proven to reach even the most stubborn of the unsaved.

Available where books are sold.

CPSIA information can be obtained
at www.ICGtesting.com
Printed in the USA
LVHW012346210520
656196LV00011B/1338